Letters To Boot Camp

By Hayden Hodges

D1619146

Copyright © 2012 by Hayden Hodges
Letters To Boot Camp Written by Hayden Hodges (2012)
Photos by Hayden Hodges
Edited by Alexandra Schmidt

To:

All the Past, Present, and Future Warriors of the United States,

Every Parent, Spouse, Sibling, and Child

Who's loved one has stood on those Yellow Foot Prints,

And to my son, JD.

Semper Fidelis.

Introduction

My Son is a United States Marine.

When JD first told me he was going to join the Marine Corps I have to say I was almost sick with terror. After all, the Marines are indeed the first to fight.

I tried to talk him into the Air Force, not because I think the Air Force is easier or less dangerous. Simply because in my "Mom Mind", 8 weeks of Basic Training sounds much better than 13 weeks of Boot Camp. Of course, deep in my heart, I knew all along he was Marine material from the very beginning and no matter how much I tried to change his mind all my efforts would be futile.

See, there was always just something about him. Maybe it was his fearless attitude, or his natural respect of others. Maybe it was the way he always took pride in himself, his loyalty to his friends and family, his great strength, gentle heart, or perhaps his ability to turn off his emotions when necessary to get an ugly job done. Who knows, but I saw all of it in him while he was growing up. So yes, even though at first I didn't like it, I knew he was following the right path even if one day it might put my beloved Son smack dab in the line of fire. And that was that.

It was his dream, his goal, and my job to back him up anyway I could. And I did just that!
This book is all about one guy making his way through Boot Camp, and one Mom doing all she could to help him and his platoon get to the finish line.
These are the actual letters between us, along with side notes of things I didn't say and explanations as to what or who we were writing about.

Boot Camp is like an 80 hour a week hard labor job with no time off, so you'll notice there are many more letters from me to him. I had a lot more time than he did and I made sure to write him daily from the time I had his address until the last week, when I knew he wouldn't receive my letters in time. The only things I've changed are the names and the dates ever so slightly. I think it's good to see the whole picture. Understand, I am by no means a professional writer... I am just a Mom with a story and some information to share. I can be rude and my language isn't always appropriate, but I am who I am and to try and change that for the sake of being proper would surely distort my message.

I heard another mother put it like this, "Our children choose the Marines, and we get drafted."

Honestly, I have never heard a statement so true. But, I would never give up the pride in knowing that my Son is indeed "One of The Few." Drafted or not, I'm a Marine Mom now, and I love all my Marines!

Semper Fi.

-Hayden Hodges

A Proud Marine Mom

And so it began....

It's hard work to just get on the bus.

In high school JD started talking to me about the Marines, and in return, I eagerly talked to him about the Air Force. Slowly but surely he made me understand that he wanted to be a Marine, not an Airman. He started talking to his recruiter when he was in 10th grade, but for my sake, he didn't actually enlist until he was almost 19. It took that much time for him to make me understand that it was the Marines, and only the Marines, for him.

It didn't help that his recruiter was actually one of the busiest recruiters in the nation! I tried and tried to make contact with him. I called more times than I care to think of. Heck, I even showed up at the recruiters' office on multiple occasions. I met every recruiter in there except my son's until about 3 months before JD was going to ship out to Parris Island. By then my son had already been to MEPS, and had enlisted 5 months earlier.

Please, don't get me wrong, I'm not bashing JD's recruiter. He was a Godsend and is a big part of the reason why my son is where he is today. Honestly, he was simply hard for me to get hold of due to my schedule. But he was, and still is, always available to his Poolees, Recruits, and Marines. I respect him for his hard work, knowledge, and understanding of what it takes to become a Marine. I also appreciated the care he showed in regards to my son's future along with the futures of all the young men and women he worked with.

These recruiters know their stuff, and JD's made sure he knew exactly what he was getting into. As the matter of fact, every Marine Recruiter I have met has had the Marine Corps along with their Poolees best interests at heart. Knowing that, and seeing it for myself, made it worlds easier to put my child's life, more or less, in their hands.

Once I accepted that JD was definitely going to enlist in the Marines, I changed my Air Force Raves into Marine Corps Cheers! I researched everything I could find on the Marine Corps, and learned a lot more than I probably needed to know. But it worked for me, and more importantly, it worked for my son. I had his back, and he knew it.

One thing I learned a little too late... I didn't actually get to be there when my son raised his right hand and enlisted in the Delayed Entry Program for the Marine Corps. Why? Because neither one of us knew I was allowed to be there. Well, it turns out you are indeed allowed to be there, and while not all parents go, many do, and to this day I wish I had.

The first thing I learned was that while in the "Delayed Entry Program" (DEP) a recruit is called a "Poolee". While waiting to ship out to Boot Camp, Poolees are expected to go to "Poolee Functions" on the weekends where they will do whatever the recruiter needs them to do. Sometimes it's a physical fitness type thing, and sometimes it's not. They're also expected to be working out (PT), on their own, every day.

Really, while it's pretty time consuming, all of it makes sense. While going to the Poolee Functions they are hanging out with Marines and getting a good taste of the culture. It doesn't matter if they are doing PT or standing around a box at the local Toys for Tots Christmas toy drive. At all of the events they will learn something new about the life they are entering. Add a daily workout to that and it will save them a lot of pain and suffering later on in Boot Camp.

Just to be able to ship out and officially be called a "Recruit", a Poolee has to be able to pass an "IST", or Initial Strength Test. That means that they have to do so many dead hang pull ups, (or stay in a flexed arm hang for so many seconds if they're a female,) they have to do so many crunches in 2 minutes, and they have to run a mile and a half in under a certain amount of time.

All that was great to know, but the IST is a cake walk next to what they'll really need to do in Boot Camp. There they have to pass many tests, including a "PFT" (Physical Fitness Test, take the IST and double it,) and a "CFT" (Combat Fitness Test.) So I thought, why bother with that IST stuff when it's less than what's really needed? Thank goodness JD thought the same way, and when he left to become a Marine he was a Beast! (At least I thought so!)

Yep, getting ready for Boot Camp was an experience to say the least. Every morning we went to the park so he could run like the wind! He often ran with a back pack weighted down with a 55 pound weight! That is until the bottom of his back pack started giving out. Then, when he knew he had the endurance, he really started focusing on his speed. I would drop him off in the park and drive to a mark 3 miles away with my stop watch in hand. Each week the run became easier for him as he became faster and stronger.

Don't think that timing him for his 3 mile got me off the hook! After he ran, we hiked for miles. Some days I thought he was going to be the death of me! I even ended up spraining a tendon in my foot! Oh, it may have stopped me from jogging, but it didn't stop me from hiking with him. To top it off, he worked out like the devil doing crunches, push-ups, and pull-ups, every night before he went to bed.

And the food! My goodness did he eat! Of course, he was careful about his diet, but the sheer quantity of food was amazing! Yes, at times I was not only certain that I would die trying to keep up with him, but that he was going to send me to the poor house as well. Of course, to be honest, I wouldn't change any of it for the world. We spent that spring and summer together, working, laughing, and enjoying life.

By the time his ship date came along JD was able to do 17 dead hang pull ups, well over 100 crunches in 2 minutes, and he could run 3 miles in 21.3 minutes. He had also memorized the 11 General Orders for a Sentry, The Marines Hymn, The Marine Rifle Creed, and the United States Marine Corps Core Values.

It wasn't easy, but he did it, and I was excited for him even though I knew the day would come and the United States Marine Corps would take my son away and make him their own. JD would spend

Thanksgiving, Christmas, New Year's, and his 20th birthday all on Parris Island.

On November 7, 2011, in a hotel lobby, I smiled and gave my son one last big hug. I told him I loved him and how proud I was of him. The last thing I said was, "You go kick some ass Baby, and I'll be there waiting when you're done." He had to go, so with that I turned around and walked out. Yes, I did look back, and yes, he did grin and wave. From there he would go to MEPS one last time and then get on a bus with all his new best buddies to Parris Island where they would be made into Marines.

I think I played my part well. Walking away from my son that day was the hardest thing I have ever done in my life. It felt like my heart had been grabbed by some unseen hand and was being ripped out through my throat. But I smiled and stood tall, for him. I made it about 2 miles down the road, pulled over at a rest stop, and cried. (This was interesting, because in all honesty, I can count the amount of times I have actually shed tears in my adult life on my hands and I still have a few fingers left over.) He never knew that, but I guess he does now. Fortunately I had my best friend Penny with me so it wasn't too bad and I was able to choke it back pretty quick.

Yeah, let me warn you right now. When your loved one goes off to become a Marine, you will know an amazing feeling of love and pride! But with it comes terrible feelings of loss, helplessness, and concern.

No one warned me about that last bit, but it's true across the board. It really is as if someone has taken your heart, ripped it right out of your chest, and given you the best gift ever all at the same time! Remember to do your future Marine a favor, never ever show them your pain. You could mess up their focus, and believe me when I say, "they need all the focus they can get!"

I found it's best to just hold on to the love and pride. The rest will ultimately take care of itself.

Receiving and Phase One

After the bus ride, all you can do for your Recruit is pray and write.

Write all the time!

I had been told by the Gunny at the recruiters' station that I would get one phone call from JD when he arrived at Parris Island, and hopefully one more phone call about 12 weeks later.

Apparently a good number of recruits get sick or injured during Phase One of training. Think of it this way, you have 60 young adults living in close quarters from all over the United States. All it takes is for one of them to show up with some creepy virus and they are sure to share it with at least a few of their new found friends. If that happens don't think the Marine Corps is just going to send them home. Nope, Marines don't give up. What they will do is everything humanly possible to get your recruit back in tip top shape. Of course, that means if your recruit needs any serious medical attention, their training will just have to wait for them to get better. It also means that they'll probably be calling you before that 12 week mark. So you see you really can bet your life that this is one of those times when NO NEWS IS GOOD NEWS.

Just so you know, that first phone call home isn't about chatting. Your recruit will call at whatever hour and they will yell as loud as they can that they have arrived safely and will be sending you a letter with their official address in 10 days or so. No worries, they're not alone! You'll hear a whole mess of people in the back ground doing the exact same thing. Fortunately, I knew what to expect in advance.

Had I thought about it, I would have left a special, "*I love you JD! No worries! You got this!*" message on our answering machine. Then he could have left me his extremely loud message, and I could have played it back time after time. Alas, I didn't think of that till it was too late.

As luck would have it, the Gunny also told me that I could get JD's address from them in about 3 days instead of waiting for the official letter home! Oh yes, you had better believe I was all over that! After all, between the first call and the last, it would be all about the letters.

I did even more research on Parris Island and the Marine Corps Boot Camp itself during those 3 days. I even found a "Training Matrix" online that let me know pretty much what the recruits would be doing every day. I must say, having that "Matrix" in my hot little hands made me feel at least a little more connected. It was indeed my very own Holy Grail! I highly suggest you get one. All you have to do is an internet search for "MCRD Parris Island" or "MCRD San Diego" and you'll find that they each have information for you regarding training, the different companies, and graduation.

It took less than a day for me to realize that I was obsessing. Work just wasn't enough to slow me down in my research. So, I also started going out and jogging on my own every morning. I gave myself a much needed goal. I already missed my son like crazy and I figured that if he had to suffer to be better and stronger, than I could too. (It didn't hurt that I also made a bet with my friend Kevin that I would be able to run an 8 minute mile by the time JD came home for his 10 day leave.)

Then, three long days after hugging JD goodbye I showed up at the recruiters' office. Sure enough, they looked up my son and gave me an address to write to! Just like that! No fuss, no muss. And I wrote....

****

Nov. 10, 2011

Hey JD!

  I've decided to type my letters because my hand writing would turn a 2 page letter into a 4 page letter and that could all get pretty bulky in the envelope....

  *I hope today was better for you than yesterday. Either way, it's a day done and a day closer to graduation! Yup, I'm just kind of guessing how things might be as you make your way through the obstacle courses, drills, and crazy pt sessions with people yelling at you guys all the time. I know your probably hating it right now, but I also know you're doing fine. Even if you're not quite sure, I am. **I am sure of you.***

  I bet you're really looking forward to getting hold of one of those pugil sticks for a little close combat and also getting out on that rifle range for a bit of distance demolition! Of course, I also suspect you're pretty tired and just about everything is sore. Trust me, things will get better. It's true, if it doesn't kill you it makes you stronger. The way I figure it, you were physically and mentally strong as anything when you got on the bus, so you'll be a super bad ass by graduation.

  And I will be in much better shape too! This is just day 3 of me going out to walk/jog in the mornings and my old legs are actually cussing at me! But hey, if you can't stop, than neither can I. What you're doing is much tougher than what I'm doing, but I'm old. All I have is my treachery. You still have youth and skill!

  Ok, Ok, I also have will power and more strength left in these old bones than I realized. It's amazing what you can do when you have a goal. That's right, like you, I have a goal, see I can't have you being all lean a mean without me being able to at least look like I can keep up. (And I don't want to look fat in all those pictures we'll be taking of us at your graduation with you in uniform!)

I'm excited for you JD! Think of Chesty Puller, and think of those guys out there, memorialized by the Iwo Jima Memorial! Those Marines and many more, have been legends in their own time!

I know it's Tough, but so are YOU!

You are going to be A United States Marine! The stuff that legends are made of Mister! Don't you dare second guess yourself and think, even for one second, that this might not have been the right choice. It was, and is right. And you will make it with flying colors. Yep, your body may scream at you to stop, but you have to ignore it. Pain is temporary, glory is forever. (And chicks dig scars.)

Speaking of chicks, your friend Kayla sent me a message asking for your address. I'll be hopping online to send it to her in a minute. And, per your request, I will also put it up on your Facebook page.

Oh! I almost forgot to tell you, I got your deposit made, your tags turned in, and your insurance canceled. So you have no worries here at all, and money in the bank if you need it.

I gotta say, I'm a little concerned that my letters may pile up on you, so, if that happens don't feel like you have to read them all at once. Take a look at the back right hand corner of the envelope, see that little "#1" there? Yup, Mom thinks of everything! So if you need to stash some for bad weather days or something it's all good, you will still be able to read them in order.

*Also remember, **I'm here for you.** Don't feel like you need to write me every day, I know your busy busting butt and learning a whole new lifestyle. Just a quick little note to let me know how you are once a week would be awesome! (Heck, honestly, if you write every day or once every other week, it all works for me.)*

Well, there's more to come tomorrow Son of Mine, so I'll end this here and let you get to enjoying the story.

I am so proud of you!!!!! Miss you, Love you, can't wait to see you in February!!

Semper Fi!

Love,

Mom

****

I should tell you here that before JD left, he and I had gone shopping for a book that he might like to read in Boot Camp. Recruits are only allowed to take a small address book and a small religious book with them. JD had his Bible, but to help give him a mental escape we decided that I would send him a few pages of "The Gunslinger" By Stephen King each day. It was a good choice, as the main character in the book is also doggedly persistent in his quest even though it's filled with all sorts of pitfalls and hardships.

Now, to understand my next letter it will help you to know that the day that JD left for Boot Camp almost didn't happen. Yup, a day before he was supposed to go SSgt. Ramos called and told my son that he was being "put on standby." It seems they didn't have enough space, or so they said, for him to be sure of shipping on his scheduled date. This came from headquarters, there was nothing that SSgt. Ramos could do. Sadly, all JD could do was go down to MEPS with the others that were "definitely shipping out" and hope 2 other people would blow it at the last minute. The odds weren't great, but it happens. Maybe someone would blow the drug test, break a toe, or get a last minute speeding ticket. It happens, but not often.

Regardless, you can only imagine how upset JD was with this new development. To me it was my first real experience with the phrase "Semper Gumby." My only goal at this point was to make it OK for JD no matter what happened. It wasn't an easy task. Here was this poor guy who had spent months getting physically and mentally prepared to go to Boot Camp! Heck, just a few days before he had made rounds saying his goodbyes to his friends and family. He even had to deal with his Grandmother crying at him! Just the thought of going through all that again every weekend until they "had room" was understandably agonizing.

 So we planned. And it was decided that if he didn't ship, and indeed returned home the next day, we would go to Gettysburg for a couple days. Not only to take in the amazing history there, but to do some ghost hunting as well! If he did ship the deal was we would try to go on his 10 days leave instead. See, ghost hunting equals adventure, and to my son there is nothing better than adventure. I almost had him hoping to return home! But, thankfully it didn't happen that way. Two people actually did blow it somehow, and JD left on his scheduled date.

******

November 11, 2011

Hi JD!

Another day down! Good job!

Don't forget to stretch out on your rack before you pass out at night. It'll help a little.

Ok, I thought about it, and I don't want to just make your mailing address public 'cause I want to be sure no idiot sends you something stupid. So! I have sent Kayla and Chris the address. I also posted on your Facebook that if anyone wanted to write you that they could message me and I'll give it to them through private message. That way I can tell them the rules about sending stuff, and I can check them out to make sure they are not an idiot.

I looked into some of the hotels in Gettysburg, the rates are still pretty cheap in February. So, you'll have to think about it and let me know if you want to go right after you get home or a few days before your leave is up. Cool?

Hey! I got a joke for you....

At the end of the night an old half blind Marine leaves a bar pretty drunk.

Outside he sees a nun. He walks over to her and slaps her in the face. Then he punches her in the stomach and knocks her over.

He proceeds to kick her several times and when he's done he bends down to her and says, "Not as tough as a Marine, are you Batman?"

Bahahahahahahahahaha!!!!!!!! Ok.. That was just WRONG!!! Hahahaha!!!!

Poor old Gary was laughing so hard he could barely finish telling me that joke!

I know it's terrible, but funny none the less. Gary told me a few more jokes that I should relay to you, but he was laughing too much for me to catch all of them. So he's going to email them to me. I'm sure you'll enjoy them as much as we did.

He also told me that it should be ok for me to send you certain things, like mole skin to help you avoid/heal blisters. Please let me know if I can send you some, and I'll get it in the mail ASAP. Yup, He is really excited and 100% positive that he will be at your graduation. (I'm telling you, Gary's almost as proud of you as I am!)

Neighbor Ralph asked me today if he'd be allowed to go too, for some reason he was thinking only immediate family could go to your graduation. I told him I was sure he could go too, but he has to get his own hotel room! Then I let him know that it would be sometime in January before I had all the details. He was cool with that and told me about what a good guy you are.... As if I didn't already know.

(Yes, I was indeed bragging about you to Creepy Neighbor Ralph too... I'm not crazy, I'm just plain proud.)

You know, this is probably the hardest thing you have ever done or ever will do, but when it's over, you will be a Marine and extremely proud of what you've accomplished. ('Course, I have always been extremely proud of you.) After this, nothing will ever be "more than you can handle" because after this the rest will be cake! Your future is not only financially ok, but it's going to be jam packed with excitement and adventure! That's freaking EXCELLENT!!!

I sure do miss you! But my incessant bragging along with my crazed workout regime is keeping me pretty busy. Yeah, sooner than we think it will be February!!! In the meantime, you just keep going JD! (Btw, my calves hate me! But I'm doing it! In the last 4 days I have lost 1.5 pounds!!!! Oh Yeah! I got this!)

Enjoy the story. I LOVE YOU!!!!!

Love, Mom

*****

** My friend Gary is also a Marine. At the time JD went to Boot Camp Gary was in "The Sand Box". Fortunately his deployment would be over and he would be back in the States before JD would graduate.

*****

Wondering what the rules in regards to sending stuff are?

 Easy, don't send anything other than regular letters or cards unless your recruit has specifically written you and asked for something different. Try to stick with plain white envelopes, later if they have asked you to send them anything like protein bars or new insoles for their boots, I found that the Flat Rate boxes at the post office are the best way to go. If you do send cards **do not send the ones that make noise.** Also, stay away from any card with glitter, you really don't want your recruit to sparkle.

Do not send anything with postage due or with a signature required.

 Never write messages or anything other than addresses on the outside of the envelopes. Remember, every night they do mail call, and it's the DI who passes out the mail, he or she has the right to read the outside of the envelope as it really is open to the public. *(Note: I did number the letters I sent JD with very small print on the lower right hand corner of the back of the envelopes and this did not cause any problems. I'm sure the DIs have seen this before and understand the idea behind such a practice.)*

For wives and girlfriends: Do NOT perfume or put a SWAK on any letters!! This will surely cause your recruit serious issues and make his already hard life quite a bit harder. Put your SWAK on the actual letter inside. That way you can be certain that it's his and his alone to enjoy.

*****

Ahh... Another tiny tid-bit of history... Just 6 months before JD left for Boot Camp our house had caught on fire from an extension cord in the basement. No one was hurt, but the basement was gutted and everything in the rest of the house was covered in soot. To give you an idea of how nasty the fire was, even though it was contained to the basement, the mini blinds on our third floor windows were actually melted!

Needless to say, the whole house had to be stripped down to the stud walls and rebuilt. Thank goodness for insurance! Alas, Servpro didn't do a good job on most of our stuff. That is except for the one piece that had been on the opposite side of the wall where the fire started. Strangely, that was the one piece that came back beautiful! Go figure, they had sent it out to a restoration specialist.

Due to the fire we spent 5 months crammed in a tiny apartment. Luckily JD had his last month home to enjoy his own bedroom along with all his new furniture before he left.

******

November 12, 2011

Hello Baby!!! It's me again! Da Momma!

Hell yes! Another day done! Another day closer to your goal!

I got your tax bill from the county for your truck yesterday. It's a whopping $13!!! Hahaha! No sweat, I'm going to go pay it off on Monday.

I talked to Aunt Mary and she is just thrilled to know you're going to be a Marine! She says they have the best looking uniforms out of all the services. Then she said, "He better watch out for all the girls, as handsome as he is, and then in that uniform! My goodness! He's going to have to beat them girls off with a stick!" Yes, she actually said that! It's true, you may have to get a stick...but to hear sweet little Auntie Mary say it!?!?! Good Lord! I couldn't breathe I was laughing so hard. Then she asked me what was so funny, she was being serious....and that just made me laugh more. She's too cute. Ya gotta love her.

Ok, get this, Servpro brought back that dresser that was in the basement, man I tell ya what, that thing looks brand new! But, believe it or not, they actually wanted me to sign a paper saying that I was satisfied with their work on all the furniture! Hahaha! I scratched out the words "completely satisfied" and replaced them with "not at all satisfied". That guy Ted apologized, but he looked like a dear in the head lights when I did that! It was awesome! I wish you had been here to laugh at him with me.

I timed myself this morning on a mile walk/jog... I'm almost embarrassed to say that it took me 17.2 minutes... But hey, it'll get better. I'm sure it took me longer on Monday than it did today. At least I'm jogging the entire half mile. (I walk the first half at a decent clip, and then I jog all the way for the 2nd half. It's actually a lot more than I thought I could do without someone chasing me.)

I'm really looking forward to your first letter home. Tomorrow I'm going to add some preprinted address labels in your letter. That way you can just stick it on there instead of writing it all out. I'll make a few with my address and a few with yours. If you want more with other addresses on them just let me know. I can send you stamps too if ya need them. All I need is the go ahead from you.

Don't let them fool you! You are doing GREAT! Believe me, no one knows you like I do, and that's why no one is more sure or proud of you than I am. Every day done is a day closer to you getting your pin and me being able to tell everyone MY SON IS A MARINE! (And you know how I love bragging about you!)

Damn Skippy Mister!

Hang in there! I know you got this. Just keep going. Sleep and eat as well as you can when you can. And be sure to go to church. When you come home you'll have an awesome dinner and your nice comfy bed waiting for you.

I'll write more tomorrow. I LOVE YOU!!!!

I hope you're enjoying the story.

Love,

Mom

****

My son had already been gone almost a week, and I still wasn't used to the empty space. I knew it was too early to expect a letter from him, but I stalked the mail man regardless. I needed something, anything, to let me know JD was assimilating at least fairly well into his new life. It was already getting tough to write. I searched for something to say in my one sided correspondence.

****

November 13, 2011

Hi JD!

I hope all is going well and that you are kicking ass! Yeah, kicking ass always means someone is trying to kick you back, but you're tough, you can take a hit and keep fighting. After all, you got Mountain Man Smith blood in you! That makes you; tough, smart, a little bit on the crazy side, and damn proud of it too!

Before I forget, I think I forgot to write a 3 on the back of yesterday's letter! So, once you get it, (you should already have it) if you have the chance, you might want to put a #3 on the back. Just to keep them in order.

I'm trying to figure out how long it takes my letters to get to you. I talked to a lady in Kohl's today whose son went to Parris Island about 2 years ago and she said that the mail took anywhere from 5 to 7 days to get from here to there... If that lady was right you could be in, or very close to, your 3rd week already! Holy smokes! That would be awesome! Of course, I'd hate to think the postal service is that slow. I hope my letters are only taking a couple days. Still, that would mean you're at least half way thru your second week! That's Sweet!!!! Every day done is a day closer to the finish line and your graduation!!!!!

Speaking of the postal service... Just a heads up, I am putting a letter in the mail every day, (even on Sundays!) but with the holidays coming up I kind of expect the postal service to get slower until after the first of the year. Don't be surprised if you get 2 letters one day and somewhere during that week one runs behind. Just try to read them in order so you don't miss part of the story.

Now! On to the amusement of the day...

Ok! I saw an ad online for a new laundry service…. It read:

Magic Dry Cleaner & Laundry Service.

We won't tear your clothing with machinery. We do it carefully by hand!

(All I could think was…. How kind of them to destroy people's clothes by hand! I'm sure it's pretty expensive to get such a wonderful service! It must be hard work…)

I know today's letter is short, I promise tomorrow's will be better!

Get as much rest as you can JD! I'll write more tomorrow. Till then, I wonder if you're sharing the story with any of the other recruits??? Have a good day tomorrow!!!! I Love You!!! Semper Fi!

Love,

Mom

November 14, 2011

Hey JD!

I'm writing this 7 days after you left here Son, That's freaking awesome week 1 is done!!!

If this letter really takes 7 days to get to you from me, You are at the beginning of Week 3!!

The shell shock is past, Time is flying by so fast!

Oh I know it still sucks, In week 4 you'll all start swimming like ducks.

Week 5 will be a gas, You will find that test easy to pass.

<u>And week 6 and 7 will be delightful, Yes, you'll be out shooting your M16 A4 service rifle!</u>

Hahaha!! Ok, no one ever said I was a poet! But I think I should at least get an E for effort!

I went to the eye doc today. Apparently I was right on the money all those years I guessed at my script! I was literally right on!! I laughed, the doc said my eyes were so healthy that there is no way I wear my contacts all the time. But I assured him that I do indeed eat, breathe, and sleep with them firmly in place.

I went jog/walking with Beth this morning again. She makes me feel good, I'm faster and stronger than she is. Before I thought I was the queen of excuses, but she has me beat in that category big time. Today she hardly wanted to walk because she "didn't eat a big enough breakfast." Hahaha!!! Right! Seems to me that a BIG breakfast would slow ya down more than a lite one would. Perhaps she's not crazy at all, but some kind of different life form that just looks like a human?

I got your phone and the charger from the recruiter's office today safe and sound. Its battery is deader than dead, so I stuck it on the charger. After it's completely charged I'll take the battery out and set them both on your dresser so the phone should be ready to go when you come home. (If I just left it charging the battery would be trash within a few weeks...)

So, all is still well here. I am making head way with my diet and pt, and soon I should be smoke free! Yup, next week people will suffer here too... On Friday the 18th, (that's when I go to the doc) I'm going to start taking Chantix to quit smoking. I can't wait to see who accidentally pisses me off!! I'm kind of excited to see what kind of hateful things I can get away with and then blame on a lack of nicotine. I'll be sure to let ya know how it goes. Hahaha!!!!

SO! How are you? Hanging in there, I'm sure. A few aches and pains can't stop my boy Damn it! You're top notch warrior material! I know it and so do you!

No sweat Mister, to save you from any more trauma, I'll try to stay away from writing more poetry... That one really sucked! Talk at ya tomorrow! Sleep well! And keep in mind that you're going to be one of the best Marines the Corps has ever had!

Love, Mom

*****

Life was moving on and I still wasn't sure if JD had even received my first letter. It was killing me! But between reading everything I could find on the Marine Corps, working out, and the friends and family I still had at home, so far I had managed to find something new to write about. But, I worried that soon my letters would turn into nothing more than "Keep Going" chants that would do nothing other than numb JD's brain even more than it already had been. So along with whatever news of the day I might have, I decided that I should send him some pictures and maybe start looking for some jokes online or something to brighten his day.

*****

November 15, 2011

Hey Baby!
It's another day done!!!
I paid off your tax bill (all $13 of it) today. I also got the confirmation letter from your car insurance that they did indeed stop billing you and should be sending you some kind of refund.
If that shows up before you get back I'll just write "for deposit only" on the back and put it back in your account for you.

I got a good laugh at Tom today. Seems he has himself a stalker!!!! Some really, really, crazy chick he was nice too has decided that he is her soul mate! He said he left his phone at the fire station on accident this morning and when he got back there were 72 text messages on the phone from HER!! She wrote him a freaking novel! He read one of the texts to me, it was hilarious! She is talking about how much she loves him and how once they are married he won't be allowed to ignore her texts anymore!!!! Hahaha!!! Best part is that he hasn't even gone out on a date with this girl, he literally just met her! Yup, it gets worse, she's friends with one of his friends. So she knows exactly how to find him! I couldn't help but laugh when he said... "Ya try to be nice to a creepy chick and the next thing ya know SHE's telling you, 'it puts the lotion on its skin'." Hahaha!!! Poor Tom... Hahaha!!!!!

As you can see, I printed up a picture for you so you don't forget what your Momma looks like! I like to think it's a good "You got this, now go get 'em Son" picture. Now that I've got color ink for the printer, let me know who you want pictures of and if at all possible I will ambush them and take a picture to send you. (I also printed the picture of you wearing Audry's sunglasses and looking like a crazed rock star. But that's for ME. I doubt you really want a copy of that there anyway!)

Jake has been mentioning going back to school! Yay!!!! Tomorrow I'm going to Strayer to order an official copy of his transcripts. I'm trying to talk him into going to the Community College so he can get more social interaction. But even if he goes to some place like Phoenix, I'll be happy.

It's so funny, he seems to think that I need him to basically live at home forever! Silly boy! One day I plan on living in my RV and visiting you, your sister, and your brother wherever you all may be! Of course, if you're in Europe, Africa, or some other uber cool place! Then I'll just have to park my RV and fly on over for my visit.

Ya know, you've given me the ability and the right to brag at everyone I see about you! And soon you'll also be the guy that gives his Mom a great reason to really TRAVEL!!!! THAT IS FLIPPING EXCELLENT!!! Hey, in case you haven't figured it out yet... I'm super proud of you!!!! And I'm super excited for you all at the same time!!! Crazy huh?

Sleep Well Son! I hope to hear from you soon!

Love, Mom

Got time for the Joke of the Day?

At school, a boy is told by a classmate that most adults are hiding at least one dark secret, and that this makes it very easy to blackmail them by saying, "I know the whole truth" even when you don't know anything. The boy decides to go home and try it out. As he is greeted by his mother at the front door he says, "I know the whole truth." His mother quickly hands him $20 and says, "Just don't tell your father."
Quite pleased, the boy waits for his father to get home from work, and greets him with, "I know the whole truth." The father promptly hands him $40 and says, "Please don't say a word to your mother."
Very pleased, the boy is on his way to school the next day, when he sees the mailman at his front door. The boy greets him by saying, "I know the whole truth."
The mailman drops the mail, opens his arms and says, "Then come give your FATHER a big hug!"

Oops!! OH NO!!!! Heh heh heh!!! **<u>I love you!!! No Worries! You're doing GREAT!! I Promise!!!</u>**

****

Friends and family are always good things to write about. Unless it's bad news, it's my humble opinion that bad news should never be given to a recruit trying to make their way through Boot Camp. After all, what can they do? Stop training and come home? If they did that it would almost guarantee that their dream of becoming a United States Marine would be lost forever. I suspect that not many Marines would tell you that they'd be happy to go back to Boot Camp again as a recruit. I believe it lacks the warm fuzzy feeling of home. Yeah, I'm sure pretty much any sane person given the choice after getting a good taste of what's really behind door #2, wouldn't open that door again if they didn't have too.

So I was quick to write JD with our friend Tom's stalker news because it cracked me up. And quick to tell him that his brother Jake was planning on going back to college because that was seriously good news! But I did NOT tell him that his Step-Dad, Brad, was going to need back surgery due to being rear-ended hard enough to total our Ford F150 pickup. Yep, I was a bit stressed, but it was MY stress, not JD's. So call me greedy, I don't care, I kept my stress all to myself, and I liked it that way.

See, even though JD and Brad had never really gotten along, the thought of a surgery like that would still have worried my son. And my whole goal here was to keep him updated, make him smile, and let him know I was right here for him cheering him on. Not to drive him crazy with concern over things he could have no control over even if he had been home and not on Parris Island battling sand fleas! Makes sense to me.

Oh, and just so you know, Audrey is my little 5 year old Granddaughter. Yes, that picture of JD wearing her little girl sunglasses still makes me laugh to this day!

****

31

November 16, 2011

Hi Baby!

Today I ran that half mile a little easier! I don't know if I'm getting any faster, but I'm not huffing a puffing as much. I know, you're probably laughing at me, but be easy on your old Mom! I think I'm making good head way seeing as it's only been a week! Hell yeah!! I'm gonna be almost as lean and mean as you!! (Kinda... But not really... Ya know, I'll be lean and mean in an old lady kinda way.)

I sure do miss you, it's strange being without my sidekick! But I'm cool, and I'm crazy excited to see you in your new uniform and to call you Marine!!!!
As of today I still haven't got your address card! I'm not sure when it actually got sent, but it's all good as long as you're getting my letters and enjoying the jokes and the story.

(And eating and sleeping as much as you can! I know you're working hard, so every moment you get to take care of yourself you need to use to its fullest!!!) *Eh, I know you already know all that... But you also know that I can't help it... After all, I'm da Momma!*

So get this! When you get back you gotta see this video Tom caught at the station! Well, he didn't really catch it, they put up security cameras to hopefully see who's been stealing stuff off the units. But what they got is just so much cooler! In the video Tom's dog Dakota is barking at the door by the bays to be let in when suddenly the door just swings opens for the dog!!! You can see both sides of the door on 2 different cameras and there is no one there!!!! When the door opens Dakota jumps back then stands there for a second as if she's looking at someone. After about 20 seconds she just walks on in!!! It's freaking cool!!!

At least whatever kind of ghostie they got, the dog is obviously ok with it. I hope they catch more crazy stuff now that they got the cameras, but ya gotta see this one! I told Tom to save it for you!

Hey, I think they should call some of those ghost hunting guys on TV! I bet that would make the station a pretty popular place! Then they could charge all the other would be ghost hunters to come investigate!!! Hahaha!
Not us though! We're members, so we get to investigate for free! Yup, or else I'll take away the karaoke!!

I love you!!! I'll write more tomorrow!!!

Love,

Mom

******

The video showing Dakota and the magic self-opening door is really pretty interesting. The fire house where it was taken has been rumored to be haunted for years. Of course they didn't put in the security cameras for ghost hunting purposes. Sadly there are dishonest people everywhere. The good news is that the video surveillance system has not only caught a good deal of strange occurrences, there have also been no more thefts reported.

Joy of all Joy! On the evening of the 16th I got my first letter from JD! It was only the form letter telling me his official address, which was slightly different than the one I got from the recruiter, along with his graduation date and the rules on mail. But JD was kind enough to write me a little message at the bottom of the letter!

What he wrote was: *"Love. JD –P.S. Send stamps, a picture, and LOTS of letters. I hate it here… OooRah!"*

*****

November 17, 2011

Hi JD!!

Yay!!! I got your letter!!

I hope you got my 2nd card with the updated return address labels and the stamps. At first I was all ticked off thinking that the recruiter gave me the wrong address for you. But he swears you're getting those first 6 letters. I don't know how much I believe him, so you let me know. I have all of them saved on the computer, so I can reprint them easily along with the story and send them all at once if need be.

It is freaking pouring down rain here! I've been keeping an eye on the basement and so far so good. It's crazy how much I despise heavy rain now! I need to go back to my Cherokee Roots and learn some kind of anti-rain dance. Yeah, if there was such a thing you better believe my happy ass would be out there right now just dancing away!

The only really cool thing about today was your letter. Other than that, since I couldn't go jog in the rain, I went out to the little gym at Wilderness. I realize though that I really like being outside more than being on a treadmill.

BTW, I love that you wrote Ooorah! After "I hate it here" at the bottom of the letter. It told me basically, "Yes Mom, I hate it here, but I'm ok and know this is where I need to be to become a Marine, so I can take it!" I smiled like a bird fed cat when I read that. Thank you JD, you made my day.

Looking at your postmark I'm guessing the mail takes about 5 days to get to you. So today should be like November 21st. That means you are just starting week 3! I really hope you got my other letters and enjoyed my poetry. Hahaha! (Yeah, it sucked, but it was well thought out I assure you.)

Thanksgiving is around the corner and your sister is demanding I make a turkey! I think that baby she's growing is making her super crazy! I figured I'd just make a turkey breast and maybe 2 legs, it's cheaper that way and there are only 3 of us here at the moment so why make a big ole bird? But NO! Even though she is making her own turkey she is still demanding leftovers from me!!!! I haven't told her yet that I'm not making a cheesecake either... She's a little too scary.

I figure I'll let her accept the lack of left overs (I mean, I'm sure there will be some, just not as much as she demands.) Then, at the last minute I'll tell her there will be no cheesecake until February when we will thoroughly celebrate all the holidays at once along with your birthday and your freaking awesome achievement! See I got this all figured out, she just needs to get off the crazy prego train!

Seriously, she'll be fine. She was pretty dang happy when I told her I was going to pay for their hotel room when you graduate. So that alone should get me off the turkey/ cheesecake hook.

Oh! Someone told your Nana about the walls and towers that you have to repel off of and she called me all concerned! I'm sorry, I laughed and told her I was pretty sure there was still a shoe print on the side of the house outside your old bedroom window. I have no worries about the tasks at hand because you've already done that out of a third story window with make shift equipment. (Yeah, those poor bed sheets.) At least now you've got the good stuff to climb with! She was a bit shocked to find out you had climbed out that window before, but not too shocked. And what's even funnier was how happy she was to know it! It was like I told her, "It's all good, JD has already been there, done that, and got a degree."

Well Son, I know you're probably getting tired of hearing it, (reading it) but I'm damn proud of you! You just keep going after your goal no matter what it takes and you'll have it sooner than you think. There is nothing that can stop you. THAT'S A FACT I KNOW! You are going to be a top notch U.S. Marine!

Don't forget! Every chance you get, sleep, eat, and go to church. And remember, I love you!!!

Oh! And enjoy the story.

Love,

Mom

*****

Yup, getting just that little line of correspondence from my son made my day!!

And yes, on multiple occasions as a teenager JD had snuck out of his third story bedroom window using nothing but knotted bed sheets like a prisoner making a jail break! I had seen the boot prints on the side of the house one day and a few weeks later actually watched him make an escape! I knew he was just going to hang out with his friends to go fishing, so I didn't say a word until the next day. Honestly, I'm not 100% positive, but I think after that he realized that the front door was easier than the window.

Don't get me wrong, JD was a good kid. No drugs, no gangs, no pregnant girlfriend. But no kid is perfect, and if the worst he was going to do was some night fishing with his buddies, well I was good with that.

*****

November 18, 2011

Howdy JD!

You got another day done! THAT'S EXCELLENT!!!

They say everyone in Boot Camp gets sick, the question is how sick? I'm really hoping that the worst thing you might get is a stuffy head. Of course, I'd prefer you not get sick at all! That's why I keep going on about eating and sleeping as much as you have time for. You were never bombarded with a mess of antibiotics so you have a great immune system. Ya just gotta do what you can to keep it fed and ready to fight. GOOD NEWS! The basement stayed dry over night! YAY! Another pain in the ass avoided.

I looked up your school because I was trying to remember exactly where it was. Now, I'm not 100% sure that the list I found is correct, but if it is... You're going to an Air Force Base to train!! Oh Man!! That will be like going to a resort after Boot Camp and then MCT! You better not get spoiled though, because as soon as you're done it's back to the Marine Corps barracks for you Mister!

Wow! In less than a year you will have stayed in no less than 3 different states! (And of course where ever your duty station is!!!) You know I like travel, so I'm jealous!!! Watch you get some paradise type place like Hawaii or something. Oh no matter! I'll be visiting you. I hear Egypt is nice in the fall as well.

Ok, wanna laugh? I busted my ass this morning 'cause I'm a super genius and went out jogging (downhill) on wet leaves! And wouldn't ya know it, I slipped. I was all sprawled out like a TV murder victim! All that was missing was the chalk outline... No worries, I'm fine, the leaves cushioned my fall. All I hurt was my pride. I kid you not, there were 4 freaking squirrels just standing there staring at me! I'm sure that's their way of pointing and laughing! (Even I had to laugh at myself.) Good thing I didn't have any donuts! Little bastards probably would've tried to rob me if I had!

(Hmmm... Jogging with donuts??? Nah... That would be kind of counterproductive...)

You'll be proud of me though! Even after such a pride crushing blow, I got up, brushed myself off, and continued my jog/walk giggling the rest of the way instead of pouting my way back to the car.

I miss my workout buddy!!! Of course I couldn't even come close to keeping up with your current workouts! Semper Fi!!!

Love, Mom

Ok! The Joke of the day is.....

As a drunk guy staggers out of the bar one Friday evening, a fire engine races past, siren wailing and lights flashing.

Immediately, the drunk starts chasing the engine, running as fast as he can until eventually he collapses, gasping for breath.

In a last act of desperation he shouts after the fire engine, "If that's the way you want it, you can keep your bloody ice creams!"

(Bahahahaha!!!! I think I've seen that guy!!!!)

November 19, 2011

Hey Baby!

I doubt you'll get much mail this week because of the holiday so I am super stuffing this envelope with extra reading material! Of course, I'm still writing every day as well, just covering the bases.

I made Beth walk 6 miles today! She was a little disgruntled, but in the end she was pretty pleased with herself for trudging on! I was pleased with her too. All her begging to turn around was ignored until I reached the 3 mile mark. Then I was kind and asked her if she wanted to rest a minute before starting back. She took 5 and then whined at me all the way back until we could see the car again. After that she was all smiles again! I guess 6 miles in one shot was the furthest she had ever knowingly walked... Kinda crazy... But she was raised in the city so she's used to catching the bus.

(Besides, I got a bruise on my butt from yesterday's graceful slip on the leaves! There was no way I was gonna let her make me wimp out if the dang boo-boo on my behind couldn't stop me!)

Again we go back to the idea that if you can't stop, well neither can I!

I went today to see about getting the Chantix to help me quit my nasty habit... But the doc said with my history I can't take the stuff... I guess it could cause me to have hallucinations and I might kill Brad or some shit like that. So he told me to try cold turkey and gave me the number for some crazy support group. I'm just gonna do it cold turkey. I don't plan on joining "quitters anonymous" or whatever they call themselves... I'm not saying those groups aren't a good thing, they're just not Mom's thing...

So tomorrow is the big day, wanna bet on how long it takes me to flip out on Brad anyway? (Hallucinations or not, I think he's still going to be in danger.)

No worries, while my letters may become more sinister for a few days, I promise, I will keep my evil plotting upbeat and fun! (What am I saying? Evil plotting is always fun!!!)

Your brother asked me today what my plan for Thanksgiving was. Funny, he was cool with eating out, but got a bit defensive when I said I'm not making that dang cheesecake! After I explained my weight loss goals and how I didn't want the temptation, he was better, but still trying to guilt me into making it!!! He even pulled MY Mom into it!!! But, I assured him, if it upsets Nanny I'm sure she too will forgive me. He had to agree and finally gave up. Thank goodness he quit when he did!!! He almost had me convinced!!!

I hope you're having a good week JD! And that they feed you guys an extra nice meal on Thursday. Lord knows you all deserve it. Never the less, remember; eat, sleep, church! And the rest will fly by! There is nothing there that you can't handle! Plus you got a great cheering section right here waiting for you to graduate and come on home to PARTY!

Love,

Mom

*****

A smoking habit isn't easy to break. But I knew it would do me worlds of good and make my fitness goals all the more achievable. Plus it would make me suffer! And for some reason that I still can't explain, I wanted to suffer. I guess knowing that my son was changing everything about his life in one big swoop made me feel like I should make changes too, no matter how tough they may be. Oh but it was going to be much harder for me than you might think. Not only because we are talking about a habit I'd had for over 20 years, but also because my husband Brad was a smoker as well. And he had no plan whatsoever to quit any time soon.

My only saving grace was the fact that we do not allow anyone, including ourselves, to smoke in the house. Had that not been the case, I am certain I would never have made it past the first day!

That evening I got my first real letter from JD! I can't even express the emotions I felt just holding that envelope! I imagine it might be the same way one might feel if they were holding a winning lottery ticket! I opened that envelope and found 3 letters for the price of one!

*****

Hey Mom,

It's a living Hell here but your letters give me strength. Sometimes I go so insane that I contemplate "accidently tripping" and giving myself a concussion or some heinous shit to get off this Island... I finally got to read some of the letters you sent. (It's the 15th I think.) Tell Jackie I said thank you for the letter. Please contact Kayla and let her know that I want her to write.

I need all the help I can get because I'm losing my mind... Pray for my soul and pray for my sins. I've got a job to do now. I'll be back when it finally ends.

I miss you more than ever.

Love, JD

Hey Mom

I don't know when I'll be able to send this… But I've received all of your letters up to the 15th that you've sent. It takes about 3 days or so for me to get them. The rest of my platoon is jealous of me because I'm 1 out of 2 that get so many letters!

It's a real mind fuck here, but with every day that passes it gets a little better. Today was the first "fun-ish" day I've had. MCMAP is fun.

SSgt Smith is a great DI, very motivational… The other 2 aren't so nice… Tomorrow is bayonet course.

Thank you for all the letters. They have given me A LOT of strength and will to carry on. I want as many letters as I can get.

Love, JD

P.S. Tell SSgt. Ramos that all is going well. I'm gonna use your address for all my letters if you don't mind… OH! And send the mole skin PLEASE!!

You're proud of me I hope. I'm proud I've made it this far.

Please send me Kayla's, Dad's, Jackie's, and Nana's addresses on the sticky things.

Thank you soooo much! - More letters on the way - Love, JD

Mom,

The biggest part I hate about Boot Camp is..... Well.... Everything for the most part.... Except sleeping....

I miss all of you.. Hell I even miss Brad! Hahaha!!

Just killin' free time writing this short letter.

I miss and love you all. I'll be happy to see you all in 11 or so weeks.

Love, JD

P.S. IT-ing is starting to get casual.... Send more letters! Gimme motivation!!

****

You'll know SSgt. Ramos better as JD's recruiter. When I caught up to give him JD's message he wasn't surprised at all. He was just a little sad that JD hadn't had the time to write him directly. It was kind of cute the way he too took pride in my son.

IT-ing is more or less punishment. It stands for "Intense Training" and what it means is basically getting forced to exercise fast and furiously, usually in a sand pit. Every Recruit gets "IT'd" at some point on Parris Island.

****

November 20, 2011

Hey JD!

I got your letters from the 15th today!!!! Yay! I know Boot sucks ass, but I'm so glad the IT-ing is getting more casual, I'm sure it won't end for a few more weeks, if at all, but casual is manageable. And I am super happy you have at least 1 good motivational DI! (I think it's the job of the other 2 to be butt heads. Maybe they're not so bad when they're not at work. Ya know, like the guy that's fun to go out drinking with but ya can't stand him when his wife is around.)
I knew you would like MCMAP! I bet you kicked ass!!!
I hope the bayonet course went well, I bet it was kinda fun too.

You want motivation!?! I got you covered! Let me tell you what I know....
I am insanely proud of you and everything you do! You are going to be one of the best damn Marines the Corps has ever known! I am positive! There are such amazing adventures in front of you and this is just the part of the road with all the pot holes! There's a reason it's so rough and it's the only way to go. See, after you clear this, the rest will be smooth sailing for you. You won't even notice any bumps that might try to get in your way! This ain't anything to you! You are tough, smart, and courageous! And that is a freaking FACT! I could prove it many times over with many examples of things you've done or dealt with in the past... But that would be a long ass list. So, simply put, to me you are a hero! And you can do anything you set your mind to do no matter what obstacles try to get in your way! You got this JD! Ain't no doubt about it!

I have an ingenious idea! I'm sending you some note cards with pre-addressed and stamped envelopes! That way all ya gotta do is write a line or two, sign 'em and stuff 'em in the envelopes! No fuss no muss! I actually tried to get them in the mail earlier, along with the mole skin and some more address labels. But I didn't make it in time. So I'll have to send it Monday morning 'cause the package needs to be weighed for the right postage. Maybe you'll get it with this letter! I can hope.

(See I write you every night, then I print and mail it all the next morning. So, while this letter will be dated Nov. 20, I'm actually writing it the night of the 19th. And yes, even though tomorrow is Sunday, I am still sending you your letter! If writing to you and praying for you is all I can do to help you, well, I am going to do it! I got your back!)

On a super scary note... I went up to Gary's house today...
Wow! God love him, or should I say, "bless his heart," that place is a mess! I told him not to buy a house on the side of a mountain! Much less one that was almost 45 years old!!! Let's just say he has a shit ton of work to do on that place when he gets back... Poor old Gary...
* Hey! I have been smoke free for 20 hours!!! I've been fiending all day!!!! I'll see if it helps my jog tomorrow morning. Somehow I think it's actually going to slow me down for a while. But at least I don't have that creepy "just quit smoking" cough. Not yet... We'll see. So far so good!*

Oh! In case you forgot,
I AM INCREDIBLY PROUD OF YOU!!!!!! I LOVE YOU!!! SEE YOU SOON!!!

Love,

Mom

****

It makes it so much easier to write when you've got a better idea of what the person you're writing to needs to hear. I was, and still am, incredibly proud of my son. And with his last letter he let me know that I was helping him some just by letting him know of that pride. I thought that was freaking awesome, even if it had to be from a distance.

*****

November 21, 2011

Hi JD!

Another day done!!!!
Another day closer to your graduation and to me changing my bragging from, My Son JD is Going to be a Marine and is busting his butt on Parris Island right now! To... My Son JD IS A UNITED STATES MARINE! (Of course all my bragging starts and ends with me talking about how hard you've worked, and how awesome you are, and of course how proud I am of you! Those parts will never change!)

Yep, the lack of ciggs is taking its toll... For now... Of course, this too shall pass I'm sure. Every time I started jogging today I was racked with wretched coughing fits! So I decided that I would just walk the 6 miles as fast as I could. That worked out just fine! I did the 6 in 1.5 hours, so I was pretty steady at a 4 mile an hour walk. Not too shabby for my old short legs! I figure in a few days the cough will go away and I'll be back to jog/walks with no problem!
It's funny how everyone seems to be avoiding me today. I'm certain they are terrified, but other than one little snap at Brad, I think I have been pretty decent. Eh, I'm glad they're scared! It gives me the advantage.

I've been watching you-tube! Those pugil sticks look like a blast! You'll be playing with those too soon I think! Sweet!!! That looks like a good opportunity to get real aggressive and take out some pent up hostility! I like releasing pent up hostility. That kinda shit makes me happy. I know it makes you happy too!! It's in your genes!!! That's them there Native American Warrior Genes! (Yup, your Grandpa loved that kind stuff too.) Sometimes ya just gotta smack the crap outta something and the whole week seems so much brighter!

I talked to Gary this evening! He said he's going to put pen to paper tomorrow and write you! He's excited for you and wanted me to tell you that "by week 6 the shit actually gets to be pretty damn fun"

He also said the redundant stuff that you guys have to do is all about making you guys detail oriented. Apparently the devil really is in the details. Needless to say, he is extremely happy and proud of you. I'd say he's almost as proud as me! (Almost, I don't think anyone could be just as proud of you as I am!)

Jackie says you're welcome for the card and she's gonna send you more soon. Oh! And I gave James your address, he plans to write you too! I contacted Kayla, and she says she's writing you too, oh and your friend Jessie. (I think she is still trying to get in shape and you're kinda like her fitness inspiration, but not in a creepy way. She just seems to really look up to you. Ain't anything wrong with that! I think you make an excellent role model!)

I love you and miss you! I can't wait to see you in February! I hope you have (or had) a good Thanksgiving!! Like I said, I'm not cooking, so at least 1 turkey is saved from my "seasoned buttering." Or should I say from my abuse??? Hmmm...

Get some good sleep tonight JD! Don't forget to stretch a bit.

I hope you're enjoying the story, the next book is even better! If you get thru this book and like it, I'll start sending the next in the series.

Love, Mom

****

James has been one of JD's best friends literally since birth. While JD is a Marine now, James is still living at home and in college. (Just like JD's older brother Jake.) I have to say, it's interesting to see how two guys so alike could grow up and take such different paths and still be so supportive of each other. After I gave James the address he wrote JD at least every other week. If you think about it, that's pretty damn impressive coming from a 20 year old guy. JD's own father didn't write him that much...

As for me "abusing" a turkey…. Well, I'm one of those strange people who enjoy cooking and more or less playing with the food during preparation. I do things like hold the bird up and pretend like its dancing and then I'll get a bit belligerent and start talking smack while I'm seasoning the thing. My children have always enjoyed the spectacle, so it has more or less become a tradition in our house.

****

November 22, 2011

Hey JD!
Another day done! SWEET!!!!!

I got a good laugh at the post office! The dude in front of me must have thought hitting on the old bitter lady behind the counter would get him a discount or something. He was probably in his late forties and the old woman had to be 60 something. Anyway, he goes up there wanting to mail something by next day mail. Well, that crap is not cheap! So he starts off telling her about how he's just got behind on some bills because he had forgot all about them. And now he needs the payments there by tomorrow.

She says something like, "it happens" and then she tells him his total is $19.98.
Right then he says to her, "I bet you get a lot of compliments, you've got such pretty eyes. I have to ask, are you single?"

To which she gives him this great evil smile and says, "No, I don't get compliments here. I've always thought my eyes were too dark. I have been married 35 years, and your total is $19.98. Will that be cash or credit?"

I couldn't help it, I just busted out laughing! He turned around and glared at me. And that made me laugh even more! But to get him to finish up with her I tried to control it. (But not well...)

Then he turns back to her and actually asks if he can come back and pay later because he forgot his wallet!!!! (This dude was special!) At that point she takes his letter pushes it back in front of him and tells him, "Sir, this is the US Postal Service, not Social Services. So you just take your letter and bring it back when you can pay up. After all I'm sure you don't want any of us going postal on you. Now do you?" And she smiled that freaking evil smile even bigger at him! Hahahaha!!!!

Heck! She even had me a little scared! I thought she might snatch him up right in front of everyone and eat him whole or something!!!
He stared at her for a second and I think he realized he was in danger, because he took that letter and pretty much ran out of there! It was awesome!!!

For the record, when I went up to her she was actually chuckling and completely normal. But then I wasn't looking for a freebie. And she does have really dark eyes... Like evil crazy postal ladies often do! I wish I had been videotaping it, I'd have sent it in to Americas Funniest Home Videos or something.

My coughing fits weren't as bad today when I tried to jogging. I'm still not 100%. But I think by tomorrow or Wednesday I should be back to normal. It's funny that I'm so used to having junk in my lungs so when I take the junk away I must readjust to relatively clean air rather violently....
But hey! I am proud to say I have killed no one! I have jumped down Brad's throat twice now, but I assure you he had it coming. At least I thought he did.

I hope you got my package of mole skin! I realize now I probably should have sent enough for your entire platoon to share... So I am going out to BJ's in the morning to see if they have a big ole package of it. If they do I'll get it and it will be in the way to all of you by Friday morning.

I think I got your schedule all figured out! Today you should have been out with the Pugil Sticks and got some Problem Solving stuff done.

Tomorrow (the 22nd) it looks like you got a 2 mile run and a class about your Commitment to Become a Marine.

So! If this takes 4 days to get to you, minus the holiday, you should get this letter on the 26th or the 28th... Let's Go with Monday the 28th. That's the Confidence Course, Knife Tech, Combat Care, and a few other things. Tuesday the 29th looks fun too! It's got the Confidence Course, Pugil Sticks, Counter to choke holds, and more Combat Care. Let me know if I'm on the right page, I think I am because the schedule I have will take me right to Graduation!! YAY!!!

I miss you!!! I hope you're trying to stay healthy!!! You better!!!

Love,

Mom

****

I know I said it before, but I'll say it again, that Training Matrix was indeed my Holy Grail! If you have a Poolee or a Recruit in Boot Camp, you really should print yourself, and your recruit, a copy. I was sadly under the impression that such a thing would be provided to them there. Well, it's not, but they sure can get it in the mail.

****

November 23, 2011

Hi Baby!!!!

Woohoo!! Another day is finished!!!
I hope the days are going by pretty quick for you. I know they keep you busy as Hell there! I also suspect you're getting to the point where it's not as freaking confusing anymore and soon it will be a lot more fun. Still hard work, but at least more enjoyable hard work.

Just remember, you are unstoppable!!!! And we're here cheering you on with all our might!!!! Oh yes, your mother is indeed insanely proud of you! And You better be proud of You too! Hell everyone is proud of you! (But I AM the PROUDEST Dag Nabbit!)

I went to BJ's and they didn't have any big ole packs of mole skin. So I figure I'll send you more every Tuesday so you should have more every Saturday! (Unless, of course you tell me not to… I know you guys have limited space.) Also if you need a bunch more, for like the whole platoon, just let me know and I will get it to you.

Ok! On to the more amusing news of the day!! Apparently last night Tom's stalker decided to prove she's the one for him! She went to the station, broke into Tom's car and got down to her underwear!!! Then she text him saying she had left a surprise in his car for him. Only one problem, Tom was out towing a car. So he called Eddie and had him go look. (Just in case it was a bomb or something.) Well, needless to say, Eddie was NOT impressed with what he saw!!

Then the chick freaked out and started screaming for Tom! (Just imagine a half-naked crazy chick screaming in Eddie's face for Tom to come save her. Poor little guy had to be scared.) Eddie told her to get lost but she just kept screaming!

So he decided to call the cops! The cops came but she had already left, and since she actually broke into Tom's car he is the one who has to press charges. But at least Eddie got her served with a no trespass… Poor

Eddie... He said that with all that flailing around, he wasn't sure if she was wearing bottoms or not! You know Eddie, he bitched for hours about how he never wanted to see something like that again!! If only it had been Jason that discovered her!!! Hahaha!! There would have been a cat fight!!! A skinny cat and a fat cat going at it!!

Hey! I got good news!!! Soon it will be February! And you will be a Marine!!! For now, eat when you can, sleep when you can, Kick Ass Always, go to church on Sunday, and don't forget to stretch out at night. Oh! And remember I love you!

Love,

Mom

*****

Then the 24th came along and the clouds cleared from my skies for a moment longer! Yes! Stalking the mailman like a cat with its prey was paying off! Another letter arrived from Parris Island!!! (I was obviously much better at this than my buddy Tom's stalker! At least I was getting what I wanted!)

****

Hey Mom

I hope my letters have reached you. I've gotten all of yours. It's getting a little tougher here on the Island. Some people keep fucking up Drills. And one kid, Cox, flipped off our 2 meanest DIs. Unfortunately, all pay for the action of one.

Hey! Send more stickers with your address!!

SSgt. Smith apparently said our platoon is his last so he's gonna make us the best Marines he's ever made. I overheard another instructor talking to some officer at the chow hall today. They were talking about his platoon and he said, "Well, I doubt we'll win all the competitions. SSgt Smith's platoon is already the best new platoon on the Island for now."

BTW, your letters give me the ability to push through all of this.

Thanks Mom! I couldn't have gotten this far without you!

But seriously, it sucks here.

I hope by the time you get this, everything will be better.

Love, JD

P.S. Sgt. Santos smacked my damn hand so hard that my thumb is giving me issues. Hurts like a bitch, but no pain, no gain. OooRah…

****

OK, reading these letters still break my heart and piss me off. But they also make me beam with pride to know that nothing could stop my son from reaching his goal. No matter what, he would hold on, and he would make it through.

*****

November 24, 2011

Hi JD!!

It's me again!! I hope you're not getting tired of me! If you are that's just too bad because I'm going to keep bugging you every day and you can't stop me!!!!! Bahahahaha!!!!

Hell Yes!!! I got your letter today!!
So.... Sgt. Santos smacked your hand??? Hmmm... He best not smack it again and hurt you. If he mucks up your hand or any part of you he can lose his rank!!! Or even lose his career!
(Sorry, had a bitchy, protective Mom moment there for a second. But I know you're ok...)
You're right, no pain no gain! And I'm so happy to hear you guys are the best new platoon so far! Between having you on their team and a SSgt. that wants to make you guys his personal best... Well JD, sounds to me like your platoon can't lose!
(Perhaps the numb nut that flicks off DIs needs to go... But I'm sure he's getting a bit of special attention for his deeds... At least I sure hope he is.)

I'll be putting this in the mail Thursday (Thanksgiving) morning. So I think you're probably gonna get it around the 28th. I'm thinking you should get two letters from me today!
It also means that you're in week 4!!! (It's week 3 on the 12 week calendar that I have for your training.) Only 9 more weeks and its graduation day!!! Yay!!! You know it, every day that goes by is a day closer to the finish line! And one big ass celebration!!!

My jog today went pretty well, only one small coughing fit.
I have been cig free for 4 days!
I'm not gonna lie, I still want one, and although Brad has been good and hides from me while he smokes.... I can still smell it!!!! And my addicted brain thinks it smells like chocolate cake!!!!
But I have also lost 4 pounds!!! So I must keep going!!! I gotta be super healthy for all the traveling I plan to do visiting YOU!

Oh! There is more to report on the Tom stalker!!! She came back to the station this evening and Eddie had her arrested!!! Tom said she went ape shit on the cop and actually slapped him!! So she got pepper sprayed too!! She really is crazy!!! He said she kept screaming, "But I love you Tom!" over and over again. Bahahahaha!!!! Poor guy... His love was taken away in cuffs... Hahaha! Maybe Eddie has actually saved her and now she'll get the drugs she seems to so desperately need.
(I know, I'm horrible, but I still think it's funny as hell!)

BTW, Thank YOU! You have given me the best bragging rights EVER!!! I am sooo proud of you!! I know some people think my incessant bragging is annoying, but I don't give a flying Fuck! You really are amazing! You got this! And anything else they throw at you! I know that for a fact! You're top notch Son, and don't you ever forget it!! I am telling you! You are going to be one of the best damn Marines ever!!!!! The stuff that legends are made of! That's you Mister!!! Ya Damn Skippy it is!!

Sleep well tonight!!!

Love,

Mom

November 25, 2011

Hey JD!!

Don't sweat the small stuff today! Another day is out of your way!
All I can say to that is, Yay!!
Ok, I said no more poetry, but I said nothing about silly rhymes!

Since the mail didn't move today, I bet you get this letter at the same time as yesterday's letter (Along with the card I sent you with more address labels!) Of course I just realized you probably have more labels than you do stamps! Hence the 2 books of stamps in this letter. That's right, your Mom may be a bit slow, but she is always thinking about you!

We had Chinese food for Thanksgiving. I really hope they gave you guys a good meal. It's actually been a pretty boring day. But, as you can see from the awful picture I sent you, I got 16 minutes on my mile and a half this morning!!! Woohoo!! Yes, I thought I was going to drop dead! But I didn't stop and I didn't die after all!! Now I'm more convinced than ever that I'm ancient... Why, just 15 short years ago I would have pointed and laughed at the old lady jogging (and huffing and puffing) in the park! Now I AM the old lady!!!! Fantastic! Hahaha!!! Honestly, even if my time stays 16 minutes, and the run gets easier, I'll be happy. Ya know, that's like a 10.66 mile. If I could keep that pace further I could do a 5k (3.2 miles) in like 30-35 minutes! Not too shabby for a Grammy!

I also killed a mess of zombies on the Xbox 360 today! Yeah, I was doing real good, whipping some zombie ass. But then this freaking electrified zombie fell in the puddle of water I was standing in and fried me. Good thing I died when I did though, 'cause I was getting pretty tired and sweaty.

The cool thing is I think Jake plans on playing the zombie game soon! He says it looks easy! Ha! Let him try! Of course, if he makes it further than I have I'll have to give him kudos! (Sure would be a good work out for him too.)

I sure do miss you. I hope you are staying healthy and those other guys don't get you sick. The mental and physical stuff there is nothing you can't handle.

You just need to stay as healthy as possible! So we go back to my requests; eat, sleep, stretch, and go to church. Oh! And remember, even from a far, I got your back JD! At least the best I can.

And that I love you and I am wickedly proud of you! Oh yeah! And that you are a super (honorable, courageous, and strong) Bad Ass! No doubt!!!!!

Semper Fi!

Love,

Mom

*****

Ok, I know I'm probably too old to be playing video games. But, the zombie killing game is indeed a serious work out! It's also incredibly amusing. If you're looking for a good way to burn some calories, have a good time, and maybe get ready for a zombie apocalypse than you should check it out!

Except for that game, the holiday was indeed a sad day. I missed my son, and although his brother was home, even his sister and her little family were held up with the other in-laws and didn't have time to come to our house.

But the very next afternoon the mailman made my holiday bright again!

****

Hey Mom,

It's Sunday!! Our free time is a little longer today.

I guess you could say I'm getting used to the Hell that I'm living in. I just look at it as "another day down." But some of the recruits in the platoon are breaking down. All I can do is let 'em know we're in it together. Shit sucks though.

Drill is good one day then bad the next. Yesterday was kinda both. So I'm hoping that today shows improvement.

I'm really sick by the way. Swollen throat, chest pains, and congested. But I have to keep moving. I'm afraid to go to medical because of my wrist/thumb. It's gotten worse. But I'll be here till I graduate, die, or they kick me out.

I miss my life back home. I hope you all are doing fine and everyone is healthy. You all are always in my prayers.

Love, JD

P.S. I hate DI Jones. He deprives us of water and head calls. One kid pissed himself because of it. It's actually a violation. But no one would believe us….

Hangin in there. Love you Mom. –JD

****

With that letter I also got a poem from my son.

****

As I walk in the valley I see the long road ahead and a cliff at my heels.

Out of the cataclysmic encounter of my old and new world, springs the prospect of pride.

With a mighty left foot on the throat of my weakness bringing me to my knees.

In a mental pain so agonizing that it transforms into a physical reality of Hell on Earth.

Transformation becomes stamped on my heart with the;

Pride, Pain, and the Strength of those before me.

I walk this valley, but I have no fear.

I walk with God.

And at the end of this valley, there is a Title.

A Title of Life, Honor, Courage, Commitment.

The Title of MARINE.

-   JD -

*****

I loved getting every letter JD sent... But, Damn! My son was sick! Just what I didn't want to hear! Plus these DIs were really pissing me off.... I had to look for a reason to make it all ok.... What to say... What to say.... I had to refrain from going ballistic....

*****

November 26, 2011

Hi JD!!

*I got your letter. Don't you worry, everyone here is fine.
I got this end covered! And I pray for you all the time Son, day and night
me and the Big Guy are talking about keeping you safe and helping you
through this. I believe Nanny is looking out for you too. She's a pretty
awesome angel.
I also got the thing you sent from Navy Fed. (I saw your note in there. I
miss you too.)*

*Let me start by saying, if my calculations are correct you should be
reading this on Wednesday the 30th. That means tomorrow is December
1st and you only have 2 months and 3 days left. (And the last week,
Marine Week, will be a very good week.)*

*It also means this Saturday is SDI Inspection day! You guys need to look
sharp for that. Don't be surprised if the DIs come in and basically berate
everyone and toss all of your stuff everywhere. All it takes is one small
thing out of place and they will jump on it like a pack of wild dogs.*

*Next week is swim week. (The cold water might help your wrist.) Even
better! Swim week also marks the end of "Phase One." The 12th starts
Phase 2 when they should stop ripping you guys apart as bad, and start
building you back up. (I hope) Oh! And you'll be out on the firing range!
(Then in Phase 3 they should be making you all see how well trained and
kick ass you really are. At the end of which you will think and fight your
way through the Crucible! They call it "Polishing")*

*I wish there was something more than just writing I could do to help you
and your whole platoon. Withholding water and bathroom breaks is a
big violation! But your right, unless the whole platoon was ready to bust
him, they will not believe a few of you guys. I know from experience, not
everyone will stand up and say what he's done (even if they claim they
will) for fear of losing their place. The best you can do is to do everything*

he asks to the best of your ability and hope he rewards you guys with these simple necessities. (Thank God it's not the middle of summer!)

As for as going to medical about your wrist and/or your cold... Well Son, if it gets worse you'll need to do something. That wrist is probably just sprained courtesy of the hit you took from Sgt. Santos. Some Motrin will probably do the trick. Just be ready, because you may have to fight to stay in your platoon. But you'll need that wrist for the firing range and for the Crucible. (Lord I hope it's getting better!)

Your health is my #1 concern and as you can tell, I'm really hoping you're feeling better. If they have Orange Juice or anything with vitamin C in it, be sure to have some every chance you get. It will help you fight that cold. And sleep all you can!

About the guys that are starting to lose it... You have always been a champion to your fellow man. And I'm ok with you helping your friends there to get thru this. (Ya know, you can always give the other recruits my address and a stamp. I'll write back to anyone of them that writes me.) Just don't let anyone drag you down with them. Their fears and anxieties are not yours to bear for them. Yep, you are all in it together, but only the mentally strongest will make it through. And between you and me, there is a good reason for that. If you're in the heat of battle you won't have time to hold up the guy that's supposed to have your back.

It's like this: I trust you to keep your cool in battle and would love to have you as the guy that's got my back. But someone like Eric (a good enough guy) is not someone I would want covering me. (Even if he was in great shape.) Simply because I know he would surely lose his cool and probably get me killed. I guess what I'm trying to say is, don't ditch your buddies, but don't take any hits for them either. Please JD, I know you, you want to fix it for them. But you can't, and you really shouldn't. They have to learn and it's a hard lesson. They will get it or they won't. Sadly, if they don't, than they weren't meant to be Marines.

"Your struggles develop your strengths. When you go through hardships and decide not to surrender, that is strength." - Arnold Schwarzenegger (Guess he wasn't all muscle after all)

Believe me when I say, YOU GOT THIS, you are strong as hell! You will never surrender and you will be a top notch Marine! But you need to let the others decide whether they will continue or give up on their own.

I am so proud of you! Boot Camp is tough! I know you're going to be an awesome Marine! I have faith in YOU! Believe it or not, you're actually rockin' this out! It's only a couple days to December!!

I bet you've been busy learning a lot of new stuff and new ways to beat the crap outta people! So, there's gotta be some good stuff there. Just let go of the mental stuff. Getting your brain washed is never fun, but you must accept it. Let them give you what I like to call "Marine Mind" it won't change who you really are, it will just take away the civilian habits. Civilian habits aren't any good to the Marine Corps anyway.

*All you really need to know is that you got this, you belong there, this too will pass, you really are awesome, you will soon be more than awesome, **you will be an awesome U.S. Marine**, God has your back, you got a Mom that loves you and would gladly kill for you, and she is indeed extremely proud of you.*
Thus no matter what, you will succeed and reach your goal. And that's all there really is to it.

I miss you!!! I wish I could be there to assist you, but if there is anything I can do, you let me know and it will be done.
Ok, enough of the concerned Mom stuff.
I love you!

Now grab your anger and frustration and turn it COLD. Your orders and objectives are all that matter right now. You have no worries. You will make it out on top. I know it.

Love, Mom

Oh! Wait! I have another joke!!

A college professor, an avowed Atheist, was teaching his class.
He shocked several of his students when he flatly stated he was going to
prove there was no God.
Addressing the ceiling he shouted: "God, if you are real, then I want you
to knock me off this platform. I'll give you 15 minutes!"

The lecture room fell silent. You could have heard a pin fall.
Ten minutes went by. Again he taunted God, saying, "Here I am, God. I'm
still waiting."

His count-down got down to the last couple of minutes when a Marine -
just released from active duty and newly registered in the class -walked
up to the professor, hit him full force in the face, and sent him tumbling
from his lofty platform.

The professor was out cold! At first, the students were shocked and
babbled in confusion. The young Marine took a seat in the front row and
sat silent.

The class fell silent...waiting.

Eventually, the professor came to, shaken he looked at the young Marine
in the front row. When the professor regained his senses and could speak
he asked: "What's the matter with you? Why did you do that?"

"God was busy. He sent the Marines."

SWEET!!!!! Hahahaha!!!

****

I wrote him twice on that day….

****

Hey Baby!

Just a quick note because I forgot to say…. YAY! Another day is out of the way!!!

The letter I sent this morning was all about me being concerned. Ya gotta forgive me. I just don't want anyone or anything to slow you down or get in your way.

I know you got a job to do, and you're doing it the best you can. Which means you are doing GREAT!

I love you and miss you, and I will write more tonight.

Now go get some rest! You need to kick some more ass in the morning Recruit! (Soon to be MARINE!)

Love,

Mom

P.S. I also forgot to tell you I really liked your poem. The title "Marine" is indeed waiting for you at the end of this journey. And it will be yours, **FOR LIFE**. *Don't you ever forget it.*

****

To tell the truth, I was still steaming…. Frist he tells me he got hit in the hand, then that he's sick! And he tops it off with a DI refusing them water? As a Mom, all these things were killing me! But, also as a Mom, I knew that he needed to suffer on that Island. For all intents and purposes, he was actually in a very "safe" environment. And I seriously doubt any enemy would stop their attack so our troops could get a drink or go hit the head. No, it was better for all of them learn these things now while no one was actually shooting live rounds at them.

****

November 27, 2011

Hi Baby!!

Yes!! Another day is done!!! Excellent!

I am going to be a "better mood" Mom today! (Seeing as yesterday my whole thought process was about… Well… How do I go about removing these Jones and Santos characters?)
What Jones did was wrong and I felt really bad for the recruit that wet himself. At least I did until I thought about it more…. I doubt they give bathroom breaks out on the battlefield.

I'm really hoping you're feeling better. It kinda sucks knowing that by the time you get this almost 10 days will have passed from the time you wrote your letter…. But I am sending you all the well wishes and all the pain free days I have! If I had a way to take the physical pain away from you and put it on me I would do it in a heartbeat. But the best I can do is pray God sends you a healing angel.

Worst case scenario, you go see the doc and they take you out of the physical stuff for a few days. I'm sure they have a way to make up for anything you may miss. But even if they didn't, the very worst that could happen is you're there an extra week. (And I seriously doubt they'll do that.)

Of course, there is a good chance that during "team week" (when you guys get put on maintenance duty) they will pull everyone's wisdom teeth. At least that will get you pain killers and antibiotics for a couple days. Hey! If they do pull your wisdom teeth, you and I will both have been wide awake for that shit. What more could we ever have in common?

My jog time really sucked today... 18.5 minutes for a mile and a half... I think it was just an off day, but I'm not timing myself again till next Saturday... I also think I'm pushing too much and not pacing the way I should, so I'm losing it about halfway through... I'll keep working on it and it will get better.

And for my next trick! Drum roll please... I've been smoke free for a full 7 days!!!! Ta! Da!

Now I'm just trying not to eat everything in sight!! Damn SEE food diets!!

I talked to Kevin today. You remember, he's that crazy retired "God only knows" what he did in the Navy guy... Even though he hasn't got to really see you the past few years... (Well he's actually seen you lots, he was even at your high school graduation, but stayed clear because he hates Brad and your Dad.) He wanted me to tell you he's damn proud of you and you will make an excellent Marine. He also said to warn you... You'll get lots of chicks, but you need to be careful because most of them are nuts! (Yes, he had his "very serious face" on when he said that too...)

Hey! I found a great quote for you!

"It's not the size of the dog in the fight; it's the size of the fight in the dog." -Mark Twain

Too true! Oh if only I had a dime for every time I was under estimated... Only to step up and stomp my opponents like freaking bugs!!! There's a whole mess of fight in this little dog! Hell yeah!!!

(Isn't it nice to know where you get it from?)

You keep hanging in there JD. And don't you worry! You got this. Every day that goes by, you're closer to the finish line!

*You know I'm crazy proud of you, but it's gonna get etched in your brain by the time you're done there... Why???? Because **I AM CRAZY PROUD OF YOU!!!!!***

I love you!!! And I miss you!!! But, I'll see you soon! February is right around the corner my Dear!
Keep kicking ass!!!!
(Don't forget, eat, sleep, stretch, and go to church!)

More to come tomorrow!!!!

Love, Mom

Ok... Today's joke of the day is freaking horrible... But funny....

There once was an old couple who had been married for thirty years.
Every morning the old boy would wake up and give off an enormous fart, much to his long suffering wife's annoyance.
"You'll fart your guts out one of these days," she always complained.
After a particularly bad week the wife decided to have her revenge and got up early, placing some turkey giblets in the bed next to the old boy's butt.
While making breakfast downstairs she heard his usual morning fart reverberate through the floorboards followed by a scream.
Twenty minutes later a rather shaken man came downstairs.
"You was right all along Missus," the old man says, "I finally did fart my guts out, but by the grace of God, and these two fingers, I managed to push 'em back in!"

GROSS!!!!! HAHAHAHAHAHAHA!!!!!

November 28, 2011

Hi JD!!!

I sure do miss you! But I'm another day closer to seeing you! And you're another day closer to graduation!

I bought you a mess more mole skin the other day, and have big plans to send you a couple packs in the morning. So I hope you got my little package with this letter and it's no later than Friday the 2nd. It looks like you guys have an 8km hike Saturday the 3rd and I want you to have everything you can to save your feet. (Heck, I think you should get 2 letters, and a package, from me all on the same day! Simply because I mailed you a letter this morning too and since it was Sunday it won't head your way till this one does.)

I would send the letter in the package, but I'm not sure if a package travels as fast as a letter. Needless to say, if you didn't get it today I'm sure it will be there tomorrow. So long as you have it before you run out of the stuff I sent already, it's all good. Like the card says, if you need more per package just let me know. I'm not trying to over load you on stuff all at once and figure its best just to send what you need as you need it. But I'm also thinking you may need like 5 or 6 packs a week, since you should be using them on your elbows too. But I'll wait for you to let me know exactly how many packs to send at a time.

Today was a pretty nice day! Partly cloudy with a light breeze and almost 80 degrees! (And it's the end of November!) I was enjoying it, but Tom (the warmth hater) must have called me a dozen times to complain! Now why would he call ME (half lizard lady) and complain about being hot? He must have been desperate.
I just hope the internet is right and it was a nice day for you guys too.

I didn't jog today because I ended up walking with Beth and her son Daniel. Ya know, that kid has gotten much better, but he still ain't right. Poor Beth had to carry him kicking almost all the way back to the cars.

(Around 2 miles at least!) And he was talking nonstop super loud at the same time!!! I am so thankful that none of you guys did that crap. Honestly, I would have beaten you all and then been locked in the loony bin years ago if any of you had acted like he does.... I guess I'll never understand...

Gary should be back in the states by the 17th of December. I think the IRS Gods hate him. Hahaha! I tried to redo his taxes yesterday and right in the middle of it I guess I pushed the wrong button or something, because the entire file just deleted itself!!! (That is the 2nd time that has happened! They either really hate the poor guy, or they hate me doing his taxes for him... The jury is still out on that one.) No worries though, I'll get them done this week. Along with all those dang receipts for the insurance, your brother's financial aid stuff for college, and your sister's paper work for her medical insurance... Yes Son, this week I will be the secretary to the world!!!! Oh! And I need to get some shit to the lawyer for Brad on Tuesday! Too funny! But hey, so long as nothing interrupts my letters to you, or my morning jog/walk, it will all be ok. Now, if they try to get in the way of that.... Well then they can kiss my butt!!!!

I told Penny what I said to you about having other recruits write me, and she wanted me to tell you that if there are any recruits there that need a pen pal she would be happy to write them. That way they don't feel like they are getting short changed by your Mom. In all fairness, she has a point. I wouldn't talk to any of them like I do you... They aren't mine, you are. Therefore, to me they cannot be as cool or kick ass as you. And while I think that anyone who goes through the Marine Corps Boot Camp should be proud of themselves... I am personally proudest of you! And not just because you are doing this, but also because of who you have grown up to be. You're; courageous, strong, smart, and driven. You have an amazing future ahead of you, and I'd like to think I may have had a hand in that.

There is nothing in this world that you can't do so long as you set your mind to do it. The Marines are going to be very lucky to have you as one of their own, Very lucky.

I hope you're feeling better and everything is going ok. I know it ain't all fun and games. But I also know a man like you can cruise right through it. **You're doing better than you think***. I'm sure of it. Just don't second guess yourself and don't stop. Soon you'll reach the finish line.*
And I'll be there to see you graduate!!!!!
Then we'll come home and have an awesome party!!!! YAY!!! I'll write more tomorrow! LOVE YOU!!!!!

Semper Fi!

Love,

Mom

****

I'm pretty sure the mailman must have thought I had a "thing" for him or something. At this point, on more than one occasion, he would find me standing by the mail box waiting for him. Most days I'd just walk away muttering about the bills or junk mail. But on those OTHER days I'd literally run into the house with my prize letter like a kid with a new toy! Those days were always the best, no matter what the letter might say, just getting it meant my son was still kicking!

****

Hey Mom,

Today is Thanksgiving. I got your 13th letter yesterday, so kudos on the accurate timing.

Sigh…. I'll be honest, I don't wanna be here but I hope that eventually changes.

I had a dream last night that I was at home hangin out with you. We went to go find me a Volvo and test drove a bunch while talking about something funny. (I don't know what exactly, but we were laughing and having a good time like we always do.)

I won't be able to send this till tomorrow, so you'll get it a day later than usual.

I miss you and love you Mom.

Love, JD

****

Ouch! That line about not wanting to be there stung! Oh well, I was sure it wouldn't be the last, or even the worst sting. So I focused of the good stuff. At least my timing was good.

****

November 29, 2011

Hey Baby!

It's me again!! I'm like a bad penny, ya just can't get rid of me!! Heck Yeah! Another day is DONE!

I got your letter today from Thanksgiving Day! Yay!!!

<u>I MISS YOU TOO JD!!!!!</u>

I liked reading about your dream! I think it was probably more like a premonition. I'm sure we're gonna test drive a bunch of cars! And I know we'll be laughing our butts off about something!! After all, we always have fun hanging out! And we ALWAYS laugh a lot!

I hope-Hope-HOPE! Things are getting better there!!!! I know it sucks, but maybe it sucks a little less each day. Good thing is, once you graduate, you will NEVER have to go thru Boot Camp again! Thank God for that! AND YOU WILL BE A MARINE FOR LIFE!!!!!

***Speaking of being a Marine, if they give you the chance to buy your Marine Corps Ring while you're there on the Island and it's less than $200 you should go ahead and order it. Then just let me know how much it was and I'll put that much back in your account.
They cost $200-$300 if ya order it after you're off the island.***

OK, the amusement of the day was....

This morning there was a group of about 8 older women in the park walking around at a good clip and yelling out evil cadences about their husbands! It was like they all had their own little mean things to say, it was actually pretty damn funny! One even screamed out about her husbands "nasty saggy things!" I realized that all that yelling must be doing wonders building up their cores! So I decided to ask one of the women if that was why they yelled so loud to which she said, "Oh no honey, we just really hate those guys!" Hahahaha!!!

She also told me they are out there every Monday and Thursday around 10am and that I was welcome to join them! (I was late for my jog/walk because I hit the post office to send your package, and I handled Jackie's insurance problem early.) While I'm not joining their hate parade, we must remember to go to the park on a Monday or Thursday when you come home so we can laugh at them together! It really is a "must see"!

I think you should be reading this on Friday the 2nd! So! You be sure to stretch a bit tonight! Sleep well and have sweet dreams! If I'm right you have an 8km (that's just under 5 miles) hike and a SDI inspection tomorrow! So be sure to use your mole skin for the hike and look sharp for inspection!
I'll be praying extra hard all day that you guys do great! (Yup, I know you'll do great! But some extra prayers won't hurt.)

Hey, I'll be doing my 6 mile jog/walk around 7am! (That's my normal time now days because that's when they unlock the bathrooms at the park. Hahaha!) Maybe we'll be hiking at the same time! Only you'll be carrying a mess of equipment and yelling at the top of your lungs. I'll be all bundled up with music blaring in my ears, and hoping my old legs don't fall off! I'll also be thinking about how strong you are! And how proud I am to be your Mom.

Yup, knowing what you're doing is helping me push myself further! If you can't stop than neither can I!!!

Hell Yes!!! I'm suffering with you!!!! (Kinda)

Really, my body hates my guts.. But that's fine, it's all mind over matter. I don't mind so it don't matter. And even though I'm sore, I know I must be getting stronger. Just like you!

Don't forget..... You ROCK!!! Just Keep Going!!

Sleep well Mister!! I love you!!!!
Talk at ya tomorrow!

Love, Mom

Time for the joke of the day!

Old Wisdom

After working on his farm every day, an old farmer rarely had time to enjoy the large pond in the back that he had fixed up years earlier with picnic tables, horseshoe courts, and benches. So one evening he decided to go down and see how things were holding up. Much to his surprise, he heard voices shouting and laughing with glee. As he came closer he saw it was a group of young women skinny dipping in his pond. He made the women aware of his presence and they all went to the deep end.
One of the women shouted to him, "We're not coming out until you leave."
The old farmer replied, "I didn't come down here to watch you ladies swim or make you get out of the pond naked. I only came down to feed the alligator."

Dirty old man!!!! Bahahaha!!!

November 30, 2011

Hey JD!!
Ha! Another day DONE!!!
HELL YEAH!!!
Looks like Tuesday starts swim week!!! Yay!! Things are gonna start moving pretty fast! Hang in there and stay with it!! Fast is good!

Before I forget! I forgot to write #21 on the back of yesterday's letter!!! If you could do it for me that would be great! I don't want your story getting out of order.
Yep, I've almost sent you the whole book. I figure you'll have all of it in about a week. Let me know if you want me to start sending the next book in the series or if you still have plenty to read. I'll just send you some comic strips if you're still working on the book.
(I really like the Lola comic strip. She kinda reminds me of myself...)

Beth told me she sent you a letter! Oh boy! I hope she didn't send you anything ridiculous! Have you gotten mail from anyone other than me and Jackie?? I hope your friend Kayla has written. She said she mailed you a letter a while ago... Oh! And your dad text me asking for your address, (I guess Nana didn't give it to him.) So he should be writing you soon too. Just remember to forgive him if he writes anything dumb, he's not as bright as us.

How did the SDI inspection go??? Was everyone standing straight and looking sharp?? Did you get asked anything?? Did they rip the place apart?

I was very busy today bragging about YOU to Becky. (She used to run the Church Café. I always called her gorgeous and she called me beautiful. I'm sure you remember her even though she left a while ago.) She was in Wal-Mart, and after saying hello the very first thing she asked me was, "Where is your son?" (It's funny how many people I see that ask me that.) So of course I immediately told her where you were and how proud I am of you!!

Turns out her oldest son is a Marine too! She said he hated Boot Camp and it took him 16 weeks to get it done because he got pneumonia while he was there. (That had to really suck!) But he finished and absolutely loves being a Marine now! I agreed, Boot Camp sucks...

She said if you get stationed in Jacksonville Florida (she actually lives there now) that you need to go see her and she will make you a good meal!
Marine Moms Unite!!!!

Oh man! Every day I look forward to your next letter!! I hope you're feeling ok!
Remember, I am super proud of you JD! You got this!
Just keep going! No prize worth winning comes easy. Like I said before, even if you don't know it, you are doing great! I KNOW IT!
I miss you!!!
I love you!!
I'll talk to you more tomorrow. Sleep well.

Love,

Mom

****

It was like a dream come true! That day I got 2 more letters from JD.

****

Hey Mom,

It's Sunday again. The schedule you got is a bit off due to the holidays I think. We've done some MCMAP, a 3 mile "hike", and a TON of Drill. The Platoon is getting better, but it kinda sucks because we got better through pain... I'm not kidding when I say we have the meanest DIs in the Company.

Every day I question my reasons to stay. BUT I'm still here... I came to learn how to be a Marine, but I see it's more like POW training.

At least our classes are interesting.

God, I can't wait for Phase 2.

Right now the day consists of; getting thrown out of bed, rushed to dress, rushed for hygiene, rushed to get gear and our rifles unlocked, rushed out of the hatch, rushed to eat chow, rushed to clean the barracks, rushed to get out in formation, rushed to Drill, rushed MORE to Drill, do some sort of activity of the day, rushed to class, rushed to the pit 2 or 3 times, rushed to formation, Drill, chow, Drill, Pain, IT/Pain, Drill, chow, Rushed to Drill, rushed inside, rushed to shower and hygiene, rushed to clean rifles, - 1 hour break-, rushed to scrub the deck, rushed to sleep. And it repeats 7 to 8 hours later.... Now accompany that with getting screamed at and occasionally knocked around, and you have my shitty life summed up....

So! Tell me, what's new with you???

I miss you lots! (Obviously) I'll be happy to see everyone in February. Prepare to be hugged to death!!

BTW, it seems to take like 3 days for your letters to get here most of the time, some take 3 to 5...

Love, JD

Hey Mom,

Sorry if the writing is sloppy. I'm using a canteen as a table. I wanna come home. lol…

But I'm doin my best to make you proud. How's everything at home? I hope you're all doing fine. It's just getting worse here. I can't say I'm OK, but hey, I'm alive. That's how I see it. I hope the remainder of these 13 weeks flies by… Even though now it's just dragging on…

I'm incredibly homesick. I should have just stuck with EMT & Fire… Too late now…

I miss you a lot.

Love, JD

*****

Oh my! This was not good… Not good at all… I think the thing that struck me the most was the simple fact that JD has always been the kind of kid who dealt with life's crap really well. He was strong both physically and mentally. And I wondered if that strength made this transformation all the harder. Oh, I knew he would make it, and I knew he would be fine. But Lord! What on Earth could anyone have done to make him seem so….. Depressed….. Nah, I had to figure out how to fix that crap, and fast.

I decided it was best to take him back to a better place… A place where he laughed his butt off at none other than yours truly.

I have a terrible habit of changing the lyrics to most songs, and I never do the tune any justice.

Well, right before JD left, the holiday shopping season was in full swing. It seemed that no matter what store we walked into there was always one Christmas song or another playing overhead. That year I changed the words to Feliz Navidad… It was so amazingly ridiculous that, even though he laughed at me at first, JD ultimately found himself singing with me!! Oh yes, and that made it all the more amusing. Here we were, a little old lady with her young adult son looking as normal as the next group, but we were singing…. Badly… And laughing like a couple of fools! (Ok… I'm not really THAT old…)

Yep, that song would be my saving grace…

******

December 1, 2011

Hey Baby!!!!!
Another day is DONE! And it's already December!!! WooHoo!!!

And I got more letters from you today!! Yay!!! Even better! It looks like they only took 3 days to get here!!!

A POW camp! Hmmm… Yep, that sucks. But I assure you, you are learning how to kill, and how to survive, anything! It's hidden inside all the repetitive crappy stuff… **Listen to me; you were called to the Marine Corps because that is what you are supposed to do. Yeah, fire & rescue is cool too, but you are a Marine!!! DON'T EVER SECOND GUESS YOURSELF!!!**
*Yes, they call you Recruit now, but not for much longer JD. Soon you will be called **MARINE!!***
OH! And FYI… You've always made me proud!!!!!
You're home sick??? I understand that! I'm sick to have you home!! It's like my right arm is gone!! But, if I can hang here (armless) all alone in the house of bickering introverts for 2 more months, (not long at all) than you can hang in there too.

I just hope I don't hug you to death when I see you! (Or try to stow away in your luggage when you go back off for your schools!!!) I will say that while you're in school I am going to be visiting you as much as humanly possible!! Hell, the people there might just give me a frequent visitor discount!!

Ya know, I can tell what you really need is a song! You know how it goes!! Sing it with me now!!!

De police day got Rob!
De police day got Rob!
De police day got Rob and he's gone to tell dem all about our job!
Day already know about Mary and Chris Yeah!
Day already know about Mary and Chris Yeah!
Day already know about Mary and Chris Yeah!
Cause day gave him a great deal!!!

Don't you feel better now? Music is so good for the soul!!
(Speaking of music, am I allowed to send you one of those musical/message cards???)

Well, that's a bummer that my schedule is off... But I'm certain swim week is around the corner. You know how to swim, and the diving board doesn't scare you, so you'll be fine there.
   Then it's off to the gas chamber.... Don't let that freak you out!!! It's really just a crazy mental challenge. The gas isn't deadly or anything. It's just tear gas. Yep, you'll all have to go in there and breathe that shit in and it does sting a little bit. The good news is that as soon as you walk out IT'S OVER! The gas leaves your system quick and any pain you may feel goes away within seconds.

Seriously, the worst part of the gas chamber is just the thought of walking in there. So don't sweat it and it will be easy peasy!!! Other than that, the best advice I have is to just breathe normal, ***DO NOT HOLD YOUR BREATH! AND DO NOT RUB YOUR EYES OR TRY TO WIPE THE SNOT FROM YOUR NOSE UNTIL YOU GET OUT!!*** Rubbing makes it sting more. And if they see you holding your breath, well, you know they don't like that...

I don't know of it helps, but the whole reason you all have to go through the gas chamber is so you have confidence in the gear. If they didn't prove that it really works you might not be as trusting in it if you ever really needed to use it. And that would suck not to trust the stuff in combat if any chemical or biological warfare broke out...

THEN YOU WILL BE OFF TO GRASS WEEK! SWEET!!!!!
You're going to really kick ass on the firing range. In the eternal words of your Granddad, "Hold that stock real tight to your shoulder Baby, just like it was part of you, or the kick will throw you off and bruise you. Now all you have to do is calm your mind, find your target, and squeeze, don't pull, the trigger. And let nature take its course. You're a born marksman." NO DOUBT! He was right on! (Funny, I can still hear him giving me that lecture time after time until I looked over at him annoyed and said, "I know Dad! I know!")

What's going on here?? Well, let's see!! Jake is just waiting on his transcripts from Strayer so he can start at Phoenix. Alas, he still won't shower...

Brad is Brad, what's funny is earlier today we took the dresser upstairs and he said, "Jeez, I wish JD was here so you guys coulda done this!' (It really was too heavy for his back... But even he admits to missing you and being proud of what you're doing for your future.)

Jackie is doing good, I went and scared the crap outta the people at the insurance place, so she now has that all squared away.
Oh! Robert messaged me and asked for your address! He must be in his school now, and will probably be writing you soon too!!

And me? I miss you, but I'm ok. I've been ciggy free for 11 days and have killed no one. So to celebrate I bought the dog a ridiculous parka!!! (As you can see from the picture) I'm sure he hates it, but it makes me laugh!

I'm going out every morning to walk/jog, and although my legs want to kill me, I believe it's getting easier. And I ain't stoppin! Dag Nabbit!! I've officially lost 5 pounds!!!! (And it helps me feel like I'm suffering and getting stronger with you. Yes, your mother is insane. But it's all good.)

Penny is the same as always, Tom seems to be free of his stalker for now, and Beth is only half as crazy as she used to be.

That's pretty much the low down here. But ya never know what tomorrow might bring!
No matter what, we just gotta keep going and doing the best we can!!!
And don't worry!! It will have an end, and it will end for the best!!!
You have my word on that Son.

*Just remember; eat, sleep, stretch, and go to church!! And of course that **I AM PROUD OF YOU AND I LOVE YOU!!!***
I'll be seeing you very soon!

Love,

Mom

December 2, 2011

Ah ha! Here I AM!! I found you again!!! Yes, you thought you could escape me!!! But NO! I'm right behind you!! Ok, maybe not right behind you... But nevertheless, you will never get rid of me!!!!!

Hi JD!

Good news! My run time today was 16 minutes flat for a mile and a half! (Much better than the 18+ I had just a few days ago.) And I really do think it's getting a little easier. I'm not huffing and puffing as much. But those hills and the slanted road are killing me!!!! I keep wondering if that park is in a flood zone or something... I mean it's not a freaking race track, so why bank the road up so high??? Maybe it was just designed by an evil bastard. Yeah, that's gotta be it... Eh, what can ya do? Damn road designing Evil Bastards! Oh well, I just laugh at my weak ass self and keep going.

Jackie told me she got a card from you!! That means you got my package!!! Yay!!!

I want you to know something very important. I know they yell a lot there. They call ya all sorts of shit and work you like a dog. But the truth is you really are; tough, smart, strong, and true Marine Corps material. There ain't nothin there that you can't handle.

See, you're not just my son, you're one of my best friends. And I'm not best friends with anyone who isn't the cream of the crop in their own way. (You're just blessed to be the cream of the crop and my son!) I hope you understand what I am getting at. The big mouthed DIs are doing a job. They aren't telling you what they really think. They are telling you what they think will make you work harder than you ever thought you could, and they're trying to make your "skin" thicker than the toughest leather..

To be able to keep going through anything and to be thick skinned is a good thing to be.

*Look at me... They call me "emotionally detached" we both know that's not always true, but I sure as hell can be that way... You are just like me so use that gift and detach as needed. Hey! I am not half rate Mister, and neither are you. I'm very proud of you, and you need to be proud of yourself too! I know a mess of it sucks!!! But, don't forget to think about all the fun shit that you're doing and learning. **You need to convince yourself that you like all the shit!!***

Your goal gets closer every day!! You're going to look awesome in those dress blues!! And you will have EARNED the title, MARINE.
Like Forest Gump said, "And that's all I have to say about that."

I've been shopping around for a good tough lap top for you. I have a few choices but the tougher they are it seems the smaller the hard drive is.... So! Here is my question, if I get you a super tough one and an external hard drive to go with it, will that work? Or should I look for one with more space that's still tough, just not as tough??? I'd like it to be able to take being dropped, and still be fast, with great graphics, plenty of RAM, and at least 500 gigs of storage... But I can't seem to find that exact thing... No worries, I'll keep looking, but if all else fails, do you want external storage, or less impact resistant????

Really, other than my jog time and window shopping, today has been pretty boring... In a way I hope your day was boring too... If not boring than at least not so freaking rushed!

Remember, I love you! Eat was much and as well as you can, sleep as much as you can, and go to church. Other than that, roll through the rest like a machine. No worries! I have faith!! You got this!!

Love,

Mom

The card he had sent to his sister basically said that, at that moment, he hated life... It drove me insane to know he had all these struggles! And to know I couldn't do a damn thing about any of it just made it all the worse. If only he could get a phone call, or a singing telegram... But no... I'm certain the Marine Corps would have frowned upon such a thing. All I could do was write, write, write, and pray my words hit a home run.

Oh, the dog? He's a 6 year old Miniature Schnauzer. He's a good sport for the most part. But he looked really disgruntled with his little parka on! It was great!

Right about this time I found a great forum online. I suggest you do an internet search for "Marine Parents", you can't miss it. It's an amazing resource. There are pages there for you to connect with other recruit parents, girlfriends/boyfriends, and spouses in the same phase that yours is in. Not to mention you can also learn a lot from the moderators and the parents there who have already (recently) been there and done that. Trust me on this one.

The next day I snatched my mail right out of the mailman's hand! Good thing too! It contained 2 more letters!

****

Hey Mom,

Gotta make this one short. Please send me a small cross on a necklace.

Did the confidence course today! It was fun! I got your Thanksgiving card and letter #17 and I think the one after.

Gotta go, I'll write more tomorrow.

MISS YOU LIKE CRAZY!!!!

Love, JD

Hi Mom,

Ok, so today SUCKED. The Pugil Sticks were fun, but the rest of the day was pure pain. Somewhere between fucking up Drills and getting IT'd for doing it right, the Platoon pretty much lost all moral and motivation.

Sgt. Jones needs to GO. He's denied some of us chow and the ability to use the head or drink water. My buddy, Roberts, was ordered to pour his Power Aid on his food today at evening chow... Poor kid gets hit, disgraced, and mind fucked worse than anyone here. The kicker is, he doesn't even do shit wrong.

Sgt. Jones does fucked up shit while SSgt. Smith isn't around.

On a different note, please send me a pen and envelopes!! I'm running out of ink.

MISS YOU MOM!!!

Can't wait to see you in February!! ...Assuming I don't fuckin SNAP.

Oh hey, sneak me like 2 or 3 Laffty Taffy things in a small envelope. I'm starving! lol!

Well, hungry, and it would be cool if you could. Hahaha!

Love, JD

P.S. Sorry about the topic of my letter, I'm just pissed right now. Today was total Bull Shit.

LOVE YA!!! Keep sending letters! It's motivation for me to carry on.

****

My God! I really hated this Sgt. Jones dude... But he was doing a job...

So, now I had to look into what HIS job really was, just so I could know how much I was going to despise him.

I researched what it took to become a Drill Instructor and what was expected of them. After getting myself good and educated on the subject I determined that while Sgt. Jones may have been out of line, his job was indeed one of the most demanding jobs in the Marine Corps. And he was doing his job. The recruits in my son's platoon, and in every platoon, were depending on the training given to them by these Drill Instructors.

When I say depending, I mean that to the fullest. If recruits came out soft, or unable to function under pressure, it could cost them their lives and the lives of those who stood beside them. I knew any recruit trained under Sgt. Jones would be able to take some heat and keep going.

I can't even imagine the pressure that must put on a person. Not to mention the long insane hours. I almost felt bad for the Drill Instructors. They have longer hours than the recruits and they run right along with them all the time! Oh, and Drill Instructor school... Wow... You can find videos of it online to get a good feel for what those guys go through to get where they are. All I can say is that it's got to be a labor of love. That being the case, I decided that I didn't have to like Sgt. Jones, but he did deserve some mad respect.

Oh, but wait! JD asked me to send him a cross, pens, envelopes, and to sneak in some Laffty Taffy! Oh my!! I could do more than send letters, mole skin, and mailing supplies! I was about to become a smuggler of candy!!

I'll admit the idea scared the crap out of me. What if he got caught? Well, I would just have to hope that didn't happen. After all, he asked, and he would know the risks better than I would...

Off to the store I went to acquire his desired sweets along with his requested mailing supplies and a small silver cross on a necklace. I planned to hide the candy in the supply package...

*****

December 3, 2011

Hey JD!!!

Hell yes!!! Another day is DONE!
I got your letters from the 28th & 29th today!!! Yay!!!

I'm so glad you had fun on the confidence course!! I figured you would. I suspect it's similar to that parkour stuff you guys used to do, is it??

Hmmm....Withholding head breaks, water, and now chow?? Yeah, sounds like that Sgt. Jones character is going overboard. Maybe his momma didn't love him enough.... Now he's got some power and he's abusing it... Sadly, there is nothing that can be done to stop him. The only thing any of you can do is to not let him win. He must want your friend Roberts to break pretty bad for some f-ed up personal reason. Maybe he looks like the guy that stole his wife... Who knows? But at least Sgt. Jones can only take it so far, too far and he will get caught by a superior. And then he'd be screwed. Your buddy needs to look at it this way, once you have all escaped the jackass's abuse by graduating, said jackass will have failed in his mission to break you guys. (The people who give up or wig out are all wins for the jackass.)
And you guys will all be stronger for it. Shit, at the rate he's going, you will all be ready for jungle warfare where the water is poison and the food is down to 1 MRE a day.

You'll all be like super Marines!!
Of course, you're already a Super Marine in my eyes!!

Yep! I was very busy today bragging at some old Marine at the park!! You might remember him, we talked to him out there once before. There I was just jogging along and he came right on up to me and asked if you went to Boot Camp yet!! I thought it was cool that he remembered you! But, he also creeped me out a little because he said he had seen me out walking or jogging in the park for the last few weeks!!! Can you say "Stalker?"

Anyway, I didn't let the creepy factor stop me! No Sir!! I went on to tell him about how you're almost in phase 2, and about how much you worked to get there, and about how proud I am of you!!! (Took me a good 5 minutes!) Yep! I guess I CREEPED HIM out too because then he said "That's great! He'll make a fine young Marine. Ok, I won't bother you anymore. Have a good day! Semper Fi!" Then he just started jogging away in the other direction!!
Oh! I also bragged at Home Depot to the weird paint guy!! Hey, he asked about you and he was more than happy to listen and agree with me!!!

I've been thinking about where and when I want to have your Graduation party. I think its best just to have it right here at the house say the Friday before your 10 days leave is up. So! I'll need a list of people you want to invite by the end of December. That way I can get out the invitations and make them RSVP by the second week of January. I figured we could have it catered for the most part if that's cool with you.

So! Let me know if that's cool with you, and start thinking about who you want there.

IMPORTANT INFORMATION.... *I ran out and got you a small cross on a chain and put it (Taped) inside a card, along with more mole skin, envelopes, (2 Laffy Taffys & 2 Air Heads in a taped envelope that says "personal" on it) stamps, a note pad and 4 pens. Lord, I hope I don't get you in trouble!! You may have to suffer for the Laffys and Heads!!!* **You will know the package because there will be a big X by my return address.**

If it seems the little envelope in there marked "personal" is going to cause any problems, don't open it, just take what you need out of the package and throw that little envelope away!!!!!

*Well Son of Mine, just in case your mind got a little hazy today, and maybe you forgot... **I LOVE YOU! I AM CRAZY PROUD OF YOU!!! AND I HAVE FAITH!! YOU GOT THIS (soon to be) MARINE!!!!***
See ya soon!!!
More to come tomorrow!!

Love,

Mom

****

I know, I blasted the DI but like I said, he had my respect, I didn't have to like him.

****

December 4, 2011

Hey Baby!!!

WooHoo!!! Another day outta the way!!!

I hope everything's going ok and you guys are starting to do more fun active stuff! (And that Sgt. Jones has either got caught by a superior or has at least cooled his jets and came to his senses.)

I also hope you got my package and that you didn't get any troubles from it... Please let me know if you did or didn't... Or if you just said screw it and tossed out the taped envelope...
Of course, I now have enough of those things to send to your whole platoon!

I thought about making a package of it with no one's name on it, just the platoon number, then driving out of state somewhere to send it. That way the post mark couldn't give me away.

But I figured the DIs would just get 'em then... And though they should, they probably wouldn't share.

It's swim week, so I gotta ask... How's it going?? Has everyone in your platoon qualified yet???

Today was pretty slow. I got my jog in, but other than that I mainly just hung out with Jennifer. I know! Big Surprise!! But she was in town to visit her mother and get away from Lenny for a while. She showed me pictures of Kim from Thanksgiving... Wow. Old Jake dodged a serious bullet there! I mean she still has a girl shape, but it's a really BIG GIRL shape!! I was actually shocked to see how BIG she's gotten! I don't know if it's a lazy thing, an over eating thing, or maybe a medical thing. But DAMN she's GROWN! It's really kinda sad, she used to be so pretty... Now I'm concerned that she could have a heart attack any day!!

Yeah, Jen ALMOST made me feel bad... She came straight out and said she was jealous of me because I have a great kid (YOU) and she has her kids... Not bad kids... But not great kids... I say she ALMOST made me feel bad, but hey, how can I feel bad about the truth???
I tried to tell her that Kim and Kelly are just a bit more like Jake, kind of late bloomers. (I was trying to make her feel better.) Not everyone can be as kick ass as JD, and that's ok... But then she pulled out the whole thing about Kelly's half assed attempt at college... Eh, no need to try and smooth it over, she'll just have to let those girls find thier own way. That too shall work itself out in the end. Besides, I think Jen was just feeling a bit down, the holidays do that to a lot of people.

You have the entire Gunslinger book now! (The last pages were in letter #25) Do you want the next book in the series, or shall I give you more time to actually read that one??
The next book is even better than the first, but if you don't read the first than the second can get pretty confusing. Whatever you want, just let me know.

BTW... I'm really proud of you!!!!!! I miss you like crazy, and I've set my sights on February for Family Day!! It's not far off at all!!

Remember! Nothing is out of your reach! Ya just gotta keep reaching!!!

I'll be mailing this on Sunday morning so I'm guessing it's Thursday now that you're reading it. I'm also guessing that most Thursday's you get 2 letters from me!! Get used to it! I'm writing you every day come hell or high water!! NOTHING CAN STOP ME!!!!!

Why?? Because I love you, and I got your back the best way I can right now.

*Oh!!! And also **because you KICK ASS!!!!***

Love, Mom

*****

Jennifer is a very old friend of mine and an amazing success story in her own rite! Yes, her life has been anything but easy, and she has had to overcome many obstacles. At this point I believe she can hurdle over anything! (Perhaps the "Life of Jennifer" should be my next book?)

Of course, Jen's two girls are both beautiful and extremely smart young women. I only hope they will eventually decide to stop using their intelligence to scam people into taking care of them. Heads up girls! I love you, but beauty fades and your mom and dad won't always be there to save you!

****

December 5, 2011

Hey JD!!!
Are you getting excited about your graduation??
I AM!! It'll be here before you know it!!

Oh yeah! I know your slammin busy with classes and drills and God only knows what else! But I tell you what, being busy is good!! It makes the time go by so freaking fast!! It's kind of hard for me to believe that it's already almost a full week into December!! Shoot by the time you get this it will probably be just over a week in!!
You're rockin this out!! **I'm so proud of you!!**

I hope you and all your friends are doing good!! Yeah, you know what? I'm sure you are all doing a lot better than you think you are. DIs lie to your face to motivate you to do even better than the best!

Ok, so, my printer crapped out and I had to go to Wal-Mart and get me an el-cheapio new one. Well what do you expect from a yard sale printer? It lasted over a year, for $10 that ain't too shabby!!

My mile and a half seems to be staying steady at 16 minutes. It seems like it's getting easier, just not faster. But I'm staying at it!! I want to get it down to 12-13 minutes. Then I'll be happy! (And I'll win my bet with Kevin!) I'd like to think it's the cold morning weather that's slowing me down. Hey! It could be!! Right?? Eh, could be I'm just old too... But like I said, you can't stop and neither can I!!!

I'll get to that 12-13 minutes!! Dag Nabbit!!!
Penny wants me to go walking with her a couple evenings a week like we used to do a few years ago. So, every other day I jog/walk 4-6 miles on my own, then on Mondays, Wednesdays, and Friday's I punish Beth! Now Penny wants me to basically punish her on Tuesday and Thursday evenings!! Of course I don't think I'll really be beating up on Penny, she's a bit too broken. And I wouldn't want to have to carry her back to the car. Poor old Penny...Heh heh heh!

Your brother said to tell you hi from him, he hopes you're doing good too, and something about a shield. (?) He was mumbling like he does sometimes so I didn't catch exactly what he was saying. But I figure you'll figure it out. (He also told me you would understand.)

I love you!!

Sorry this is so short today. I'll write more tomorrow!!!! Keep going JD! You got this!

Love, Mom

*****

   The next letter I got from my son wasn't really a letter at all, just a little note in a small envelope. The envelope also had his high school diploma and birth certificate folded up in there. All the note said was....

Hi Mom! I miss you! Love, JD

OooRah!

*****

December 6, 2011

Hellooooo!!!!

Hey JD!!!

Dats right! Another day says goodnight!!!
(Corny, I know. But I couldn't help myself.)

I got your note today from the 18th?!?! I guess it was slower than the others because it had your diploma and stuff in there.

Assuming that you get this letter on the 9th... How did the MCMAP qualifications go for you and your buddies??? Enquiring minds (mine) want to know. I bet you smoked it!
AND, how was the swimming?? Cool and refreshing??
(Probably more like freaking freezing!!! Brrr...)

Gary will be here in about 11 days! (8 days if you're reading this on the 9th.) If he didn't write you from Kuwait I assure you he will write you from here. I'm supposed to go get his car from the shop, but the schmuck hasn't told me if the mechanic is done with it or exactly where the shop is!! I guess I can't really be mad at him, it's his car... (And I still haven't finished his taxes.)

It's supposed to rain tomorrow and Jackie is bringing me the girls in the morning, so I'm going to have to go for my jog/walk in the afternoon. It's all good though, I'm really not a fan of being out in cold rain early in the morning. I figure your sister should pick up the girls no later than noonish. By then the rain should be gone (I hope) and all I'll have to look out for are evil squirrels!

Ya know, it is really crazy how fast the time is going by! I'm pleased every time I walk into Wal-Mart and see that "Christmas Count Down" sign they have up. All it really means to me is less days till February!!!

Hell yeah Mister!!!

Oh!!! I think you'll be taking pictures sometime soon too! Make sure you get a decent package! We'll all want a picture!!! Of course, I can also make copies up to an 8x10 on my printer. So you don't need to go too crazy.

Wow I miss you!!! These people here make me crazy!!! I can't wait to have my right arm back for a little while!!!

I love you and miss you bunches, and at the same time I'm so insanely proud of you!!! You're going to be an awesome Marine!!! Don't you ever doubt it for even a second! You got warrior blood!!
Keep up the good work (soon to be) Marine!! I can't wait to see you graduate!!!
Oh Yeah! And of course, bring you home so you can show off to all your friends!

I'll write more tomorrow!! Maybe something exciting will happen that I can tell you about... Hahaha! Well it could!!!

See ya soon!!

Love,

Mom

P.S. Those damn squirrels at the park have been following me. I'm sure they are waiting for me to trip again so they can mug me or something. No worries, I'm wise to their tricks!

****

Just in case you're wondering, I have a problem with squirrels... It all started many years ago when I lived in an area where there just wasn't any place to buy a really good doughnut. Thank God my mother loved me, and on occasion she would "next day mail" me a dozen fresh Krispy Kreme Donuts to help satisfy my demanding sweet tooth.

As soon as I received my sweet treasures I would put them in individual plastic baggies and freeze them for later. Then I could take one out as needed, microwave it for 10-15 seconds, and just like that I had a yummy piping hot fresh doughnut! Ahh, the good old days...

During this time I had also made "friends" with what I thought was a sweet little squirrel that I kindly named George. It was cute, George waited outside my sliding glass door every day for me to come home from work. At first I would just go outside and feed him a few peanuts or something. But it didn't take long till I thought George and I knew each other well enough for me to allow him in the house. It was like I had a pet squirrel! Or so I thought....

At first he would just come in and help himself to whatever nuts or acorns I had placed in a small bowl on my coffee table for him. Yup, he would perch himself right on that table with the bowl in front of him in the evenings and even seemed to watch TV! But then he started becoming more demanding. He had even made a small hole in the screen door outside of the sliding glass door so that anytime I opened the glass he would come right in. Much like a vampire, I suppose since I had invited him in he figured he was welcome at all times.

Anyway, on one particular morning I was a bit late for work, and more or less running around like a chicken with its head cut off. The night before I had actually dreamed of enjoying one of those doughnuts for breakfast, so the very first thing I did was heat up my last doughnut... It was a beautiful day so the second thing I did was to open that damn sliding glass door to let in some fresh air. I took my shower, got dressed, and walked out to the kitchen to start my coffee.

Then I took my damn doughnut out of the microwave and set it on my dining room table to cool a bit. After that I went back in the bathroom, put on my makeup, and dried my hair never suspecting anything was amiss.

I'm sure you can see where this is leading... I was finally set to walk out the door with my coffee in hand and a plan to grab the breakfast I had been dreaming of when I saw him... There he was, George, that little bastard, sitting on my dining room table, and eating MY LAST DOUGHNUT!!

Needless to say, our friendship ended that day. I was so angry I actually snatched him up and tossed him out the door! But that didn't stop him from stalking me for the rest of my time there. The thieving little rodent even brought his friends to stand and stare in my back door on a daily basis!!

Now you know. It was my last Krispy Kreme Donut... And simply put, that is why I despise all squirrels.

****

December 7, 2011

Good Evening Son of Mine!
This is letter 29!!
Don't you worry, the days they go by so fast!
I promise you, soon this will all be in the past!!

How ya doing JD?? Hanging in there? Kickin ass and takin names??
Stayin in the middle of the pack?
It's Tuesday night, I think you should have gotten my package tonight.
And I am busy praying like crazy that the laffys and heads did NOT cause you any pain!! Oh boy does that have me worried!! I definitely don't want to be the cause of any extra suffering for you!!
And I hope you liked the necklace.

The package I'm sending you in the morning is completely safe!! As will all others be. (Unless of course you tell me to send more munchies, I'll be scared, but I'll do it if you say so!)

Hey!! I took a full minute off of my jog time today!! I got 15 minutes flat for the mile and a half!!! That's a 10 minute mile!!! Not too shabby for these old short legs of mine!! Sadly, I think the fear of getting rained on played a part in it. (We shall see what my time is on Friday. That should let us know if it was me or my fear of getting soaked that got the 15 minutes...)
Yeah, it pretty much rained all day off and on. I think I was lucky to have an hour of no rain to get out and do my thing. (Ok, the rain actually caught me, but only a little ways from the car... So I got rained on for about 2 minutes and actually ran a bit more than normal!)

The girls hung out here for a while as your sister went to her doctor's appointment. Yes, Alexis still thinks Jake is very scary. But she seems to really like me now!! That's cool, she can learn to like us one at a time. Audry helped me make a little banner for you!! You'll see it in one of the pictures I sent in your next package. (It's kinda blurry, I'm not sure why that happened, but it's got Jackie and Jake holding up an important message for you!! Of course Jackie is holding Alexis. The weird thing is a strange bubble like shape at the top of the frame. Maybe a ghostie wanted in the pic too. You'll see it. I think it's pretty interesting.)

I ran into an old friend of my Dad's today! His name is Paul Richards. Him and his wife, Martha, saw you last when you were about 2 years old!! So I told him all about you! He said, "Well ya know Roger and Mary Jo must be lookin down here and I know they're dang proud of him too!! Heck, if your boy is half as tough and a quarter smart as your Dad was he's gonna have no problems beatin anybody or anything!" I assured him that you were indeed just as tough and just as smart! Then he laughed a good laugh and said, "Well you tell that boy Thank You from me. He's gonna do his country proud!" Ya gotta love them old mountain men.

Gary actually text me tonight!! He is back on US soil and in Indiana. I don't know why that's their landing spot, but I think he'll be here before the 17th now. Funny, he's normally always late! Now that his taxes still aren't done of course he shows up a week early! So I'm gonna send you a sticky with his address. That way you can question the hell out of him if you wish.

I hope you're staying as healthy as possible!!!
Remember!!! Just keep going JD! You got this! I know you do!! Be sure to Eat! Sleep! Stretch!! And go to Church!!!!

I'll talk at ya more tomorrow!
Miss you!!! Love you!!!! See ya soon!!

Love,

Mom

*****

December 7th was also my dad's birthday. Alas, he passed away in 1984 at a very early age. In life he really was incredibly strong and amazingly intelligent, as was my mom. I count myself lucky to have had them, though neither lived past 50, they were better parents and better people than I'll ever be, although I can always try.

So when one of their old friends wants to talk to me, I make a point to listen to what they have to say. Of course, Dad's friend was right; my parents would most definitely be just as proud of JD as I am.

The best part of the day was the letter that I got from JD! Oh my goodness!! He was going to give me a mission!! Something I could do to make his life a bit better!! Yes, this was just the moment I had been waiting for.

*****

Hey Mom!!

Things are still pretty tough here, but I'm hangin in. I'm getting used to dying every day, but hey, no one said this would be easy.

Sgt. Jones and Sgt. Santos have lightened up, sort of, so they're tolerable.

SSgt. Smith said that if we write home asking for protein bars that he would give them to us every day! Kicker is, there are 55+ recruits. So, if you could, buy a bulk of protein bars, PLEASE.

Well, I gotta go.

Miss you a whole lot!

Love, JD

PS. I need more envelopes.

*****

SCORE!!! He asked for protein bars!! Joy!! I had something to do! A way to actually better the lives of not only my son, but of all the recruits in his platoon!!

AND the 2 DIs that I "didn't have to like" had lightened up as well!! All good news!!!

I can't even express how happy this letter in particular made me that day. Of course, I realized that 55+ protein bars weren't going to be cheap, but I didn't need that specialty coffee in the morning after all. Nope, my son and his buddies were more important than my indulgence.

Oh yeah, I was all over this request.

*****

December 8, 2011

Hey Baby!!!

That's right! Another day is OVER!!!
You're another day closer to having your very own EARNED Eagle,
Globe, and Anchor!!!!
Wanna know what I say to that?!
OohRah!!!!

I got your letter today about the protein bars!!! Consider it DONE!! I
don't know exactly how many I can get, but I'd say at least 60. The next
question is packaging.... Hmmm.... They said no large packages... I'll go
ask the Gunny here and have that in the mail tomorrow, Friday at the
latest.

I hope the other recruits write home for some too!!! I wish I could send
enough for everyone to have one every day!! Alas, I haven't won the
lottery yet. But I should be able to pull off 60 a week. That's at least a
bar a week for all of you, which works for me.

(Yay! There is a message board online for the parents of your platoon!!! I
see there are brothers in your platoon! Looks like their Mom is sending
some protein too!! Sweet!!)

Yesterday was your Granddad's birthday!! (And of course it was Pearl
Harbor Day too.) But that means I had to go get a little cake.... I love my
Dad, but I only had a small piece. It was store bought and it's pretty dry,
it won't tempt me. Hey! I've lost 6 pounds!!! I couldn't have some yummy
cake messing me up!!! I'm sure Dad would understand. See, I gotta go to
the doctors tomorrow... I must show them that they are stupid and with
a little hard work I don't need their damn drugs!!! Yeah!!! I'll let ya know
how it goes tomorrow.
I bet my one doc is gonna cry!! She has been telling me all along that I
needed the "Synthroid" or I would just continue to gain weight!! That
there was no way I could keep going because my energy levels wouldn't

allow it... Blah... Blah... Blahhhhhh!!!!
She's like a crazy drug pusher!!! Ha!! She's wrong! And I'm one day away from proving it to her!!!

It rained like the devil today!!! Thank God we built those barriers. The basement got a little damp, but nothing like it would have without our handy work in place.To avoid further water also I built a damn and made that low spot, where that tree was, into a small pond.

It's good to have a Mom that ain't afraid of a little mud! The picture is of my handy work! Heh heh heh... I really think going out and jogging every day is helping me get stronger all around! Seeing as you're at Parris Island becoming even more awesome then you already are, I had to do all that by myself and without my right arm!!
If I was not staying as active I'm sure just that little job would have wiped me out. Yeah, I'm pretty proud of myself.

As the matter of fact, I am almost as proud of me as I am of you!! Almost... OK... You got me... I'm actually way prouder of you!!!

Of course since I was battling the rain all day I had no opportunity to find someone to brag about you too today... I guess I'll just have to find extra people to tell about you tomorrow!!

I love you JD!! And miss you like crazy!! I'm glad that you're hanging in there. Keep up the good work Recruit, (soon to be) MARINE!!!!!

Remember! Eat, sleep, stretch, and go to church!!!!
Oh!! And listen to your Mother!!
Chat at ya more tomorrow!!

Love, Mom
Yup! Time for tonight's joke!

Q. Did you hear about the blind man who went bungee jumping?
A. He loved it, but it scared the hell out of his dog.

****

Ok, I guess I should explain the doctor visits... JD went to boot camp knowing that I had regular doctor visits because my thyroid was more or less dying. At least that's what my doctors said. Of course, I decided to be stubborn and take control of my health without medicine. Mind you, my thyroid was not dead, it was just lower than it's supposed to be.

I have to admit, it was no easy task forcing myself to get out and go jogging. But, knowing my son was in Boot Camp becoming a warrior (and suffering) really helped me get my sorry butt out of bed and moving. The best part is, surprisingly enough I have been successful in keeping a good weight without the drugs.

*****

December 9, 2011

Hey JD!!!

Yay!!!! You're almost half way!!!
If the US Postal Service is moving in a timely manner, you should be reading this on Monday the 12th or Tuesday the 13th!! That's crazy!! It kinda seems like you just left. I hope the time is flying by for you too!!! I'm so happy!! I'll be seeing you soon!!!!

Oh!! Gary told me he sent you a letter from Kuwait. I hope you get it sometime soon. But Lord only knows how long that mail takes.... I'm sure you'll get it before the Crucible.

Nana called me today and told me you had to send my letter to her, and that you had it taped shut. So, she is just mailing is straight to me! I guess I didn't get the envelopes to you in time...
(Do you need more address stickers??? Let me know whose addresses you need and I'll get those to you.)

I just hope that "special package" didn't get you in big trouble... No more worries!! Since I can send you guys protein bars now there is no need to risk anything again. (Thank Goodness!) And I'm going to start putting 2 stamped envelopes in with my letters. That way you have them without having to wait any extra time for packages.

Oh! Speaking of protein bars! Great news! I sent you guys 66 Snickers Marathon Bars this morning!!! The post office claimed you should have them on Saturday... But if not than they ought to be there today at the latest!
I hope everyone enjoyed (or enjoys) theirs. Especially YOU!

** From that message board I was telling you about it looks like another Mom has sent bars and vitamin C drink mix too!! I think she is sending Special K bars. Apparently Cliff bars are a good deal, but I don't know how they taste so I'll have to give them a try before I go buying them. Regardless, I hope you guys got them too!! (Between the 2 of us Recruit (soon to be Marine) Moms you guys might get spoiled!)**

The Marathon Bars were a touch costly, so if you really liked them let me know and I'll send more of those a few days before the Crucible. In the meantime, I found another bar, they're called "Pure Protein", they are a bit smaller, (cheaper to mail) but have the same amount of protein. And, on the second bite, they taste like peanut butter cookie dough covered in chocolate!! I think you'll like 'em. I'll be sending those out on Saturday!

Ok!!! I know you're wondering... Yup, I went to the docs today! She didn't cry, but she tried to accuse me of getting Synthroid from "somewhere". Ha! That is until my blood work was done!! Then she had to apologize for her accusations! And I made her admit that SHE WAS WRONG!!!

I lost 6lbs from my last visit and I have gained more muscle mass!!! I'm in all around better shape! And I'm doing it without her dang drugs! Be proud of yourself for that too Son!! I'm inspired to be healthier, seeing as I'm gonna have to do all that traveling to visit you!! Damn Straight! (I ain't gonna lie, most days I would prefer to just stay in bed... But then I think.... Yeah, JD is gonna look super sharp at his graduation!! He can't have a chubby little Momma show up!!!

Nah, what I really think is... JD can't quit, so I can't either. Besides, even though I'd love to just lie around all day, I actually prefer being out and about... But we already knew that! Mmmhmm...

Just so ya know... Now all my docs and my tech know about you being in Boot Camp and about what an awesome Marine you're gonna be!!! OH! And how proud I am of you!
They were all super impressed with you! Tough and Smart!!!! That's you JD!
Heck, even the pusher was impressed! As she should be!

Your Dad called me tonight. He wrote you a while ago, but he needed to go get envelopes. So he is going to be sending that out to you no later than Saturday. He actually feels pretty short about taking so long. I guess he's had a lot of stuff going on. I harassed him about it, but he seemed to really be ashamed, so I eventually let him off the hook. Nevertheless, I told him to get that in the mail ASAP or I'll put him back on the hook!!!

Ya gotta forgive him, he ain't all there. I think Nana dropped him on his head as a baby and now he's a bit slow... Hahahaha!! (Alas, she's never fessed up to it...)
Let me know if you need ANYTHNG, how everything is going, and a list of people for your party.

I love you and miss you like crazy!!! I can't wait till February!!!!!Just look out!! I could crush you with a giant hug!!!! Keep your head up!! You're almost there!!!!
YOU GOT THIS!!! I know you do.
Talk at ya more tomorrow!!! Semper Fi!
Sleep well!!!

Love, Mom

*****

Later that day my blessed Mailman brought me yet another treasure ....

And just inside the envelope flap JD wrote:

"Hey Mom! I'm proud of you! You're my hero!!! Thank you!! I still hate Parris Island."

*****

I qualified for swim today!!!!!

Hey Mom!

Well, for the past 2 days the platoon has finally shown effort as a team via drill. We battle the other platoons all the time. They march tighter than us, but we freaking stomp them at poppin sticks! (Just look up "left shoulder arms, sling arms, right shoulder arms, etc... etc...)

In the morning we suck, I think it's because we have just woke up and feel sore as shit, but we get better around chow time. We're not "IT'd" as much, but still... I hope we stay loud, intense, and motivated.

By the way, it's the 6th and I still have yet to get "the package"...

*Could you send 56 protein bars? As for the talking card... **NO!!!** Any noise during free time will get me killed!*

BTW, I MISS YOU! Tell everyone at home I miss them a lot! Send more letters!

No more book though because I don't have much time to read it now. (But long letters are still good!)

Well, I'm guessing tomorrow's gonna suck. But I hope you have a good day!

I miss you Mom.

Love, JD

(P.S. My buddy Williams let me use one of his envelopes, he's pretty cool. Send a message to Marc and tell him to get people from the square to write too please).

December 10, 2011
Hi JD!!!!!!!!!

Yay!!!!! I'm so proud of you!!!! You musta qualified for swim pretty quick!! SWEET!!!!!
You Rock!!!!

As you can tell I got your letter from the 6th!!
Please tell your buddy Williams "thank you" for me!!!

I'm so proud of you guys for kickin ass at poppin sticks!!! I hope, with the addition of the protein bars, you guys will all start feeling better in the mornings!! Your marches will be perfect!!!! Yes!! I believe you guys should completely crush the other platoons in all things soon!!! Going against you, they are doomed!!!!

Thank You!!! I smiled big time to see your little note inside the envelope!! When you get back we can be heroes together!!! But I don't think we should wear spandex costumes, I'm thinking our costumes should be more like a Men In Black type thing. Of course all super hero gigs are part time, but just imagine all the Shit we could get into even part time! After all, you're a hero to me too JD!! (Not to mention, we really do make a freaking awesome team!!!)

I checked out those Cliff Bars... I personally don't like most of them. But the chocolate chip ones are good, they kinda taste like oatmeal cookies with chocolate chips!!! I'll get those and send them on Tuesday. I think sending you guys stuff on Tuesday's and Saturday's is probably the best I can do for now. (I also like the Pure Protein bars more because they have 20 grams of protein, the Cliff bars only have 10 grams...)

Oh! I'm also sending you guys the Propel water mixes because the other Mom online said you guys could have them too!! And the more vitamin C the better!!!

So expect 2 shipments of bars a week and 2 shipments of water mix a week too!!
You'll have to tell me which bars you like the best.

Hmmm.... I'm thinking you guys may have lined up today or maybe yesterday, and faced the gas chamber..... Yeah, I know that sucked!!! But the good thing is... YOU'RE OK. And they proved your gear would work. Oh! And it is OVER.

Hey! Next week is going to be a blast!!! It's Grass Week!!
I'm pretty sure you guys will have to move barracks for the week. And you might have a bit less privacy there, but it will be well worth it! You're really going to enjoy it!!!! And you're going to do great!!! I'm excited for you!!

Jake is now enrolled back in school!! Thank God!! I thought I was gonna have to beat him!!
He's doing good. I let him read your letter and now he is thinking about going to the square on Monday. He's gonna see if he can talk Kenny into going with him. I think that would be cool. Not only will it get him out, but just in case your friend Marc doesn't answer my message, Jake plans on asking people there that know you to write.

I didn't run the 1.5 today... I just did .5 and walked the rest of the 5.5 miles at a decent clip. My old legs were still pretty sore from all the digging I did the other day. I'm so old!!! I actually thought about just cutting my distance in half. But then I thought.... NO!!!! I am on a mission! I must continue no matter the lack of comfort!!! I'm sure your legs are sore on a regular basis, but you too are on a mission!! An honorable and courageous mission. If you can't stop, NEITHER CAN I!!!
I love the pain!!!! It lets me know I'm making more progress all the time!!! (Ok, yeah, you caught me...I'm trying to convince both of us... Pain is GOOD!!! Right?)
Eh, it ain't so bad. I'm gonna run the 1.5 and time myself tomorrow morning. I'll let ya know how it goes. I'm thinking 16, but will be stoked to see 15 minutes again!

I miss you JD. I'm really getting excited about all the cool stuff you have ahead of you. But most of all I'm crazy excited about your graduation!!! Heck I'm like a kid waiting for Christmas!! Next week I'm actually going to go ahead and make our hotel reservations.

Gotta make sure we get good rooms!!

I hope you're getting all my packages!!!
I love you!!! And I'm BRAGGING EVERYWHERE about YOU!!!
Remember!!! Eat, sleep, stretch, and go to church!!! The rest will fly by!!!
No worries!!! You got this!

Talk at ya more tomorrow!!!
Sweet Dreams!!

Love,
Mom

Wait! It's joke time!!!

A man was struck down by a bus on a very busy street.

As he was lying near death after being pulled up onto the sidewalk, a crowd of spectators began to gather around him.

"My God, a priest! Somebody get a priest!" the critically injured man gasped.
A policeman checked the crowd, and yelled out, "Is anyone here a priest?"
Out of the large crowd stepped a little old man of at least 80-years-of-age.
"Mr. Policeman," said the old man, "I'm not a priest or even a preacher, I'm not even a Christian. But for 50-years now, I've been living behind the Catholic Church on First Avenue, and every night I've overheard their services. I can recall a lot of it, in fact, most of it. So, maybe I can be of some comfort and assistance to this poor injured man here?"
The policeman agreed and cleared the crowd away so the old man could get through to where the injured man was lying.

The old fellow knelt down beside him, leaned over him, and said in a solemn voice... "B-4, I-19, N-38, G-54, 0-72"
Ummmm.... Hahahahahaha!!!!!!!!!

December 11, 2011

Hey JD!!!

I'm back!! That means another day is DONE!!! EXCELLENT!
I mailed you guys the Pure Protein bars and the Propel drink mixes this morning!!
Oh boy! I hope you got them already!! I realize packages must take longer than letters. But hey, I can hope. I also mailed you more mole skin in a card, and of course, your daily letter.

I think I'm starting to figure out how to get over on the post office!! To mail the Pure Protein was much cheaper than it was to mail the Marathon bars. All I had to do was take them out of their original boxes and put them loose in the "If it Fits it Ships" box!!! And the water mixes fit in one of those padded envelopes like I normally send you stuff in. Not a bad deal at all if ya ask me!

I got hold of another type of Cliff Bar. It's called something like peanut butter crunch and it tastes like a really peanut buttery preachers cookie. (You know, oatmeal, peanut butter, and chocolate.) And they have 11 grams of protein. So those are the ones I'll send on Tuesday. Then more of the Pure Protein ones next Saturday...

So here's my plan...
Monday's = Drink Mixes sent
Tuesday's = Cliff Bars sent
Wednesday's = Mole skin sent
Thursday's = Drink Mixes sent
Friday's = A QUIET card for you
Saturday's = Pure Protein Bars Sent
And of course,
EVERYDAY = A letter to my Son!

Please let me know ASAP if any part of the above needs to be changed. I figure you should have gotten the "package" by now. I am still crazy concerned...
Every day I pray, "Oh Lord Please look out for my Son JD. Give him more strength than he knew he had. Keep him calm in the face of anger so he

may harness his own and use it as a driving tool. Give him peace of mind and clarity to help him learn all he must learn. Lord Please give him restful sleep and wonderful dreams and keep him as healthy as possible. Do not allow his progress to be impeded in any way. Send him his angels that they may ease any pain and assist him as he needs them. Please help him reach his goal and become the US Marine You created him to be. And also Lord, Please don't let that package cause him any serious problems. Please!!!! Amen!!"

Yeah, I talk to the Big Guy all the time. No worries, I pray for me too!! I pray every day I'm out jogging that no one sees how much I huff and puff, that my legs don't fall off, and that I can keep on running! So far so good!!

Speaking of running!! Today's time for me was 15.38. So maybe my 15 flat did indeed come from the fear of getting rained on. But it's all good, I'm still happy with being able to actually jog the full 1.5! And to be losing weight without drugs!! (Even if it is slow going. At least it's going!! Right?)

Penny made me go to a Pampered Chef party at her boss's house today. (Pampered Chef is overpriced but really nice kitchen stuff sold at parties like Tupperware used to be.) So I spent like $30 on 2 things.

But most important I had new people to brag at about you!! Even Penny was bragging about you!!! There was another lady there whose son is in the Navy. Apparently, before he enlisted, he flat out told her and his dad that the Marine Corps were too hard for him to even consider!!

I gotta ask!!! Well Son, how did MCMAP qualifications go?
(I hope your prior training didn't mess you up.)

And how was your initial drill and written test??
(I hope they let you guys get some sleep and food before throwing tests at you!)

Oh!!! Just in case you forgot...
I AM INSANELY PROUD OF YOU!!!

Yeah, I miss you lots, but in my own way I still get to talk to you every day! (Hey! That rhymes!) And that works for me!

I LOVE YOU!
Sleep well and have sweet dreams!!

I'll chat at ya more tomorrow!!!

Love,

Mom

****

That was the last letter I wrote to my son in Phase One of Boot Camp. During that time I learned a lot. First and foremost I learned that there really is nothing fun or glamorous about The Marine Corps Boot Camp. Contrary to popular belief, it's not like going to summer camp, or even a fat kid camp. Even the videos online don't do it justice. Its work, a lot of extremely hard back breaking, mind breaking, work with only one real prize at the end.

That "prize" is ERNED. It is most definitely NOT GIVEN to just anyone who stands on those yellow foot prints. Once they have completed all the training, passed all the tests, and lived thru all the mental and physical stresses then, and only then, will they receive a small (EGA) Eagle Globe & Anchor pin along with the title of - <u>United States Marine</u>.

Admittedly, its one hell of a title and it means so much more than words could ever express. It also means that the holder of said title has faced and overcome many treacherous trials and hardships in order to become part of the finest fighting military service in the world. They do this for their Country, for their fellow Marines, for themselves, and above all for your freedom. Their honor and commitment is that of which most of us will never know, but something all of us should respect and cherish in our fighting few.

I also learned that they have a slightly different vocabulary than the rest of us. The "head" is the bathroom, the "deck" is the floor, and "chow" is any meal of the day, not a cute furry dog. The vocabulary list goes on and on, but that's an entire book all on its own…

At some point I had figured out that JD's letters home were his only way to vent any and all of his frustrations. I was not only his Mom and cheerleader, I was his sounding board as well. After all, he sure as hell wasn't going to complain to his DIs. He wanted to be there, he wanted to become a Marine, but he needed to blow off some stream somewhere. All I could do was respond and be as supportive and positive as humanly possible. So I kept at it.

****

Phase Two

It's not easier; it's just a little different. All you have to do is keep going.

   I was under the impression that phase two would be worlds easier and that soon I would be getting letters of joy from my son. Boy was I way off base. Although I did get some "better" letters and apparently things did indeed change a bit... But in all honesty, recruits are still treated pretty much like scum. They're just scum with even more stuff to learn and less time to learn it in.

****

December 12, 2011

Hey JD!

*Just in case you didn't know.... **YOU'RE IN PHASE TWO!! YAY!!!!!***

I'M SOOOOO FREAKING PROUD OF YOU!!! YOU ROCK!!!!

Oh boy was it cold this morning!!! I kid you not, the snot in my nose was frozen!
I assure you it was a wonderful feeling!!
According to the internet it looks like your weekend was a little wet. But it also looks like this week ought to be pretty decent. It says the lowest low for you guys in the next 10 days is 45 and the highest high is actually 70!! Not too bad at all... (If they're right.)

Well, on my part, to avoid further snot freezing I decided to invest in a $1.00 bandana. Tomorrow morning I shall look like a criminal jogging thru the park!!
It's all good, ya burn more calories heating up your body in the cold anyway. Shoot, by the time I was done today, my sunglasses were all fogged up and I was sweating like the devil! So I must have burned something!!!

The fact that the sun had kept the car warm was a pleasant surprise. I suspect stopping and getting in a cold car while covered in sweat would have really sucked.

Gary should be here tomorrow, so I cleaned all his guns today. I figured since I'm going to make him help me with his stupid taxes, cleaning his guns was the least I could do.

Other than jogging, walking, shopping, and cleaning Gary's guns today, all I did was get me some car church in! Oh My! Talk about inspirational! There was a great screaming preacher on!! I wish you had been with me to listen to him!! He was wild and super loud! But what was really important was what he was saying...

It went something like this,

"WHEN YOU ARE GOING THROUGH HELL, yeah we've all been there, YOU CAN NOT! I SAY, CAN NOT, BE AFRAID!!! NO! GOD didn't give us FEAR!!!! YOU gotta KEEP on GOIN! See, JESUS has been there before YOU! THAT'S RIGHT! HE HAS CUT YOU A PATH!! He HAS been there and DOUBLED BACK! Right now HE IS RIGHT BEHIND YOU lighting your way!! That's right I SAID JESUS is LIGHTING YOU A WAY IN THE DARKNESS!! HE'S GOT ONE HAND ON THE FLASHLIGHT AND THE OTHER READY TO PICK YOU UP IF YOU FALL!!! CAN YOU SAY AMEN!?!! HALLELUJAH!!!!!!"

I have to admit, I grinned like a bird head cat listening to that man. I liked his message, but his delivery was so loud and fantastic I had to go online and find his sermon just so I could share it with you!! (The ALL CAPS are where he was screaming so loud his voice was cracking!) But I think the message is a good one just the same and it hit home for me in more than one way.

So, I'll be mailing this Monday morning along with 60 little drink mixes! I really hope at the very least, that you guys have gotten the Marathon bars I sent. It would be really awesome if you already had them and the Pure Protein Bars and the water mixes I sent on Saturday as well! Has the platoon received packages from other parents?? I would think "The Other" mom's package should be there by now too. I hope so!

I'm thinking you outta be reading this on the 15th (maybe) I hope you guys had time to get your pictures done!

Have you guys had the chance to order your rings yet? Remember, if it's less than $200-$300 you should order it there!! And tell me how much it was.

A USMC Ring is a must have!! Way more important than any other ring!! (Except for when you get married. Then that ring will be the most important. But your USMC Ring will still be a close second to it!)

Well Son, I think you know all this but, I love you, I'm crazy proud of you, and I can't wait to see you!!!!

Soon you'll be in Grass Week!!! Even though that will be fun, don't forget!!! Eat, sleep, stretch, and go to church.

Hopefully some interesting stuff will happen tomorrow!!

Or I'll just have to tell you all about the boring stuff!!!!!

Until tomorrow!
Sweet Dreams!

Love,
Mom

*****

I love that preacher and have since made his broadcast something I listen to regularly.

JD and I used to go to a local church. But then we realized that although they seemed positive enough, and they seemed to do a few little things in the community, the truth was that the people who ran that particular church were only looking to get rich…

So we figured that since we were already out jogging on a daily basis, we'd start "going to car church" on Sunday's before hitting the park.

We would literally sit in my car, eat a light breakfast, and listen to whoever was on the radio giving a sermon. It was much better that way, the messages were better, and we could enjoy a variety of personalities and perceptions.

I know it's a bit surprising that I would call myself a Christian and still use profanity, or laugh like I do at the world in general. But I am a Christian and I am also a very real person. I am a far cry from perfect, but I like myself this way. After all, perfect would be boring. Besides, I think if God didn't mean for us to enjoy life than surely he wouldn't have given us the ability to laugh, sing, love, and of course smile.

Don't get me wrong, I do my best to follow those 10 Commandments, and I am indeed grateful for every blessing that comes to those people in need. I am quick to help where I can, just as we all should be. I try not to be a hypocrite, and I pass no real judgments on anyone. However, if something or someone amuses me, I am not going to deny it. If something or someone angers me, I'm not going to deny that either. All in all, I'm a pretty simple person, and I am doing the best I can.

Oh, and yes, the snot really did freeze in my nose but I kept going. The question is; does that make me driven, or a moron? I guess we'll never know.

More importantly, that day I got a letter in the mail. It was the one that JD had sent to his Nana and she had forwarded to me. It may have been a little back dated, but I was dang happy to have it to add to my collection. Not to mention, it was the best letter yet!!

*****

Hi Mom,

So today is Sunday, Thank God!
   The platoon is no longer the best due to a mix of loss of morale, pissy demotivating DIs, and idiots that are showing up from inside the platoon. So needless to say, the heat has been turned up.

 BTW, Thank you for the mole skin. I have plenty now.

   During SDI Inspection, (which consisted of 4 DIs from different platoons) all hell broke loose. Racks got flipped, recruits stripped, assault packs scattered, boots tossed out the hatch, and people getting screamed at. I prayed that they wouldn't mess with me. I'm glad I did because then a sense of calm came over me... No DI even looked at me. None of my stuff was fucked with. It was like I didn't even exist. I was the only one to not get fucked with. I think Nanny was there with me, I don't know how or why, but I know she was.

 Can you please send me a training schedule so I can know what's in the future?

Furthermore, I got a letter from Brad of all people! I was actually pleased to hear from him. Let him know I said thank you.

 Tell Jackie I got her letter and I thank her for the support. Also please tell Beth I got her letter too and I said Thanks! So far I've gotten letters from Chris, James, Nana, Brad, and a few others I can't think of right now. Please thank them all for me.

 So how is everything at home? Are you okay? I hope Jake is back in college by now, he is destined for something...

BTW, DI Jones is damaged, he couldn't pronounce my last name to save his life and it's pretty annoying. Unfortunately, I've been fucking up a bit on Drill, so I'm getting blasted every other day.

So back to the topic of Home!

Keep running Mom! I'm so proud of you. In all honesty, you are my hero. Without you I woulda never made it this far... in anything. You should sneak down here and work in the chow hall so I can see you every day! (It's ran by civilians.)

The 5 mile hike was cake. Just BS because we got IT'd when we got back.

How's the house? Basement still dry?
I miss my bed btw. I miss you all and I look forward to your next letter.
Thanks for everything Mom. Now, stay healthy, keep running, and do what
you do best, be the greatest Mom in the world!

Love, JD

PS. It's still a living HELL here.

****

WOW!! What a nice guy to try and give me some of the credit. Of course, the credit is all his, I just did what I could to distract him a bit.

Hmmm…. He didn't have the Training Matrix! Damn! Ok, I could fix that…

****

December 13, 2011

Hey JD!!!!!!
Another day is OVER!!!! SWEET!!!
Grass Week is around the corner!!!

I got your letter that you sent through Nana today!! I am so glad no one messed with you during the SDI Inspection!! I am certain Nanny is there looking out for you as much as she can! It's funny how ya get that calm tingly feeling every time she's about to "step up to the plate" so to speak. And the more concerned or hurt you are the more she seems to be able to pull off. It's really pretty impressive. I'm sure I already told you this, but in the past I have screamed out to her in my head and had that exact calm come over me. Only to have all the pain I was in literally became a small ache. Yeah, there have been many times that your Nanny has come to the rescue, too many times to get into. And I'm sure right now you have pretty much all her attention.

(She's probably got your Granddad looking out for your brother and sister right now. Yeah, she'd let him handle her light work while she's hanging out with you!)

I hope the schedule I put in here has the right dates. I know I was off before. But it's at least very close. I honestly thought they would have this posted for you guys, or I would have sent it a while ago!!

I really want you to know something....
*I love you, and in a way you're right, without me you wouldn't have made it very far. **But only because I gave birth to you.***
Everything I do for you is because; I love you, I take a great deal of pride in you, I believe in you, and I want you to have the best!
***But, if you weren't as strong as you are, as smart as you are, and as all around amazing as you are**, then all my efforts would have been lost.*
* Don't get me wrong, I LOVE being your hero, and as far as heroes go, I'd like to think I'm not a bad choice. But you need to know that you are a*

HERO in my book too!!

You have overcome stuff that would have broken a lesser person. You came through every wrong turn, test, trial, and even the mistakes of others, all with your head held up high and you humor intact. (And you know how important it is to laugh at just about everything.) Bottom line is...

You have never let me down.

I am proud of YOU, and proud that You are My Son!
Don't you ever forget that!! BTW, it makes me really happy to know you're proud of me too!
(That's why I'm still running!)

DAMN!!! I wish I had known civilians ran the chow hall! I would have got me a job there before you even left!! That would have been Excellent!! But if I applied now I'd probably start about the time you were graduating!! Damn government jobs take forever to get!!

Besides, I probably would have gotten fired the first day you pointed out that Cox kid. They probably frown on the lunch ladies smacking the crap out of the recruits...

Please, try not to let your morale slip. You are going to be a US Marine!! And you are going to be a freaking awesome Marine!! Remember, this is the hardest part!! After this NOTHING will seem difficult again!! You are becoming even more amazing than you already were!! It's not easy, as the matter of fact, it's hard as Hell!! But it's worth it!! And it's NOT TOO HARD FOR YOU!! So no matter what! You keep that drive to rise above all the obstacles they throw your way, never forget you're fighting to reach your goal, and always give it all you have! Even if you or anyone messes up something, you just keep going till you get it right!! Because you were born to be a Top Notch United States Marine!!!
And you got this!

Ok, I didn't time my 1.5 today, but I did time the 6 miles and got 80.2 minutes! That's about 13.3 minutes a mile!! Not too shabby. I figure I'm walking about 4 miles an hour and knocking my 15 minute miles down

to 13.3 with my jogging.
And it is getting a little easier every day!! Slow and steady wins the race!!! Today was extra fun! I looked like a robber running around the park!! Notice the picture!! Bahahahaha!!!! But in 26 degrees your old Momma needs to cover her face!!! Frozen snot in my nose is not my idea of a good time.

I'm gonna try to contact people on your list and let them know they should write you! And if they don't I will go put fleas in their houses!! Yeah!! That'll teach 'em to ignore me!!
Seriously, did you know you can actually buy flea eggs online? Yup, but other than to mess with someone, or maybe to study the little fuckers, why in the world would anyone buy freaking flea eggs?
Hmmm…. It's gotta be all about messing with people...

I guess Penny didn't realize that anyone can write you!! But she asked me earlier today if she could write you and if I would give her your address. So of course I did!!!
However, I must warn you, Penny writes some crazy shit!! But it's usually funny crazy shit.

Have you guys gotten any of your protein or drink mix packages from me? I hope so!!! More Propel water mixes got sent today and I'll be sending Cliff bars tomorrow!!

Of course now that you're good on mole skin I'll have to think of something else to send along with your letters on Wednesday's!! Hmmm…. I'll think of something!

You sleep well tonight!! Don't forget to stretch!!
I'll chat at ya more tomorrow!!!
I miss you!
But, I WILL SEE YOU SOON!!!!

Have sweet dreams!!!

Love, Mom

****

Yes, you can really buy flea eggs online. What wonderful news!

****

December 14, 2011

Howdy Son of Mine!!

Another day down!!! Sweet!!!
Look out! If you thought time was moving fast before... It's about to
really start flying by!!! I think it may be more work... But it's the kind of
work that's gonna be a lot more fun!
Then before we know it I'll be there watching you graduate!!!!!

I hope the DIs are delivering your packages. The Cliff Bars went out to
you today! You know, I'm doing what I can... I wish I could do more, but 2
yummy bars and 2 tasty drinks a week will have to do for now... I'm
hoping other Moms are doing the same or better.

I can't wait to get your next letter!!! I'm still worried about that dang
taffy.... I hope you either didn't get caught with it, you didn't really get
hammered over it, or you just had the chance to throw it away... I should
have never sent it and now I'm kicking myself! Of course, now that I can
technically send you munchies (protein bars) I'm busy looking for the
tastiest!!

It's like sending "good for you" candy!! It makes me happy!! And no
worries, I'm completely cool with sending enough for everyone. It's just
like having more than one kid, ya just can't do for one and not do for all!!
That would be crap!!

Beth came out today and ruined my jog!!! Lord have mercy on that girl!
She can only jog about 20 feet and the starts wheezing!!! So I just made
her walk my 6 miles and then take 3 different trails!! "Sadly," she told
me she's just going to go to the WMCA for the rest of December... THANK
GOD!!! Apparently the hills were just a bit too much for her... She
actually called me a machine!! Eh, she's a wimp. But she means well.

Oh boy!! Gary is all excited!! He bought himself a new shot gun!!! He says the thing has a bayonet on it. That's insane!! A shot gun with a bayonet on the end!?!? He's so excited he had me on the phone just telling me about that gun for a good 45 minutes!!

Between you and me, all I really got out of the whole conversation was all I've already told you.

Oh, and that he plans to get a new stock for it with some kind of special something...?

I showed Gary where you are in the training schedule. He agrees that the rest is going to scream by and most of it oughta be pretty fun. He's excited about coming to your graduation too!!!

FYI, now all three of the ladies that work in the front of the post office know all about you and about how proud I am of you!!! Hey! I told you I brag at everyone!!! And they see me at least 3-4 times a week!! So now they have started asking if I've gotten any new letters from you! I must be good at making my point because one lady in there says she's never been so excited for anybody she's never met before as she is for you!!

She told me today that she's told her husband about the "lady with the wonderful Son who is at Parris Island becoming Marine!!" She said it made his day! "He was real happy to hear that there are still wonderful Sons and proud Mommas in the world."

(Damn Skippy Mister!!!)

Oh! Just a heads up, I think you'll basically be dry firing for Grass Week. Don't let it frustrate you. It's all about learning how they want you to position yourself and your weapon. But from Table 1 Firing Week on out to the Crucible, I believe you guys will all be live.

I hope the schedule I sent yesterday got to you and that I have the dates right on it!! If you didn't get it yet then somehow this letter passed the one I sent yesterday..... I'm sure you'll have it at your next mail call.

I LOVE YOU!! I miss you!!!! And I AM INSANLY PROUD of YOU!!!!!

*** You better be eating all you can, sleeping all you can, stretching, and going to church!!!***

And enjoying at least 2 protein bars and 2 vitamin packed drinks a week!!!

Let me know which ones you like the most! Even if they're ones sent by someone else that way I can send more of your favorites.

I'll talk at ya more tomorrow!
Stay Strong (soon to be) MARINE!!! You got this!!!

Love, Mom

****

It was another great day at the home front! That wonderful mailman delivered just what I needed!

****

Hey Mom!

Today was hell, but not as bad as the past week. I qualified for my tan belt, so that was cool.

Got your "special package" <u>*Send More!!!!!*</u> *Laffy Taffy and Air Heads are AMAZING.*

Can't say much this time, I'll write more tomorrow.

Love, JD

PS. Got the picture too! It made my day so much better!!

*****

All I could think was, "**OH THANK GOD!**"

*****

December 15, 2011

Hi Baby!!!!

Joy!!! One less day to go!!!
I got your letter today!! EXCELLENT!! I knew you'd qualify for the tan belt with ease so long as your other training didn't mess you up. You could also probably take MCMAP much further if you want too. But tan is all you need for now.
I'm super happy you liked the picture!!! That's only a small section of your cheerleaders!! You got a ton of em here!!! And I'm recruiting more every day!! They're even in the post office now!

<BIG sigh of relief.>
I'm even more glad that the laffys and stuff didn't get you in trouble!!! You really want to risk it for more?

Ok... This time I will send 2 Air Heads in a little envelope, taped shut again, inside a card. You will know the card because again there will be an X by my return address. It will not be your Christmas card. So, I'll send you a Christmas card tomorrow morning and the other card Friday morning. It's so clandestine. Sneaky and dangerous!!! Please!! As soon as you get it let me know the outcome ASAP. I was suffering with worry that I may have gotten you in trouble the first time.

Wow!!! I really miss you!! I've resorted to talking to that little Treasure Troll in the car, and boy is he rude!!! Just this evening he was talking smack! He even cussed and called me names!! So I started slapping him around and then he said something about how "A Marine gotta have a treat!!" I decided he was right about that so I stopped smacking him around. Instead I have tied him up and taped his mouth shut until he learns some manners!! Yeah!! That foul mouthed Troll won't be back talking me anymore!!!! (Unless he manages to work himself free... Hmmm.... Maybe I need to tape him better....)

Yay!!! I came in today at under 14 minutes!! That's like a 9 minute mile!!

It's funny, I was pushing for a better time today, (it was 37 degrees, much better than 27 of yesterday) and I could just about hear you say, "Keep running Mom!!" I thought my lungs would explode and my legs might fall right off! And just when I could see that 1.5 mile mark I got one of those God awful stitches in my side! Pain is weakness leaving the body... Right?

I tell ya what, when I saw 13.something on that stop watch, I was so pleased with myself that the rest of the 3 miles I had left to walk seemed like, well, like a walk in the park!!! Heh heh heh!

That's right!! We are suffering together!!! Say hello to the pain and goodbye to the weakness!!!

I know this week has probably pretty well sucked. Drills, gas chamber, tests.... Ugh...
But next week will be freaking GREAT!!!
And you guys will have a bit of a break from your regular DIs!!! At least while you're on the range. Of course you can't be completely free of their company.

I think of them as crazy stand-in parents. They'll be there to wake you up and put you to bed no matter what. But hey, at least they bring you your mail, without them all my letters would just be me thinking I was talking to you while I was really talking to myself. Yep, so in some strange way, those Dang DIs make me seem a touch more sane.

Did I mention that I'm BIG TIME PROUD OF YOU?? Well, I am!! EVERYBODY KNOWS IT TOO!!!

As the matter of fact, I have bragged so much that I had to promise the post office lady that I will take you in there when you get back so she can meet you!! Oh, and my ladies at Wal-Mart are all excited to see the new you when you get back too!! I could go on... The women at both Fas-mart, and the little Hispanic girl from the 7-11, and the lady at Vinny's too!!! There are more, but I'll surprise you with your new fan club later!!

OH!!! BTW, Gary says that the Thrift Savings Plan is something he wished he had done. And he thinks you should sign up for it. I doubt you'll get this in time to make a difference though... That was probably something you guys went over yesterday. Gary said it would have stopped him from spending all his money on women and beer!! Hahaha! (Right...)

OK! My questions of today are;
A. How did the written test go?
B. Was the rappel tower fun?
C. How was the 10k today? (I'm guessing you get this on Saturday)
D. Did you sign up for the Thrift Savings Plan?
AND
E. Can ya make me a list of names to invite to your grad party?

February is around the corner!!!
Keep up the good work Son!!! I LOVE YOU!!!!!
I'll talk at you more tomorrow.

Love,

Mom

Wait!! I got jokes!!

A man goes to see the Rabbi. "Rabbi, something terrible is happening and I have to talk to you about it."
The Rabbi asked, "What's wrong?"
The man replied, "My wife is poisoning me."
The Rabbi, very surprised by this, asks, "I'm sure you're wrong."
The man pleads, "I'm telling you, I'm certain she's poisoning me. What should I do?"
The Rabbi then offers, "Tell you what, let me talk to her. I'll see what I can find out and I'll let you know."
A week later the Rabbi calls the man and says, Well, I spoke to your wife. I spoke to her on the phone for three hours. You want my advice?"
The man anxiously says, "Yes, please."

"Take the poison!"

OH MY!!!! She must be a lovely lady! Hahahahaha!!!

****

Ok, so I have a little green haired Treasure Troll in my car. And maybe on the odd occasion I could be caught talking to, or playing with, said troll. I'm not really crazy, I have a perfectly good excuse! The troll was left in the car by my grand-daughter, and sometimes I need to do something childish to stop my mind from becoming much too serious. Besides, it's fun.

****

December 16, 2011

Hi JD!!

Yay!! You've officially made it to Grass Week!!! You're on the downhill slide now!!!
I'll be mailing this in the morning. So I'm thinking you'll be reading it on the 21st!! That's the half way mark!! You've made it thru the shitty uphill climb!! Now it's time to start having some fun!! Like I said before, you still got hard work to do, but it's a lot more fun hard work. (I HOPE!)

Oh, before I forget, I thought I had some Air Heads still, but I guess Audry took the bag home with her. No worries though! There are 2 Laffys in the special card. (Just look for the X and toss out the envelope if it looks like it's gonna cause any trouble.)

I didn't get to jog today.

 It was "run errands for everybody day!" Joy! I'll just make sure to go a bit further than normal tomorrow.

Your sister started it by texting me at 7am asking me to bring her a spicy chicken biscuit! I tell ya, that baby she is making loves him some spicy chicken! Then Tom actually needed me to go help him handle some stuff. After that Nick called to tell me he needed to touch up the paint on the back door so Harvey would pay him the rest of his money!

(Umm... ok.. I just wanted the paint touched up, I didn't know Harvey was holding out on his favorite "douche bag".) So I had to run home for a bit.

Then Brad called and asked me to pick up papers from the docs and take them to his lawyer. After that Gary called and asked me if I could go to the Hospital and meet this nurse, Dorothy, (she's actually an old friend of mine and his) so I could pick up some stuff he had mailed to her while he was deployed. Of course, Dorothy is a motor mouth!! So I was there for almost an hour!! And of course, I bragged to her all about you! Needless to say, she was pretty damn impressed.

THEN Penny called to tell me that she got off work early and wanted to hang out. Well, I had to go to the station anyway, to pick up equipment for your sister to use at a party tomorrow night, so I just snatched up my girl and took her with me. I saw Tracy there and he asked for your address! So you might get a letter from him too!

Good thing I hit the post office first thing to mail your package of waters right after getting your sister her biscuit!!! Because by the time I got all that other shit done and the equipment to Jackie and Dave it was already 8 pm and I am Beat!!!

But hey! I bet your day was even crazier than mine!!
I also suspect your new barracks are a bit more close and personal than the other one was. But those guys are all your brothers too now. Don't worry, any idiot brothers (like Cox) will ultimately be disowned by the family...

Tom thinks it would be really cool to have your party at that Marine Corps style restaurant in Stafford. It's a pretty nice place, so I'm at least gonna call and find out what the cost would be. But, honestly, for a number of reasons, I'm still thinking a home party will be better.
My number 1 reason is; I know for a fact the food at home is good.

Well Son, Mom's gonna catch some shut eye!! I LOVE YOU!!
Have fun out on the range!!!!

And no worries!!! I have faith in You!! You got this!!!
Sleep well!!
And don't forget you still need to; eat, sleep, stretch, and go to church!!!
Till tomorrow!!! Sweet Dreams!!!

Love,
Mom

*****

Harvey is the contractor we hired to rebuild our house after the fire and he is the one who refers to Nick and his favorite "douche bag." Honestly, their relationship seemed very much like that of two very bitter old people who have been married for an abundance of years. It was very interesting to watch them work together, but regardless of their playful nagging, they did an excellent job on our home.

I'm sure you're wondering why I referred to JD having "new barracks". Well, that's simple, like I said before; I did a mess of research about Parris Island and Boot Camp. So I knew they would be staying closer to the firing range and that those barracks are not as, shall we say, big, as their regular barracks. But it must be better than hiking all the way out there every day. Yeah, you have to give it to them, the Marine Corps has all this planned down to perfection.

I was in a particularly good mood later that day. Why? Oh, come on, you know why... But what you don't know is that I got TWO letters from JD that day!!

*****

Hey Mom!

Boot Camp still SUCKS! I miss you like crazy. I've been having dreams about home the last few nights. Last night I dreamed that you all came to the island and picked me up. A lot of family and friends were there. The odd part was when I came home I was afraid of "getting comfortable" because I was in the "civilian world". Then you came to me and said "SSgt. Ramos said that if you go back to Boot Camp you'll get dropped to a different company." So I freaked out and yelled, "NO! Then I'll just stay here!" LOL!
But it was good to see your face… I almost cried….

Initial Drill and testing are on Monday and Tuesday. So stress is high and shits getting harder, but I'm hanging in the best I can.

Bad news, I think I might have asthma. I'm hiding it, but I'm a bit freaked out that sometimes it gets hard to breathe….?

The pugil sticks were fun by the way! First round I got my ass handed to me. But in the second round I hit him so hard I knocked his mouth piece out!! Automatic Win!
Soon it's rappel, gas, and shoot.

I miss you all so much. I wish I could just call home. Please send me more photos.
How did the doctor's visit go BTW?
Tell everyone I said hello and keep writing me! Every letter helps!
Thank you so much Mom!!

Love, JD

Hi Mom,

So long story short... We came in last place for initial drill. Another platoon came in first with a record breaker. Needless to say, my life is now a new level of hell.

The gas chamber was... Fun.
My eyes slammed shut, my nose became covered in snot, my throat felt like razor blades were lodged in it. And my skin burned... Oddly enough, I thought it was pretty cool! LOL!

The rappel tower was fun too, aside from the rope harness... It was too tight.

Sneak a single protein bar for me. We only get them when the SDI deems it useful. So not every day, more like every other day, but that's alright.

Grass week isn't all that great. I heard its boring and the DIs fuck us up more. And we move to a more "isolated" barracks...

BUT! It marks my halfway point! BTW, 2ⁿᵈ Phase is crap...

OH! I got Gary's letter as well as Dads.

I'd be so happy if Jake went to the square. He could maintain my reputation in a sense. Hahaha!

Table week (Firing the weapon) will be fun. I heard good shit about that, and after that Boot Camp should be smooth sailing.

So what if we're the worst platoon at the moment... Not really, we're just lacking confidence. Come graduation day we're gonna stomp the other platoons in the fucking dirt!
* I felt so bad though.... Our senior DI had to walk away because he didn't want us to see him cry after we fucked up initial drill... That sucked.*

I'll send you a list of people to invite to the party in my next letter! Gotta go! Love you!

Love, JD

****

WooHoo! He had the right attitude! And he was kicking ass!! SWEET!

****

December 17, 2011
Hi Baby!!!

Yes!!!!!!!! Another day is done!

I got your letters from the 11th and 13th today!!!!
I'm so proud of you for smacking the mouth piece right outta that guys face!!!! That's my boy!!!

*UGH!!! I'm sorry that other platoon beat you guys at initial drill... But no worries!! You'll freaking smoke 'em next time!! **Stomp the fuck out of them all!!***
But remember, <u>you</u> can only make <u>you</u> perfect. If someone like Cox fucks up the drill then all you can do is NOT let him fuck you up. And don't sweat it. You are going to be a Great Marine!
All ya gotta do is get to graduation.

Don't worry. I don't think you have asthma. You never have before. But sharing a room with 60 people isn't the best thing for anybody's overall health. I think you probably still have a bit of a cold. If you had active asthma, I assure you, the gas chamber would have locked you up. And it didn't, or you'd be in medical right now. And you most definitely would not have liked it!!!
Speaking of the gas chamber... Only a full blown, born to be, US Marine would say they enjoyed that shit!! HAHAHA!!! That seriously tells me you're on exactly the right path!!

I think, other than the extra closeness, and extreme lack of privacy, you're really going to enjoy Grass Week! Ya know, a little bit of boring might be a good thing for a week.
(What a crazy dream you had!! Of course if SSgt Ramos said some crap about sending you to another company... Well, all I would be telling you was that we had to leave town... Fast... Hahaha! (But I guess you know

that and that's how you could tell it was just a dream.)

*   I miss you!!! Seriously, when you get ready to go off to SOI after your 10 days.... If you don't see me, and if any of your bags seem really heavy... Just do me a favor and don't drop me... Because that will be me hiding in the bag!!*

I'm definitely going to be visiting when you're at your school!! This lack of JD and Mom time sucks!! Neither of the people who live with me shares my sick humor!!! Brad has no humor, and Jake is actually too sick!!

Yeah, I got that picture of you wearing Audrey's sunglasses and it makes me smile every time I look at it. But ya know, even I get choked up sometimes missing you. Then I just think of how freaking proud I am of you and of all the great adventures you have ahead of you!! And of course all the great places I WILL HAVE TO VISIT so I can come see YOU!! Then I go jogging, walking, or shopping for you!! And I feel much better.

(BTW, my jog this morning went pretty good!! The rain waited till I was as far away from the car as possible to start!! Hahaha! That's my luck, but it was just a sprinkle so it didn't bother me much at all.)

I guess I understand them holding out on the protein bars for now. Maybe they just want to make sure they can give you all one every day the last few weeks before the Crucible... Are you guys getting shipments from other parents too?

I hope the DIs are at least giving you guys the water packets as they come in!!! Your body can really use that extra vitamin C!! Yeah, I'm going to start sending 3 packages a week of Propel mixes instead of just 2...

I know you're strong enough, and tough enough, to make it through without it. But any edge I can give you I WILL. And if you can get rid of that dang "community cold" you will all be way ahead of the game. Besides, colds don't just mess with your breathing; they can cloud your mind too!!! I bet a number of the guys in your platoon are having the same problem. Heck, it wouldn't surprise me if that played a big part in that initial drill going bad.

*   As far as sending an extra protein bar... I wish I could figure out how to hide that, but they are so big... I just can't see how to do it without them finding it and you suffering... What I can do is send you a vitamin C*

strip with all my letters! They're like the Listerine strips, but orange flavor and packed with C! I can put it in a little wax envelope inside each letter.

Ya know, Gary has always come back from all his deployments with what I call "kennel cough." It's from too many people and their germs flying around in a confined space. No sweat! With some extra C we'll take care of that and get your lungs back in tip top shape.

It's kind of funny how we are both thinking about the same things. (It's our psychic link!!!) Like the fact that YOUR HALF WAY DONE ALREADY!!!!!
THANK GOD!!!
Seems to me though that you're already well past the middle mark seeing as in all reality **on the last day of the Crucible you'll be an Official United States Marine.** *The last week is just small detail stuff and of course FAMILY DAY AND GRADUATION!!!!*

I'm so excited!!!!! February is right around the corner!!! And then I get to bring you home!!!
(And don't worry about feeling weird in the civilian world! If you start to I'll just have Gary use his best take charge Marine Sgt. voice and order you to relax! He's pretty good at that stuff. Giving orders and relaxing that is...)

YOU'RE DOING GREAT JD!!! DO NOT DOUBT IT FOR 1 SECOND!!! NOT EVEN 1 MILLISECOND! BECAUSE I KNOW YOU ARE AND SEEING AS I'M STILL MOM, I STILL KNOW BEST!

I AM DAMN PROUD OF YOU SON.
Now you sleep well, and have Sweet Dreams about car shopping, and ice cream at Baskin Robbins, and the lunch special at Vinny's, and about showing off to all your old friends and acquaintances in your uniform!

Heck! Have yourself a dream about being the Marine that saves the masses!!!! Those dreams are always good!!

Talk at ya more tomorrow!!!!
I love you!!!!

Love, Mom

*****

I was really enjoying sending the protein bars and drink mixes to these guys! It made me feel like I could give them something to look forward to on a regular basis. I knew the extra protein and vitamins were good for them and it didn't hurt that they were pretty tasty too!

Early that morning I had sent yet another shipment of drink mixes to them. Later that day I got a short note from my son... And I just had to laugh...

*****

Mom!
Don't send anymore drink mix!
Had to write this in a hurry... The protein bars are still OK though!!
Love you!
Miss you lots!
Love, JD

*****

Well, what could I say? Too late! Hahahaha!

*****

December 18, 2011

Hey JD!

Yay!!! We have made it thru another day!! Ta-Da! You on the island, and me among the weirdoes!!

I got your note about the drink mixes. Of course I had already put a package in the mail that morning... (Too Funny!) Gotta love snail mail... I'm thinking you guys won't have much time to be mixing waters, but maybe you can just open and eat a protein bar?
Oh well... I'll just use the cash I save on the waters to get a 3rd box of bars to you each week. I think that will work out just fine!

Your sister and I went to the station for their "Kids Christmas" party. It actually had a pretty good turn out! Audrey made me and Jackie get in the picture with the poser Santa!! But it's a decent enough picture... Cole, Tracy, and Tom were all there, and really all we talked about was the stuff you're doing and about how proud we all are of you!!
If they can all get the days off all 3 of them are coming to your graduation!! As you can see from the enclosed picture, they are all giving you the thumbs up of approval!

Since I was at the station I also talked to your old friend Max. (The little skinny curly haired dude.) Poor kid!! He seems smart enough, but he has 2 kids and another on the way!!!! At least he has a plan. He's going to college to get his RN and his Medic. He's also thinking about the military after he gets an associate's degree. (That poor kid seems to really be jealous of you and proud to be your friend all at the same time.) I hope it works for him.

*   Anyway, Tom, Cole, and I all decided to go out to dinner at Logan's.... You'll never guess who we ran into there... TOM'S STALKER!!! Oh My!! Talk about a total nut job!! She came right up and started questioning ME! Yes Son, she was certain that I must be Tom's new girlfriend! So, of course, I told her that I was!! Hahaha!!*

*   That didn't go over well because then she went off about how I am too old for him and how I could never love him the way she does!!*
(I agreed with that as well, no JD, your mother could never become an obsessed lunatic over anything... Except maybe my coffee... Hahahaha!!!)

Well, I guess I was in a mood or something because I started egging her on. I know I should be ashamed of myself, but I couldn't help it!! She started really going on about me being some kind of creepy cougar lady! Ummm... Tom is only like 8 years younger than me! But she was making it sound like I was a good 20 years his senior! So I informed her that older women know much more about men than little brats like her...

Ok... I said a lot more, way more than I should have, but at least I stayed calm and didn't flip out. She, on the other hand, went completely ballistic!!! She started saying she was going to beat my ass and shave my head!! (Now why would she think shaving my head was a good idea? I know! She must hate me and my lovely hair because I'm beautiful!! LOL!!)

Finally Tom and Cole decided things were getting too serious and told her to go away... (I swear! I wouldn't have hurt her... Much... Heh heh heh!)

It was insane... Even Tom and Cole couldn't really convince her, so the bartender had to threaten to call the cops if she didn't leave... All the way out the door she kept telling Tom about how much she missed and loved him.

Honestly, she was kind of sad... She never made a really aggressive move towards anybody; she just yelled and screamed... A lot... Hahaha!!!
I hope she moves on soon... For Tom's sake... I'll keep you updated! LOL!

I guess now that she knows what I look like and she thinks I "stole her man" I should be on the lookout for her. Eh, it's all good, if I see her again I'll just start bragging about you immediately. Ha! That oughta fix her!!

Ya know I talk to everyone about you, and the cool thing is everyone has good things to say about you!! (What else is there to say?) I'm not sure if they really know how amazing you are, or if they know that I'll kill them if they say anything cross. Either way it works for me!!!

You honestly deserve a boat load of praise. I'm wickedly proud of you!!! And you've earned every bit of it.

I hope you like the pictures!!!!!
I miss you!! Love you bunches!!!

Don't forget!! Eat, sleep, stretch, and go to church!!!
I'll talk to ya more tomorrow!

Sweet Dreams!!!

Love,
Mom

*****

 I wasn't nice to Lorna, aka Tom's stalker… But then again, I didn't even raise my voice, I simply told her some things that weren't true, and some things that were… Tom is one of my best friends and a generally good guy, so when she came at me out of the blue like that just for being in his presence… Well I have to admit, I went on the defense and didn't handle the situation as well as I could have.

******

December 19, 2011

Howdy JD!!

Today was Sunday! That means by the time you read this it should at least be the 21st!! The crazy gift giving, over spending, and totally misrepresented holiday is less than a week away...
And the 21st is the exact middle mark from you getting on the bus to Parris Island and your Graduation Day!

Past the Crap and into the Fun, soon you will be all the way done!

Heck you ought to be half way thru Grass Week!!! Excellent!! So has it really been boring? Or was the pace actually a nice change for a bit??

I went looking for those dang vitamin C strips that CVS has carried for years! And suddenly they don't have them!! So I have ordered them online. As soon as they get here I'll start sending you one a day inside your letters unless you tell me not to. I thought about sending you a vitamin gummy in each letter, but they might be easily noticed... The strips are paper thin and will just melt in your mouth! No need to even chew!!! They should be here in a week, so if for any reason you don't want them just let me know in a quick note.

Gary is staying over tonight. He's making his way to Florida for Christmas with his folks. Poor old Brad is trying to be Mr. Hospitality!! Hahaha! I think he was sad that Gary didn't have a beer with him. But getting a buzz going and then trying to get up at 7am to drive 13 hours just doesn't seem like a good idea. At least it doesn't to Gary and me!!

Of course, Gary wanted me to make sure and tell you that HE WILL BE AT YOUR GRADUATION! He's only going to be in Florida for the next 2 weeks. (As if there was ever any way he'd miss you graduating from USMC Boot Camp! No Way! Ha! As proud as he is of you, I'm certain he'd have to be strapped down to his death bed to miss it!!)

(I made the guys take a picture for you! Gary and Jake look normal, but Brad looks like he's waving hi or something with one hand and giving you the thumbs-up with the other! Well as you can see, he just looks goofy, doesn't he?)

Now I figure I'll be sending you bars on Mondays, Wednesdays, and Fridays! That might help you all a bit more.
I think it's funny. The ladies at the post office have started calling me Miss Parris Island!! Hahaha!!! Works for me!!

I also think it's cute that the little lady there told me yesterday that she's got you locked tight in her prayers. It's sweet. And hey, all the prayers anyone can get are helpful!!
Alas, perhaps she should pray for me... I'm afraid my nose is going to freeze in the morning again. The weather man says it's going to be 22 degrees at the time I'm out running!!! Eh, that's ok I'll be the masked jogger again!!

I'm glad your weather looks decent.

I hope your move to the new barracks wasn't too much of a pain in the ass.
I'm so proud!!! Look at how far you've already made it!! There is no stopping you!!

YES!! YOU REALLY ARE JUST THAT FREAKING AWESOME!! That's MY BOY!!!!!!

I love you and I miss you!!! But I'll be seeing you real soon!!!!!

Sleep well tonight Son.

Love,
Mom

December 20, 2011

Hi JD!!!!

*How's Grass Week goin? Today you're not only a day closer to graduation, but you're also only 1 month away from 20!!!! ** Of course, we'll just keep that to ourselves. ***

I got a note from "the other" Mom on the message board asking if your last name starts with an H! Apparently her son is racked next to you. I hope he's a decent guy.... I'd hate to be making friends with the mother of a rotten kid.

BTW... It's lucky for me you have enough mole skin! See, I decided today to go a good deal further on my walk/jog and gave myself one wicked blister!!! (Yes, I'm a super genius) Ah! But the mole skin I still have here will save me from further damages!! Yay!!!!

That damn Treasure Troll worked himself loose and has started making fun of me for jogging like an old lady!!! It ain't right I tell ya!! Just this morning right out of nowhere he jumped out of his hole and started pointing and laughing at me saying shit like, "You're an ole bitty! Jogging! Pffft! Go on with your huffing and puffing like the little engine that could!! Where does it get you? Now you have worn a hole in your foot!! You have no sense and that's why you do all this stupid shit!"
So I snatched him up and smacked him around a bit till he was quiet again!!
Yeah!!! I kicked some Treasure Troll Ass!!!! Hahaha!!! Hmmm... Can ya tell I miss you??

I hope you guys are all enjoying the bars!! After tasting them all, I believe my personal favorites are indeed the Pure Protein Bars. I'm gonna see if I can find another type that's even yummier and send them. I just like the idea of you getting 20 grams of protein instead of 10.... But I believe taste and enjoyment are important too.

And while Cliff and Pure Protein bars are good, they must be getting old... I think you need a new yummy thing to munch on!! Maybe some of the Balance Bars... I'd send the mint chocolate ones, I know you like those! But they're hard to find in quantity... Hmm... OK, I don't know what they'll be, but I'm sending more tomorrow! And they will be yummier than the Cliff bars I sent this morning!!!! Promise!

I'll keep my fingers crossed that you guys get them by Saturday and they can be like a Christmas Eve treat!! (Or, a "whenever the DI gives them up treat.")

Just so ya know, Calvin and Beth have proved that...
THEY HAVE GONE COMPLETELY WACKO!!
You know they were on the outs. But now she thinks he's a devil worshiper and he's planning to sacrifice Daniel or something! And he thinks she is a hard core bitch who plans to take all his money and run off with the boy!! It's almost comical the way they are both pleading their cases to ME!! As if I will agree with either of them....

(I'm still trying to figure out why they both decided to call me... I guess they figure I'm a good mediator or something...) Seriously, first it was Beth who called me crying, then it was Calvin who called me up yelling!!! I hate to say it, but he posed his case much better than she did hers. She has no proof of his devil worship or his evil plans to sacrifice the kid... (Yes, I wasn't joking, she actually accused him of that shit.) But he can prove she got passports just last week for her and the boy...

Yeah, I doubt she's going to leave the country with the kid in tow. Of course, I could be wrong... After all, to save the boy from being sacrificed to the boogieman by his dad I'd flee the country too!! Bottom line is that they are both nuts!! But Calvin, as usual, seems less nuts. It's really quite an amusing drama that they are playing out!!! I can't wait to find out which one is the real killer!! Is Calvin in leagues with the devil? Or is Beth a truly crazy gold digger? Tune in next week for the thrilling conclusion of 'Who is Nuttier Than Who?' Hahahaha!!!!

I got a good list of names for your party now!! The invites are going out in a few days, but if there is anyone you may have left out, don't worry, we'll get them an invite the first week you're home.

Speaking of you being home, Gary was talking about stealing your bed!!! When he stayed over the other night he apparently woke up without all his normal aches and pains... Then he started plotting on how to sneak it away and make it his very own!!

Ha! No worries, I told him that I'm going rig a bomb to the bed that will blow up as soon as it gets 100 yards away from the house.. So now he's thinking that maybe he should just go buy his own. See, I got your back. For a Momma to rig a bomb just to make sure a comfy bed is waiting on her son is a true sign of love!!

I hope you have fun out there on the range!! I know you'll do great!! Yup, in case you forgot, I'M CRAZY PROUD OF YOU!!!!!

Sweet dreams!!!!!!

Love,
Mom

*****

In all fairness to Gary, JD has a really nice bed. I almost feel bad because it's so seldom used. But hey, perhaps one day he'll be stationed somewhere where he can live outside the barracks. And of course, there is always those times when he comes home on leave!

*****

December 21, 2012

Hellooooo JD!!!!

Almost done with a week in the grass!!! I bet you're learning so much so fast!
The rest of your tests will be easy to pass. Oh yes! Don't forget, next week is going to be a BLAST!!! (It's a silly rhyme! Not a bad poem! I swear!! Hahaha!!)

I wish I could come down and go shooting too. Or just hang out.

Well Son, today was pretty boring. I went for my jog/walk. (The mole skin worked great! I hardly noticed the nasty blister on the side of my pitiful baby toe.) I got those Balance Bars in the mail for you guys and chatted with Gary for a bit. Then I went to Wal-Mart and people watched for a while. There were all sorts of freaky people in there doing their holiday shopping, so it was extra amusing! Yep, I could almost feel the flames of Hell licking my feet because of all the things I was thinking. (Perhaps I should be ashamed... But I'm not.)

Then I talked to Tom for a bit, poor guy got food poisoning and was sick as a dog all day... But, he's got a strong constitution so he was much better when I talked to him this evening. That's what he gets for eating at a hole in the wall sandwich shop that he said smelled like dirty feet and curry... Nasty!!!

Of course I got stuck talking to Beth for a while as well. And she was just as nutty today as she was yesterday....
THEN, Brad and I went to Firebird's for the company's holiday dinner... It sucked. The new finance manager hammered back 10+ mixed drinks in less than an hour. (4 of which were Long Island ice teas) Sadly, all that liquid courage made him even more of an idiot then he seemed to be to begin with.... So instead of choking him to death I decided that we needed to leave. After all, I have no need to go to jail for killing an old drunk ass. I also had no need to be on the road with him...
Oh!! And!!! Brad took the Venza and got the bumper fixed. It looks pretty good too. So letting a drunk crash it right now would probably just piss me off.

I'm thinking that you should be reading this on Christmas Eve. I hope you guys have a really nice day, a good church service, and a nice dinner. I think you deserve it!!! Maybe they'll give you an extra hour of free time or something too. (I doubt it, but hey, I can hope!)

My plans for the holiday are.... Well... To go to church; then jogging, goof off, maybe win 2 or 3 dollars off of a few lottery scratch tickets, and write you!!
I'm sure Jake, Brad, and I will have a decent dinner too. Probably Chinese food!! Heh heh heh!! Jackie, Dave and the girls are going to be at Dave's sister's house, so they'll stop by on Wednesday to get their gifts.

Oh!! Btw, you got Audrey a Zhu-zhu Pet, and Alexis a Pop Up book. Amazing how you can get that kinda stuff done all the way from Parris Island!! Heh heh heh!

I'm super proud of you, and I miss you. I wish you could call home... But honestly, February really will be here before we know it!! And I'm EXCITED for that!!! Heck Yeah!! Gonna have my hotel reservations on Monday!!

Gee I hope something interesting happens here tomorrow so I can tell you all about it. If not I may just write you a "story" about my day!! Hmmm... That's an idea! I'll let you know if that's the case.

Don't forget!! Eat, sleep, stretch, and go to church!! I got your back here!! And you got all that there.
You better believe me when I say, there ain't nothing in this world that you can't do!!! You know I am right!

Till tomorrow!!! Have sweet dreams!!!

Love,

Mom

I have not been a fan of the holidays for many years. So for me to say this was a busy and fun filled time at home or with loved ones would be a complete fabrication. The only reason I have ever bothered with any holiday tradition or gift giving is so that perhaps my children, and now grandchildren, would not turn out to be like me in this regard. People have a right to enjoy themselves no matter what their parent's issues are.

Of course seeing as all my children are grown now, and my grandchildren don't live with me, I really had nothing extra to do. My days were long and empty. But I had to write about something. I had to send JD his daily escape somehow.

****

December 22, 2011

Hey JD!

I hope you all had a Very Merry Christmas!! Next is New Years!!! Then 20 days later is your 20th! After that, 8 days later you will have finished the Crucible and then it's off to GRADUATION! WooHoo!!!! You're cookin with Napalm now Baby!!!

So, as you can tell, I'm assuming that you're reading this on Monday the 26th. Weird thing is that your schedule is empty for the 26th?? Bizarre... I wonder if you're actually getting a day off... Yeah right, I seriously doubt that. Hey, I know! That must be the day they teach you guys the secret Marine Corps hand shake!! Yeah, that must be it.

Well, a whole lot if nothing happened today... I went for my jog and barely beat the rain back to the car. Then Jake and I chatted for a bit. He wanted a burger so we went to see Jackie at her restaurant, and by the time I got back from that Brad was awake... Since then we've just been watching the rain..... So!! The next section of this letter will be my completely fictional day!!!! Hahahaha!!

* * I woke up early this morning determined that today would be the day I took over the universe! I had all my penguin minions scattered, everywhere around the world, armed with laser beams and ready to attack anyone who stood in the way. They merely waited for my signal...
Looking back, I see now that I should have held on to a laser for myself as my defeat for the day was eminent without one....

Yes, the day started perfect!! But then as I came out of my layer I noticed a terrible smell!! It was like burning plastic and dog shit all mixed up together!! I had to find the source of the hideous odor so I immediately began a thorough search of the house. It didn't take long before I found my once trusted evil lap dog Smokie and my remote signaling device!! He had stuffed it in the fire place and was burning it to bits to thwart my plans!! (He had also shit in the middle of the floor! Probably in fear of what I would do to him once I discovered his treachery!) Just as I was about to beat the living hell out of the tiny traitor, that talk show doctor guy leaped out from behind the couch and told me Smokie had been on his show last week and told everyone about my master plan!!

Damn!! If only I had kept a laser handy I would have fried them both right then!
But I had sent all the lasers out with the penguins... And well, you can only imagine my surprise to think that Smokie could talk! Much less that he had ratted me out to the public on that damn show!!!

Alas, I knew the plan for the day was ruined. I was going to be stuck in conversation with a complete nut who thought a dog could talk! Ha!

But he knew something... And I had to find out what it was and how he knew it!!
So I tossed the rotten dog outside and asked.... "You're telling me that little jerk can talk?! What did he tell you?" To which the good doc said, "Well, he doesn't actually talk, we used a pet psychic. And through her he told us everything!! Now I'm here to stop you from releasing your midget army!!!" I smiled at the poor mistaken doctor, "Midget Army you say?? Why, I have no midgets."

At this point the old talk show host was making himself useful and cleaning up the dog shit. I was pleased with his servitude, but still confused by his presence. Do pet psychics really work?? I think not!! He asked where he might find the carpet cleaner and I told him it was over the sink. I sat down to watch the creepy little guy clean. Then he asked, "Do you really expect me to believe you have no midget army? I saw the dang signal device!" I tried to look dumbfounded. "Nope, no midgets. And you destroyed my TV remote, that wasn't some crazy signaling device. I personally think you're crazy." (Of course it was!! But how did he know???) 'Tell me, what did the dog say?"

He cleaned the rest of the shit up in silence and then wearily responded. "He told everyone about how you captured the little people, dressed them in tuxedos, and then brainwashed them to do your bidding! And I want you to know that what you have done to those little people just isn't right! Your poor dog told us about how you made them swim in freezing water, eat raw fish, and about how you strapped light sticks to their chubby little arms! Then he told us about how you were planning to take over MY SHOW!!!" The dude had worked himself into a serious frenzy with his speech and accusations! His whole head was red with anger and I thought he might have a heart attack right there!!

So I did my best to calm him. I needed more information before he died!! After all, while I had no little people, I now understood, the pet psychic just messed up in translation...

"Hmm... You look upset, let me get you a glass of water and then go into my, ummm, basement, where we can discuss this further."

He accepted the glass, and followed me to my secret lab!!! Bahahahaha!! Little did he know that I had laced the water with E!! Soon I would be able to turn on all my party lights, hand him a glow stick, and he too would be under my control!!

But he was sipping it so slowly! It was maddening!!! I decided to continue our conversation...

"First of all Doc, I don't even like your show. So why would I want to take it? And second of all, how do you think I brainwashed a bunch of midgets? I'm merely a lowly suburban Mom with 3 amazing children, one of which is going to be a Freaking Kick Ass Marine!!! That's right! Ain't no little bitches here Doc."

He tried to say something about wanting to pet my head! That's when I noticed that he already had that stupid dreamy look on his face that all druggies get on E!! So I quickly shoved a glow stick in his hand, turned on that God awful techno music, and ran to flip the switches that control the light show!!

He was, and still is, in the secret lab, petting a blanket, playing with his glow stick, and dancing like an idiot... I see my mistake; I got him too wasted too fast... Too much E... Now I must wait for some of it wear off so I can question him... It's almost my bed time and that bastard is still dancing!!!

*But that's ok, I am patient... My penguins are still in place, waiting... I am building a new signal device... And as soon as I know what the good doctor "thinks" he knows, and where I can find this "pet psychic".... I will complete my mission... AND TAKE OVER THE UNIVERSE! Bahahahaha!!! ***

Now, wasn't that a much cooler day than just watching the rain fall? Notice how I even brag about you in my completely fictional day too!! That's how proud I am!!
I know you're going to have fun this week!! Let me know how it's all going!!
I love you!! And if tomorrow is boring too..... I'll let ya know what happens with that creepy talk show host.
Sweet dreams!!!!!!!
Love, Mom

*****

Am I really insane? Maybe... Would I do whatever I could to make my son's life a little better? Even if it meant portraying myself as a complete lunatic? Absolutely! It's not easy to write someone, anyone, every day. At least it wasn't easy for me, especially when all I could share was mundane, good, or amusing news. Had I chose to tell him about all life's curve balls and pit falls that had been coming my way it would have been so much easier. But, that was never an option.

Thank God that day the mailman was my best friend again! I really don't know how I would have continued with my fictional days, but the two letters I got from my son fixed that problem.

*****

Dear Mom,

A) *I scored 3rd highest in my platoon for testing! (I got a 95, the platoon average was an 87.)*
B) *Rappel tower was fun aside from the normal screaming and the tight rope harness that hurt like hell.*
C) *The 10k was more like a forced march to our new barracks with no a/c. It's a small, dirty, crammed, rusty, crap-hole atmosphere.*
D) *Remind me to sign up on Family Day for TSP.*
E) *Invite anyone you want!! LOL!*

It's December 18th and I'm holding up good here, but Sgt. Jones saw me look to the left in chow hall. So he "has something special planned for me"

The barracks is a really rusty place. Red floor, rusty racks on both sides, humid, hot, and hasn't been renovated in years.

During grass week we will get IT'd at least 3 times a day, no time to eat, and over all messed up. But rifle week should be easier.

Thank you all for the Christmas card! That, along with the "Go JD! Go!" picture made my day! Can you send like a family portrait of you guys?

I can't really grasp that I'm about half way through. It's strange to think about because I feel like I've been here for years, but at the same time it feels like only days... Makes no sense...

I hope our platoon gets 1st on the PFT. We got last in everything else so far...

Our DIs HATE us now. I just pray I can make it through the next 2 weeks... Grass Week will suck... I don't know what's going on for Christmas though.

I miss you all so much, I still have dreams about life back in the world. By the way, congrats on the run time! Keep pushing! You're the best Mom in the world!

Love, JD

Hey Mom,

I need to let you know that you CAN send more drink mixes and the WHOLE platoon thanks you for the power bars. You are known by all now! LOL!

Grass week will suck simply because of the 880 yard dash, obstacle course, and strenuous PT along with the elevated stress of the DIs. However, team week is... Soon-ish. I look forward to it.

This place still more or less sucks but hey, I've made it so far, I'm not backing down now. All the fights, all the pain, tears, blood, SWEAT, agony, and the constant hazing/screaming.... And somehow I'm still here. I've been fucked up, beat down, thrown to the back of the rack, practically shit on, and somehow I know I'll never quit. I'm going to make it across that parade deck come Hell or High Water.

I have literally held on to pure faith with no hope of anything else and I'm still here. This is the hardest shit of my life. So close, yet so far away.

I love and miss you. Tell everyone I miss them too and to keep writing me.

Every letter helps, every picture helps, every moment I can read those words from home helps.

Love, JD

P.S. I think I'm gonna love Team Week! Much more relaxing, no one is screaming, just some manual labor. Plus it's a time that we'll get to march ourselves to chow and do shit on our own!

Merry Christmas!!! Love You!!

Not too shabby. He was doing much better than I think he ever realized. But above all he was where he wanted to be and he knew it.

The "Go JD! Go!" picture was of his brother and sister holding up a banner that said exactly that. It was the same banner that my Granddaughter Audrey had helped me make for him, and it was a big hit!

Ah-Ha! And I could send more drink mixes!

****

December 23, 2011

Hi Baby!!!

I got your letters from the 18th!!! The post mark is the 20th, so if my letters are moving as fast as yours, my after Christmas letter about "My fictional day" was probably in your hot little hands on Christmas Eve!! Hahaha!! Nevertheless, I'm certain this is an After Christmas read for you!!

I'm so happy!!! I told you that you were doing great!! And having the 3rd highest test score (95!!! Sweet!!) is freaking FANTASTIC!!! I can't wait to tell EVERYONE!!!
I already told everyone about your tan belt, the swim qualification, the fact that you thought the gas chamber was cool, and how you knocked some dudes mouth piece out!! THAT'S RIGHT YOU ROCK!!!!!

Oh man, I'm so glad you guys are enjoying the bars. I sent more this morning. Of course now I'm going to go back to sending water mixes too!!! I'll get some more of those out tomorrow.

I really want you guys to have whatever edge I can give you so you can start stomping the crap out of those other platoons!! With some extra protein, more vitamins in your water, and little more focus, I know you guys can turn it around and make your DIs love you again! AND CRUSH THE OTHER PLATOONS!!! (Or you guys can be like Robert's platoon, (insane) and just get your butts to graduation any way possible. And still be bit healthier than the others. Really, either way works for me.)

Yes!! I will make sure you have a family picture within the next 5 to 7 days! The trick will be to get everyone together. Jackie, Dave, and the girls aren't coming over till the 28th to get gifts. I should have a chance to get a picture then.

I'm a little surprised that they are still being so hard on you guys during grass week. I was really under the impression that they would lay off a bit so you guys could focus more on learning all the shooting tricks they have to teach you!

Eh, every Marine I know was in your place years ago and they all had different DIs that punished them all differently. So although it ain't easy for anyone, everyone has a slightly different experience... Shoot, Tracy said he got stuck searching for a bug in the sand once while his DI screamed at him to find his damn bug!! Hahaha!! He said it's funny now, but he assured me that back then it sucked!

I know for a fact that what you are doing right now is one of the toughest things for anybody to do! That's why they call guys like you "a special breed." The reason you keep going is simple, You, My Dear, ARE A MARINE. That is what you were meant to be all along. (I'm pretty sure that's also why you brutalized all those GI Joe's when you were little. They were Army guys and the Marine in you just couldn't relate to them... Hahaha!)
You WILL be a FREAKING AWESOME MARINE!!
SEMPER FI MISTER! ALWAYS FAITHFUL!!! THAT IS YOU. And don't you ever doubt it.
Besides, I think I make a pretty good Marine Mom too.

My run today went pretty well, but I think my little toe boo-boo is slowing me down. I didn't time it or anything; I'll do that on Saturday. It just felt slower, so I made a point to take an extra trail. The way I see it, if I can't go quick, then I'd better go up!! So I took the uphill trail to the spot where we were planning to build a house under the cover of darkness!! Heh heh heh! I tell ya, that hill is steeper that it looks... But I made it!

I know exactly what you mean by "it seems like you have been there forever, but then it also seems like you just left here yesterday!!"

Yep, I'm pretty sure that yesterday I was 22 years old, but it also seems like I'm over a thousand years old. Ok, that's a bit of an exaggeration, but you get the point. I am like 22 and I must be some kind of vampire or something because I've actually been around a mighty long time!! (As a sad vampire who's back aches from sleeping too long, and who keeps growing these crazy gray hairs on her head!)

It's all good JD! You're getting closer every day!! I sure do miss you! And I sure am proud of you!!
I'll be seeing you real soon, and when I do, you will be a full fledge US Marine!!
Remember, No Worries Son, they ain't got a damn thing that you can't handle. And that is a fact.
Come on team week!!!! JD needs a little JD time!!

I love you!!!! Sleep well!!
I'll chat at ya more tomorrow!!

Love,

Mom

****

To my surprise I received yet another short note from JD that day. It was written on the back of one of the envelopes that I had sent him! On the back of envelope #39 to be exact.

****

Mom,

Long story short, grass week SUCKS. There are two points to this week... Train us on the M16 A4, and FUCK up recruits. Yeah, grass week is said to be the hardest week in boot camp. But I'm doing alright.

Of course today after shooting, our platoon laid covered in sweat half dead from getting IT'd so hard and for so long... It is what it is.

Yeah, the shit sucks, but oh well... I'll write more tomorrow.

Love/Miss you A LOT, JD

****

Wow.... Well at least they weren't going to get soft.

****

December 24, 2011

Howdy JD!

It's me again!! Ya know what that means? You've made it!! Grass (Hell) Week is over and another day is just about done!!! Yay!!!!!

I got your note today. (The one on the back of the envelope.) That sucks! Grass week was supposed to be a bit more relaxed...
Eh, this too shall pass... And you will make it through. As the matter of fact, it's Friday night! So by the time you get this, you will have already made it through! Sweet! Good job Recruit!

Now you're in Table 1 Firing Week. I certainly hope the freaking DIs lay off a bit now.
Ya know Team Week is actually the last week of phase 2. Time is moving insanely fast!! Every day brings you closer to your goal and closer to home.

I can't wait to see you! I've been trying to figure out how I could sneak on the island and just say hi, but I'm pretty sure the Marine Corps would frown on that if I got caught.
Seems they have even made a point to not have any real blueprints or even complete maps made public!! Sneaky, sneaky... (Actually they are smart, smart!) That's fine...February isn't far at all!!

Of course, Team Week is also the when they have all those dental surgeries' planned. Ugh!! Well, if they come after your wisdom teeth, I hope they do it real early in the week. That way you'll have some time to heal just doing regular manual labor instead of being out on the firing range and trying to heal. I think BWT/Table 2 Week actually has belt fed weapons. It could be fun if I'm right. But, if ya just had your teeth pulled.... Then the vibrations might really suck!! Hmmm..... Let me know if and when they pull the wisdom right out of ya. And, how you're doing.

So, tomorrow is the Saturday before Christmas, and somehow Tom has talked me into going to the MALL!!!! He needs a gift for his new

girlfriend, and he can't get there to get it because he has to work. Wow!!
I'm a sucker!!! At least I know exactly what he wants me to get, and
exactly what store I can find it at!! But I still may have to throw a few
elbows!
After all it's the SATURDAY BEFORE CHRISTMAS!!
I hope I don't kill anyone...
No sweat! If I get arrested I'll just have Jake write what I tell him to write
to you until I get bailed out!! Then we'll be right back on track!!

The ladies on the message board said that you guys should have had a
long church service on Christmas Sunday. And another woman whose
son was there last year said that they gave the recruits a nice dinner for
Christmas too. I really hope that they did the same for you guys.

You all deserve a little something extra.

It's almost New Year's Mister!!!
*But most important is **IT'S ALMOST FEBRUARY!!!***

OH!! Just so ya know, I got water mixes out to you guys this morning, and
tomorrow morning I'll be sending out more Balance Bars along with this
letter.

Keep going JD! You're almost there!!!

Remember... Pain is Temporary, GLORY IS FOREVER!!!

Eat, sleep, stretch, and go to church. I love you!!!
I'll chat at ya more tomorrow!
Keep Kickin' Ass (very soon to be) Marine!!!

Love,

Mom

****

I was wrong about BWT (Basic Warrior Training) week. Alas, I was relying on information from a Marine who had been on Parris Island almost 20 years prior, but times change and The Corps changes with them. So now day's recruits don't get to really learn belt fed weapons until they move on to the next phase of their training after Boot Camp. That was a real bummer for me. I knew JD would enjoy learning about, and firing the big guns, but he would just have to wait until he was officially a Marine before they would teach him those things. (On a side note, JD did indeed have a blast at SOI learning and firing the big belt fed weapons. Good things really do come to those who wait after all.)

Yes, I am a sucker, and I did go to the mall for my friend Tom the weekend before Christmas. It was bad, but not too bad. At least I accomplished my mission without getting hurt or hurting anyone in the process. Yeah, to make it out of the Mall unscathed that close to Christmas is a win in my book.

Of course, like I said, I'm not a fan of the holidays. But damn, I sure missed my son like crazy! My comic relief and faithful assistant was many miles away. I knew his birthday was really going to suck for me too, but then I also knew it would be worse for him.

****

December 25, 2011

Hi JD!!!

I made it! Oh the crazies at the mall tried to swarm me! But I busted right through them!! Straight to the Jewelers where I purchased the necklace that Tom wants to give his girl.
Personally, I think he's going a bit over board, they've been dating maybe a month, and that necklace cost over $80. But hey, out of all the chicks he's dated, this is the (oldest) best one yet.

So it's Christmas Eve and Brad got off work early. But not too early. I still had plenty of time to go to the mall for Tom, swing in to Target, get you guys some more Balance Bars in the mail, and go for a 5 mile jog/walk. (I'm huffing and puffing a little less each day!)
I timed my 1.5 mile... It sucked... 14.5... Yeah, I'm blaming my tiny almost completely healed blister.

Eh, I was probably just having an "off" day. Besides, a month ago I would have been thrilled with 14.5!! But ever since I got in the 13s... Well, you know how it is... I'm spoiled and expect to always have the speed on... That's how it should be... Right?

I know your new barracks suck, but I'm seriously hoping this week is more fun than last week. At least you should be really shooting!

Hey, I found out today that freaking Chuck Norris is over 70 years old! All I could think was... Holy Shit?!?! Really?!?! And yes!! Really!! The dude may have had some plastic surgery, but what really impressed me is that he still looks to be in fighting shape! Crazy!! Ya know, I don't think he ever did drugs, or drank a whole lot like most other fighters turned actors did... Heck, some of those guys have turned into serious chubsters thanks to the booze.

Just goes to show what staying active and living kind of healthy can do for ya. Kind of like you're Pawpaw, I dare say that dude is still in fighting shape too!! So, I figure if I keep up the jog/walking and just generally stay active and live more "healthy" than not... Perhaps I too can grow up to be just like Chuck Norris! (Except in chick form... Hahahaha!)

It's a little crazy how fast December has flown by! But hey, it works for me. The faster time goes, the quicker I get to see you!! I got a neat little gift for you for your graduation. Something that will fit in your pocket and you can take ANYWHERE!! I think you'll dig it. (Now you're probably thinking... Hmmm... Fits in my pocket!? I can take it anywhere??? I'm gonna dig it!?! Hmmm... What could it be? Well, you'll find out when ya get it!)

So! I was talking to your sister this evening and we got on the subject of laws and punishments for fucking evil people. Now I distinctly remember her being a bit of a bleeding heart in the past... NOT ANYMORE!! She even agreed that people who drive under the influence should be broken right then and there when they get caught. None of that going to court stuff!! Let the officer just break the damn drunk's leg right there beside the road!!! Yeah, I was impressed with her new found cruelty for the evil bastards. Of course, in light of her new "Hang Em High" attitude, I am now certain that she is making a baby boy this time!! (Or a really mean ass girl!!! Hahaha!)

Ya know, I am a lucky Mom!!! I have 3 children, and all of you are really cool. You all have big hearts and not one of you is afraid of shit!! Yup, I'm proud of Jackie, she's a hard ass worker and a great mom to her girls. I'm proud of Jake, he's a smart guy, and can find a loop hole in just about anything to make him seem like he's right about most stuff. And I am SUPER PROUD of YOU!! You're smart, a hard worker, tough as nails, and driven. I see a lot of my attitudes in you, nothing can ever stop you. You got the best of all the family traits!!! Bottom line, you Rock, and I am really lucky God gave me such awesome kids!!!

I really hope you had a good Christmas!! I assure you, the New Year is going to be GREAT!!!

KEEP GOING JD!!! YOU'RE GETTING CLOSER EVERYDAY!!!!

Sweet Dreams!!!

Love,

Mom

*****

I've never claimed to be a particularly forgiving person. Christian? Yes. A good Christian? Probably not. See, I have no tolerance for anyone who takes advantage of, hurts, or endangers the lives and welfare of innocent bystanders. The way I look at it is simple, we all have to share the same world and sadly there are evil, thoughtless, self-centered jackasses everywhere you go. When one of them decides that he or she is for some reason allowed to affect the life of an innocent bystander, well, I think they have proven themselves in need of a hard fast lesson.

Don't get me wrong, the Marines may have a need to endanger my son and put him in harm's way. It's not the same thing. First of all he volunteered thus he's not just an innocent bystander, and second, someone has to teach the evil jackasses of the world their lessons. Luckily, our Marines just happen to be perfect for the job.

*****

December 26, 2011

Hey Baby!!!!

Well, I made no cheesecake, and no fudge... But I had to make something, so we all settled on some gooey brownies and reindeer stew. (Ok, it's venison stew, but close enough!!)

This morning I decided to go out to Wilderness Park for my jog/walk... Don't ask me why... I know it's nothing but huge hills out there. But for some reason I just decided to change up a bit... Well, I got out there and was sitting for a moment listening to the preacher on the radio before I actually got out of the car to go and get moving... Anyway, right before I got out, this guy with a chiwawa in a little Santa suit shows up. He says hello then asks me if I have any family members going through a trying time... I said, "Well, I have a son in Marine Corps Boot Camp. I suspect that's pretty trying." Then he asks if it's ok for him to pray for my son!!! Well, I'd never turn down more prayers, so I told him, "Absolutely!"

I was thinking that he may bow his head and say a little prayer, but NO! This dude was pure preacher material! He was loudly thanking God for you and your service. Then he was sending blessings and asked God to send you 12 angels to protect you and give you strength. Ok, all that was cool... Then he thanks me!!! He said he was sent to that park, and he knew he would meet a lady there because he needed to pray for the person in her family who was facing a "trying time"!! Crazy, huh!?! And it's not my "normal" park... It was truly bizarre!! But it was kinda cool too. Honestly, him and his little Santa dog made my day. I hope his prayers along with mine and everyone else's are helping you along. Seems to me that his were so loud there is no why God missed them!!

I gotta say, it was a little strange too... Eh, whatever works! Right? Besides, I think you already have some seriously kick ass angels lookin out for you anyway.

Tomorrow I'll be getting more drink mixes out to you guys! I talked to Nana yesterday and told her that she too could send you guys' protein bars!! I even told her how many, and the best way to send them. (Flat rate boxes are freaking great!) I think she was under the impression that you could only get 1 shipment... But I cleared that shit right up!! I figure if I can talk her into sending 2 shipments a week and I send 2 or 3... And maybe that other mom from the web sends a shipment or 2 a week... Well you guys should be set!!! I can hope!! (Nevertheless, I will always have your back!! So you can COUNT ON at least 2 shipments of bars and 3 shipments of drink mixes a week!! I'll try for 3 of the bars some weeks... But I can only guarantee 2.)

BTW, you still haven't told me which bars are your favorites!!?? And if I should send the Marathon bars again around your birthday or around the Crucible...

It's my understanding that you'll be shooting 500 to 800+ rounds this week!!! Ok... Now that has to be kinda fun!!! I hope so!

Ya know, I've been thinking, I might start another eBay business... I have so much silly stuff in the attic space over the garage, I'm sure I can make a few extra bucks with it. And it amuses me to watch the end of the auctions. Heck, I'm so familiar with the post office now, I pretty much have the shipping rate thing down pat! Plus with an eBay business maybe I can make more money and still set my own hours.

Yep!! That might be my next plan!!
ALSO, with an eBay business I'll be able to travel anywhere and still keep working!!! (See, Momma thinks of everything!!!)

I'm really, really, really, looking forward to February!!!! I'm so proud of you!! And proud to be Your Mom!! Tomorrow I will have my hotel reservations in place!!!! Yay!!!!! I'm going to be seeing YOU, My Son, The Marine, SOON!!!
(I'm a little excited... Can ya tell?? Hahaha!!)

Just do not forget!!! Eat, sleep, stretch, and go to church!!

I'll talk at ya more tomorrow!
Sweet Dreams! I love you!!

Love,

Mom

*****

There is no other way to put it. The guy at the park was both odd and kind of cool at the same time. Of course, it was his little dog in the Santa suit that made him obviously completely harmless.

*****

December 27, 2011

Hi JD!

Woohoo!!! Another day done!!!!
It's almost the New Year!

I got my reservation for February at the KOA camp ground in South Point SC!! It's about 30 miles from the island, but I was able to get a little lodge big enough so Jake, Jackie, Dave, the girls, along with me and Brad can all fit in there comfortably!

Yup! Gary, Cole, Tom, and Tracy can get a cabin at the campground to share too!! Even Penny is thinking about getting a cabin there!

I'm not sure what Nana and Papa's plans are, but I'll talk to her about it tomorrow. Of course, since the reservation is only for two nights, we'll be snatching you up right after you're released, going to do some lunch, and

*then riding on home. That way you can sleep in your own bed ASAP!
I know you'll have a few sea bags with you too, so we're bringing the
truck. Yup, it'll be a nice comfy ride home!!*

*Well, as it turns out the post office was closed today. I guess since
Christmas was on a Sunday they just had to take Monday off... But that's
ok. Just means I'll be putting water mixes and protein bars in the mail in
the morning with this letter.*
*(I'm looking at the bright side! Since I'll be mailing them together, I'm
stuffing the water mixes in the same box as the bars. That will save me
like $2 and change. And saving always makes me a bit happier!)*

*Do me a favor, check the postmarked date on the next box of bars you
guys get from me and let me know how long they seem to be taking to
get to you. I'm trying to figure out when stop sending them. No need for
any to arrive while you're off doing the Crucible. BUT, **I wanna MAKE
SURE you guys have a bar each day the week leading up to it!!** So if I
know how long it takes, I can know when to start sending daily
shipments*

*Now that I'm thinking about it... You're probably slammed with mail
today since the postal service was down for 2 days instead of just the
normal Sunday.... Hmmm.... I'll keep this letter short....*

*Just so you know, I have a ton of blank address labels. So, since I know
you guys are getting busier every day, I'm printing up return address
labels that anyone in your platoon can use. I hope they come in handy for
someone... I have the terrible feeling that some of the guys there may
not have the same resources at home... So anything to make it a bit
easier all the way around should be a good thing... (I hope...)*

*Needless to say, tomorrow I'll be sending them in a package. What I'm
doing is making pre return addressed envelopes... Well you'll see... Then
you can share them.*
Hey, it's all about the team.

I'm still running! Not getting any faster... But I sure can go further! I jogged 3 miles straight this morning without stopping!! HELL YEAH! (I thought maybe I was off on my distance, so I double checked with the odometer on the car and it was 3.1 miles!! Excellent!)
And my lungs didn't even explode!!! Hahaha!! But my legs still hate me... Eh! They'll get over it, they're stuck with me anyways.

Hmmm... I said I was gonna keep this short... Heh heh heh!

You're almost there JD!! I'm really proud of how far you have already come!! Keep it up!!

You have an amazing future waiting for you!!!!!

Sleep Well!! I'll chat at ya more tomorrow!!!!!

See ya soon!!!

Love, Mom

****

JD really appreciated the address labels I sent him. It saved him time and energy, both of which are in high demand at Boot Camp. For him I sent labels with our home address, his return address, and addresses of other friends and family. For the rest of the platoon I simply sent return address labels with "RCT _____" at the top so all they had to do was fill in their last name and that seemed to work out well too.

To say that I enjoyed being able to send them stuff was an understatement. Every day that I could put a package in the mail was a good day as far as I was concerned. The only days better than those were the ones when a preprinted address showed back up in my mailbox.

*****

Hey Mom,

Today is the 22ⁿᵈ. The photos from your letters #40 and 42 made my day!

Today was also the first "decent" day this week. The platoon actually behaved for once. Thankfully grass week is almost done. The next week flies by, or so I've been told.

I hope I qualify expert.

It's still pretty tough though. But I have good news! I've lost weight, am getting stronger, and I'm another day closer to graduation!

By the way, have you ever crawled a mile in wet sand while occasionally doing MCMAP and then got the shit ran out of you running and doing dips for 1 ½ miles? Somehow they fit that in 3 hours this morning. It might not sound tough, but it is.

I miss you a lot! Thoughts of our times hanging out and having fun get me through all the hard shit.

Keep writing!

Love, JD

*****

I have always taught my children to speak freely to me because I never wanted them to feel the need to hide anything. I also taught them that it was best for me to learn of all their good and bad deeds directly from them. One way we could talk it over, the other way, well it wasn't going to be a decent two sided conversation....

But looking back, this is the one thing that JD could have kept to himself... See, my son is 5'9 and he weighed 170lbs when he left for Boot Camp. He was truly in great shape! To think of him losing weight didn't equal "good news" to me no matter what he thought! For crying out loud! I'm a Mom! I didn't want them to turn my boy into a skeleton! But he also said he was getting stronger, so I didn't freak out too bad...

I also got a second letter that day. It was written on paper that looked like it had been through the ringer, twice. But I loved it just the same.

****

Dear Mom,

Well, as you can guess... Today was a bad one... Our PMI loves us, but some idiots in the platoon fucked up during drill... over... and over... and over again... SSgt Smith was pretty pissed so we got destroyed and didn't get to eat or drink much either, but oh well...

I hope you had/have a good Christmas. I know we won't... lol!

Oh, and the Propel drink mix (or any drink mix for that matter)... Yeah, it's a definite no no now...

Hey, like I said in my last letter, yesterday was actually good. And tomorrow the platoon is going to GET SOME! OooRah!

How long does it take for my letters to get home? How's life at home? Who is coming to my graduation? And how is the best Mom in the world?

Love, JD

P.S. Please message Chris – "Hey Dude, I got your letter on the 23rd. Congrats on the job! I'm hanging in here but it's still hell on earth. I sure wish you were here with me that would make shit a lot easier. But alas, we'll chill at a later date. LOL! I'll get a letter to you when I get more time. Semper Fi buddy."

They were killing me by going back and forth on the drink mixes. But it was their show to run, all I could do was to try and keep up with the changes in the program.

JD's buddy Chris had originally planned to join the Marine Corps with him, but his family ended up moving to Australia before he actually had the opportunity to enlist due to his dad's job. I'm certain had they gone in together it really wouldn't have been any easier for JD, but it's nice to think that misery really does love the company of old friends the best.

Of course, I'm sure should the day ever come that Chris comes home and decides to join, he will also make an excellent Marine. After all, he too left boot prints on the side of my house.

*****

December 28, 2011

Hey JD!!

I got your letters today from the 22nd and the 23rd! It seems to me that your letters normally take 2 to 3 days to get here from the day they're mailed.

You're killing me! First it's no Propel water mixes, then its ok, and now it's a no again!!!
(After you graduate, is it ok for me to smack your DIs??)

Well, the box I sent this morning has Pure Protein Bars and in a separate envelope inside there are 60 more drink mixes.

The DIs can throw them away if they want to, it's really no biggy as long as you guys get the bars. SO! No matter what they say, I'm only sending the bars!! Sheesh!! They're like a bunch of wishy washy women!! (Kidding.... Kinda...)

I sent Chris your message!
  Poor Chris, I know he really wishes he was there with you. But maybe he'll still enlist one day. And then you can send him letters giving him as many pep talks and helpful hints as you can!! Or, maybe you'll get stationed near him and you guys will be able to hang out on your days off.

Wait! Chris has already responded!
[Thanks, let him know I'm still cheering him on! He has come this far and there is no turning back now, good luck!]

Hmmm.... I have crawled 500 or so yards in stinky mud... And that sucked enough for me. But, Nope, I have never crawled a mile in wet sand... And I hope I never do. Then you add on jumping up to fight?? Holy smokes!!! Yup, you got me beat!!!
(Remember, you can use the mole skin on your elbows too! It will help protect them from the sand that will ultimately work its way up your sleeves and save them from being rubbed raw.)

IMPORTANT NEWS FLASH – Brad accidently gave your account number at the bank to his HR department for his direct deposit... Now there is $906.15 in YOUR account that we kinda need for bills... (Yes, Brad is a super genius.) So, I need your permission to get that money out of your account to give him...
If that's not cool with you than we'll wait till either you get back or the bank corrects his mistake. Oh, and he says he is sorry for the mix up. And I believe he means it...

NOW BACK TO OUR NORMAL PROGRAMMING!!

Hmmm.... So, some people keep messing up during drill...
That sucks! Tell them NO MORE BARS FOR THEM!! Ok... I guess they can
still have some... But they better start focusing more Dag Nabbit!!!
(Actually, I totally understand a screw up here and there... Everyone has
an "off" day now and then. I just hope you guys all have some ON days at
the same time soon.)

I hope you qualify as Expert too!! I bet you will! Just stay focused and do
exactly what your PMI tells you to do. Those guys are damn good at what
they do. They really are some of the best instructors in the world. Take
their knowledge and your natural skill... Yeah, you're going to do great!
Heck, by the time you get this you'll probably already be done
qualifying!! Of course, it looks like there are 2 more qual days next week
too if I'm reading the schedule right.

Its Tuesday night, I'll mail this in the morning.
I think you'll get it on the 30th or 31st!!!
HAPPY NEW YEAR JD!!!
2012 is sure to be one wild ride!!!
Hmmm... Another holiday that falls on a Sunday.... I wonder if the post
office is going to be closed again this coming Monday. I hope not... But I
think it's possible.... So, I'm gonna send out your next shipment of bars on
Thursday instead of Friday, just in case.

I didn't get to run this morning because it was raining like crazy!! It's all
good. I'll just have to go a little further tomorrow. But on a great note,
all my ditches and the dam I built worked!!! No water in the basement at
all!!! Yay!!!

I'm glad you're getting stronger and faster. And I'm glad you maintained
your weight before you went in!! Seeing as you're losing weight now,
Good Lord! If you had gone to Boot super skinny that would have been
bad!!! No worries!! We'll go to Vinny's and I'll make you a cheesecake!!
Yep! We'll get you looking healthy again!!

February is around the corner Mister!!!! Keep going!! You got this!!!
I'll write more tomorrow!!!
I miss you!!! Semper Fi Son!!
Sweet dreams!!!!

Love.

Mom

December 29, 2011

Hey Baby!!

HAPPY NEW YEAR!!!!!

Well, it's Wednesday the 28th, so maybe you're reading this on New Year's Eve, but it's probably January 2nd or 3rd. If it is the 2nd or 3rd....That also means.... It's Team Week!!! Week 9!! Holy Smokes!! That is freaking Sweet!!

I think you guys will get your graduation packets to send out this week too. Please send it as soon as you can!! I'm so excited to see YOU and all the stuff you've been doing! I will be diligently looking for the packet in the mail.
ME and, I believe; Brad, Jake, Jackie, Dave, the girls, Gary, Tom, Cole, your Dad, Nana, and Pawpaw are all coming to your graduation. Still in the maybe box are Tracy and Penny... They are both not sure if they can get off work or not yet. So you have 12 adults (possibly 14) and 2 children. That's a nice little cheer section!! LOL!!!

I was almost thinking about ditching them all so that on family day you could just show ME around. I figure all they really need is to be there for graduation!! Heh heh heh!! Right???

Eh, ok ok ok... I know that was kind of greedy of me... They all miss you and want to be there to congratulate you... So, well, I guess I'll let them come along...

(Even though I miss you most Dang it!!) BUT, if any (or all) of them over sleep on family day it's not my fault!!! I'll at least make sure they're up on time that Friday for graduation.

Ya know, we probably should ditch them at least after a couple hours. Say around lunch time. Because, I'm positive we will need to get a mess of shit done, like getting you signed up for TSP and whatever else. It would be best if that was just you, me, and maybe Gary. The rest of them will probably just be in the way then....

Let me know what you think. I have no problem chasing them off. (Actually, I'll be happy to chase them off.)

Hey this week you can look down on all the new Recruits!! Seeing as you guys are now Senior Recruits. Maybe you can give some good advice to a few new guys and save them a little pain somewhere along the line... That would be nice... Or you could scare the piss out of them somehow... Hahaha!! And that would be mean... Funny, but still mean...

It's also tooth yanking week...

If they get ya, take all the drugs they offer. No kidding. Enjoy the pain meds and take care of the holes they leave behind exactly as they say!! No straws for drinking!!! That can pull out the blood clots. And stay hydrated, you definitely do not want dry sockets... If you can, gently rinse with salt water every chance you get. AND AGAIN, TAKE THE PAIN KILLERS! Trust me. It won't hurt for long, but that first day can be a bitch.

Tomorrow morning I'll be sending more Balance Bars. They have more protein in them than the Cliff Bars do. And they are like a dollar cheaper

per box too!

I sent you the extra labels I printed for anyone in your platoon, and some extra envelopes today. I hope some of your brothers there can use them. If not, there is no need for you to keep them. They'll just take up valuable space. Best off to throw them out if no one can use them.

But... If they can... Well, I've noticed on the message board that some people haven't got any letters in weeks... If this helps some poor guy to just send a quick note home saying he's alive... Well, that would probably be a good thing.

(Of course, those people on the message board could be full of it. Or maybe they don't understand how busy you guys are and are just exaggerating.)

*My jog today was cool!! Until I realized how far I had gone...
I parked at the first parking lot (next to the bathrooms) at Bloody Angle. Then I walked to the 2nd lot, and decided to jog the trail thru the field there down to the Landrum house site. I hung out there for a minute and decided to walk back out down the path to where that pull off on the one way road is, from there I went to the other end of the park out to Courthouse Rd. - I turned around and started jogging back. I made it to the same place where I came out from the trail and started walking again. I walked all the way back to where we normally park at the dead end. Sadly, as I was walking back I realized that I didn't know how far I had jogged. So I started jogging back towards the car and jogged the same 3 miles that you used to jog. Well, by then I was beat to shit!!! That last hill back to the car was like climbing a freaking mountain with rubber legs!!
I blame Jimmy Eat World. As I had them in my ears today instead of my normal Pink tunes.
I also blame Chuck Norris... Because he's over 70 and still in fighting shape!!!!! <and I'm jealous!!!*

Other than my crazy jog/walk, mailing you the labels, chatting with a few people, and getting some groceries... Well, it's Wednesday, Brad was off... I suspect you get the picture... Hahahaha!!
He's a bum....
Hopefully something cool will happen tomorrow!!! Maybe I'll win the lottery or something!!!
No matter, I'll be writing more tomorrow regardless of what the day brings!! I just hope I'm not boring you!!
It's really too bad if I am!! Cause I ain't stopping!!!
Hey!!!! Just in case you forgot....
I am proud of you Son!!!!!!!!

Sweet Dreams!!!

Love, Mom

Wait! It's joke time!!!!!

Seems this hillbilly came to town carrying a jug of moonshine in one hand and a shotgun in the other. He stopped a man on the street, saying to him: "Here, friend, take a drink outta my jug."
The man protested, saying he never drank.
Unimpressed, the hillbilly leveled his shotgun at the stranger and commanded: "Drink!"
The stranger drank, shuddered, shook, shivered and coughed. "God! That's awful stuff!"

"Ain't it, though?" replied the hillbilly. "Now here, you hold the gun on me while I take a swig."

I'm sorry!! Hahaha! That so reminds me of your dad!!! Hahahahaha!!

****

JD's dad is indeed a hillbilly. I still think that joke was written about him.

That evening I got three more letters from JD! It seemed they got a little extra time to themselves for the holiday after all. To me, it was all good.

****

Hey Mom,

Well today was alright. We actually had time to eat for once.

I ran the PFT today and surprisingly, I did good.

Crunches – 128

Pull ups – 14 (could have been better)

Three mile run 21 minutes!!!

Score – 250 (First Class)

We're the strongest platoon! LOL!

So, all day today I was thinking about the fun stuff you and I used to do. I kind of imagined that your Venza was on the road next to me on my jog with you cheering me on! Hahaha! Yeah, shit like that gets me through.

Thank God tomorrow is Sunday!

Today was the first day that we didn't actually piss off SSgt. Smith in a long time.

How are you? I'm always eager to read your letters and hear about your day.

Miss you Mom!!!

Love, JD

P.S. Please message Kayla- "Hey, I got your letter. It's good to see a pretty face in this hellish place. I hope you had a good Christmas. Please write more, every last letter helps my days go by faster. As for cookies and stuff, thank you, but please don't send them, we can't have them here. I miss talking to you and hope you're doing alright. I look forward to seeing you in a little over a month. –Your Buddy – J

Mom,

So today is Christmas. Right off the bat we got fucked up. I only got to eat one pancake and some rice before Sgt. Jones made me throw out my food. Then we had to scuz the whole deck in a "timely manner"… We were drenched in sweat within an hour of waking up… But whatever…

I miss you and the whole family. Tell everyone I said hello and to keep writing.

Love, JD

****

So nice to know my son and his platoon didn't have time to actually eat breakfast on Christmas. Of course, I'm sure homesickness was probably not helping any of those guys including the DIs.

****

Hey Mom,

So far today has been pretty chill, but that's going to change around 1300 due to the fact that because of the holiday we haven't done much today. So the DIs are sure to mess us up to make up for lost time.

Hey I have an idea! In the next yellow package you send, you should send a small recorder in an envelope with a quiet message on it. It would be nice to hear your voice. Then I could mail it back with a message of my own. LOL! It just has to be small and thin enough to conceal in an envelope…

Gotta go, love you.

Love, JD

****

OK, all in all, not too bad. Christmas day might have been a bit much, but JD's scores were fantastic and it seemed that the day after Christmas the guys got a bit of a breather.

I wasn't so sure if hearing my voice was a good thing or not, but I decided I would indeed try to find a recorder that I could smuggle in to him. My only concern was that such a thing might make him even more homesick than he already was.

****

December 30, 2011

Hey Baby!!!!

I got your letters from the 24th, 25th, and 26th!!!! A 250 on the PFT is freaking AWESOME SAUCE!!!

SO!!! Let's look at the big picture...

You qualified for swim really fast, you got your tan belt and qualified for MCMAP, you got a 95 on your written, and you got a 250 score (1st Class) on your PFT!!!!

YOU FREAKING ROCK!!!

I know the platoon as a whole didn't do as awesome on the written, or on the previous drill... And I know you are all one "unit"... BUT!! Don't forget!! You're bringing up the average! Even if you too have made mistakes in drill once or twice, or even three times, it's all good!!

Without you, and the few others that did well on the written, the platoon might all look like idiots.

Your strong, smart, and got mad skills JD!! Don't forget it and never second guess yourself!

And, although I know you should qualify as Expert, you guys are under a lot of pressure at the moment, so Marksman, and/or Sharp Shooter works just as well for any of you. Of course, it's Thursday, so you've already qualified. But no worries! I'm going to be praying extra hard tonight and all day tomorrow that you have a calm clear mind, and a decent weapon, so you get that Expert title!!

Hey, I watched a video on the CFT.... WOW! That looks to be about a bitch!!! But, it also looks like they only ran the poor guys in the video for about 3 minutes. A grueling 3 minutes... But nothing any harder than what you've already done, so of course I'm positive you'll kick ass with that test too.

I got those Balance Bars in the mail for you guys! The ladies at the post office ask me all the time if I've heard from you!! It's really sweet. They're rooting for you too!!

It's funny that you imagine me there with you.... Because I do the same thing and imagine you're here hangin out with ME!! Yup, I "channel" you whenever I'm goofing off, and when I'm out jogging in sub below zero temperatures!! Heh heh heh! Yeah, you harass me often, but it makes me smile!!

Why just this morning, I swear I heard you say, "Keep running Mom!!" Then when I started slowing down... Well, I could have sworn you called me a wimp!!!! And I agreed!! LOL!!!

Ok! So in the morning I'm going to go on a mad search for a super skinny recording device... I'll let you know of I find one that will work. I'm thinking about cutting up one of the "make you own message" cards... But I'm not even sure that'll work... I'll figure it out, and send you "the plan" as soon as I have one...

The rest of boot camp is gonna fly by!! Really Fly!!! So hold on tight and keep on getting on!!!

Never doubt yourself!! You got this shit!!!

In the mean while!!! I hope you know I am Wickedly Proud of You!! I miss you!!!

But I got mad plans to be there in very soon!!!! Semper Fi!!!!

Sleep well JD!!

Love, Mom

PS. I hope they can keep up with you! Yup, you know I am one Super Proud Mom!! Go JD!!! GO!!

****

Not only do recruits have to deal with a complete change in their routines and of course the constant yelling, berating, and exercise, they also have many tests to pass in order to become Marines. Thank goodness the Marine Corps knows that the key to teaching just about everyone is repetition and hands on experience. I had no worries in regards to JD being able to pass any given test. But, I could see how some people may have had problems if the DIs didn't pretty much brand all that muscle memory and information into their recruits.

Nevertheless, I was exceedingly impressed with JD's scores. I knew he was sleep deprived, but he smoked his initial written test. I knew he was physically beat to hell, and still he pulled out a first class PFT! Between all the work he did prior to leaving for Boot Camp, all the work the DIs had put into him, and his desire to become a United States Marine there really was nothing short of a serious tragedy that could have stopped him.

On occasion I really did imagine JD jogging or hanging out with me. After all, he had pretty much been my right hand for the past year and it wasn't easy suddenly going it alone all the time. I know it must sound odd to some people. I guess you could think of it more as remembering, or just knowing what someone would say to certain things and then laughing out loud about the conversation you just had in your head. Yeah, it might be a bit strange, but it worked for me, and apparently it had worked for him as well.

****

December 31, 2011

Hey JD!

I hope this week is going good!! You're almost free from that crazy place!
I got a message back from James asking when you're coming back... He says he's "so board all the time now!!" Poor guy... So I told him when you graduate and that he could go down there with us if he is able, but to be sure to leave the first week of February open so you guys can hang out. Then he said...
- Yah I'd love to but we're having car problems and I wouldn't trust ours if they worked anyway. lol! But I'll keep that open cuz I definitely wanna hang out when he gets back.
< Sounds Excellent!!!! Look, I've already made plans for you on your first week home!!>

I got a decent laugh... Brad asked me what I thought you would do if I missed a day writing you... (HA! Like that would ever happen!) I told him that if I missed one day, you would probably just figure the mail got jammed up somehow. But if it was 2 or 3 days you might get pretty concerned... And I'm not gonna let you worry about shit here! Not if I can help it. Yeah, He's a dummy sometimes.

I was out today searching for one of those recordable cards. Well, I found one!! Now all I have to do is rip out the actual recording device, place it in smaller packaging, and figure out how the get it to only play my message. Right now it plays the original version of "De Police Day Got Rob" first, then you push a button to hear the personal message... Ha! But, I bought 2 of them just in case I thoroughly muck the first one up! (And they were 50% off. Heh heh heh!) So, once I've perfected it, I'll give you the heads up. I would go buy a super thin recorder, but those things are like $150.00 and up! That's like a week worth of bars... So, I must make this card idea work somehow!!! Wish me luck!

I also sent out invites to your graduation party! But like I said, no worries, anyone I missed we'll invite as soon as you get back. The party will be on the Saturday before you leave for your next month of roughing it.

I ran into Marsha today... <there should be creepy music playing here...>

She asked how you were doing, so I proceeded to Brag Big Time!!
Then...... She asked... For your address!!!!!!!! Ummm.... Forgive me Son, but
I told her I didn't have it on me (Yup, I lied.) And then I told her I would
try to get it to her.... (Lie #2) This is the second time she's asked... The
first time I told her I believed only actual family were allowed to write...
But she researched it.... Oh well!! She'll never get the address!!!! She's
really much too nutty.

Speaking of nut jobs, Penny said she wrote you. But she also said she was
very tired and her letter is that of a crazy lady! Hahahaha! I hope she
wasn't too nuts!! And I hope she made you laugh. I know that was her
intention.

Tomorrow night I'll be doing a party at Widewater... I suspect I'll see
those punk ass kids that messed up my amp at the last party... I don't
know why those kids always show up to hang with us old fogies...
Hmmm... Well, they can piss off for all I care, but I'll be decent. Unless
they mess with my equipment again... Then I'll try not to go to jail. I'll be
sure to let you know how all that goes!! I'm positive it will be amusing. I
just wish you could be there with me!

It's funny, I miss you a lot, but I'm so insanely proud of who you are, all
you've done, what you're doing, and of the great future you're going to
have!! So, I'm good with just sending out my daily reports. For now.

Hey!Iit's question time!!
A. How's team week going so far??
B. How did ya do on the range?
C. Are you excited about next week?? (Is that the BIG BELT FED GUNS
WEEK?? If so, I am so Jealous!!)
D. Have you got to check and see about how long it takes for the boxes of
bars to get there?
E. Which bars are YOUR favorites!?!

Ok Son, remember to eat as much as you can, sleep as much as you can,
stretch, and go to church. And never ever forget, I got your back.
It's bed time for Bonzo!! Talk to you more tomorrow!!!
***{{GIANT HUGS}}** I LOVE YOU!!!!! Have Sweet Dreams and Sleep Well!!*
Semper Fi.
Love, Mom

Time for the joke of the day!

Bob and his three golf buddies were out playing and were just starting on the back nine when Bob paused, looked down the fairway and began to sob uncontrollably.
The other three gathered around him and asked: "What's wrong?"
Bob looked down at his feet, sniffed and dried his eyes some, then apologized for his emotional outburst. "I'm sorry, I always get emotional at this hole - it holds very difficult memories for me."

One of his buddies asked, "What happened? What could have gotten you so upset?"
Bob stared silently off in the distance, then said in a low voice, "This is where my wife and I were playing 12 years ago when she suddenly died of a heart attack right at this very hole."
"Oh my God", the other golfers said. "That must have been horrible!"

"Horrible?! You think it`s horrible?" Bob continued still very distressed. "It was worse than that! Every hole for the rest of the day, all the way back to the clubhouse it was hit the ball, drag Alice, hit the ball, drag Alice..."

Soooooo WRONG!! Hahahaha!!!

January 1, 2012

Hi JD!!!

OK!! Another day is DONE!!!

Before ya know it, you'll be testing everything you've learned and going through the Crucible!!! Honestly, it won't be bad for you. You're awesome when you're put on the spot and under pressure. Plus, after all those "camping trips" that you and Robert and Chris went on... Well, minus the potential for some beer.... Let's just say, you've already done the "light" version of the Crucible all on your own.

First things first, Gary told me that it would be GREAT if you qualified as expert on the range! And at first he couldn't remember what he qualified as... He must really be getting old! Hahaha! But then he remembered... Turns out he got "sharpshooter" back then and only later did he manage to get expert. (He swore me to secrecy, but said I was allowed to tell you. Just NO ONE else!! Hahahah!)

I got a "schedule of events" for your graduation in the mail today! On family day I'm going be on base by 6am getting me some coffee and waiting to see you run by on your motivational run!! HELL YEAH!! But don't you dare look for me unless they say you can look at the crowd! Just know I'm there.

I'm not sure what I'm gonna wear, but I assure you it will be LOUD!!! That way when (if) they let you guys look you'll be able to spot me pretty fast!! And I'll probably be standing next to Gary. Yeah, ya know, he's damn tall and normally easy to spot.
Nevertheless, once I have exactly what I'm gonna wear, I'll send you a picture of me wearing it!! That way it'll be even easier. (Best to know what you're looking for as I suspect the crowd will be pretty big.)

This morning, after my jog/walk, Penny and I hung out for a while. It's killing her to know if you got her letter, and if it made you laugh or if it just convinced you that she's completely insane. I let her know that she shouldn't worry so much! We love her even though she's insane. I made her go for a "short" walk in the park with me. (It was really more like a stroll in the park.) After a whopping 2 miles she was dying!! I feel bad for her, she needs to get her knees and back fixed. Once upon a time she and

*I would walk the neighborhoods for at least an hour and she was ok....
But yesterday in the park she was limping by the end of the first mile so I
just turned around. And by the time we got to the car she was plain old
done!! NOT ME THOUGH!! I'M BECOMING BAD ASS AGAIN!!!! I'm used to
doing at least 4-6 miles. Heck! At her pace I probably could have walked
all day. (Unless I died from the slowness...)*

*Well I told ya I was doing the party at Widewater tonight... And that's
exactly what I'm doing right now!!! Heh heh heh! GOOD NEWS!!! Only
members 21 years old and up were invited!! No idiot kids! Yay!!! They
banned all the under 21's from even being in the station tonight! Works
good for me!!*

*So about 15 people showed up for the New Year's Eve Bash here! Earlier
Jason was bitching because he thought they didn't buy enough booze.
Ha! He must have been expecting a lot more people, because they have
enough alcohol to poison everyone here twice! (Of course I think what's
closer to the truth is the fact that Jason just likes to bitch.)*

*At least the little party is going well, and all (except for me) are good
and drunk! They've even been dancing!!! (Badly, but dancing none the
less.) Tony is currently working up some nerve because right at midnight
he plans to propose to his girlfriend Tara. He's too young in my opinion
but, God forgive me, they're both pretty "simple", so maybe it'll work out
ok. I'll let ya know how it goes and what she says tomorrow.*

*The chief (the old guy, Jack, Not the fire chief, Hail) just requested Johnny
B Good!!! SWEET!!! Reminds me of us blasting the oldies cd in the car
and watching the other drivers as they looked around all confused! Yup!!
We'll need to jam more oldies in the car!!!That was great!!!! It's true, we
really are easily amused. Hahahaha!*

*Speaking of the Chief! He wanted me to tell you that he's proud of you
and you're on his prayer list! (Wow!! I've known Jack for years and never
knew he was a praying man. I actually have a lot more respect for him
now than I did before.) That's all good stuff JD!*

*I hope you guys slept through the date change!!! It's 11:30pm, way past
my bed time!! I'm just praying that you're resting peacefully, and not on
fire watch or something! But hey!! Tomorrow is the first day of year and
the first day of TEAM WEEK!!!*

Well, it's almost midnight....
HAPPY NEW YEAR SON!!!!
(Ha! Even though you're probably reading this on Wednesday or
Thursday, NOW YOU'RE technically THE FIRST person I said HAPPY
NEW YEAR to!! SWEET!!)

I'm gonna have to drive home soon. I'll write more tomorrow!!
Keep up the good work!!! And try to enjoy your week of manual labor.
I LOVE YOU!!!!

Love, Mom

****

 I used to own a DJ company a few years back and sometimes I'll still
go out and play for private parties, but mostly just for friends and
charities. Needless to say, now you know what I mean by "doing a
party."

****

January 2, 2012

Hey JD!

It's weighing in my little mind... How ya feeling Son?? Tough as nails and
strong as steel I hope!
I'm seriously hoping this week is giving you, and your platoon, a chance
to recharge a bit.
You guys have been going, and going... Yep, you've officially made the
Energizer Bunny look silly.

I know it's not easy for any of you guys. But, you got to know, every
Marine who went before you, along with a whole mess of other people,
are all proud of you and impressed with all you've done and will do.
(Heck! Even the mail ladies are proud of you!!) Yup, they weren't kidding
when they said, "The title of U.S. Marine is Never given, Always earned."
And once you've earned it, its forever."
And that, my Dear is extremely impressive!

Hey, has that Cox dude cleaned up his act yet? Gary said that usually those types of guys get weeded out, but the "ass clown" in his platoon, a guy named "Parks", apparently made it all the way to graduation somehow..... To this day Gary still finds that to be a bit shocking.

He also wanted you to know that drill is actually a test of how well your DIs are doing. Not how well you are doing. The only stuff that goes into your record are your personal scores on stuff like the written, swim qualification, MCMAP, PFT, CFT, and the range. (HA! No worries!! You're doing great! Told ya! You got this shit!!)

I've also been wondering if you plan to come home and do some recruiting, or if you plan on going straight to your MOS school after your Marine Combat Training? Have you given it any thought??

Oh!! Before I forget to tell you... Last night Tony's girlfriend, Tara, said yes! And then the party turned into some crazy crying drunk filled hug fest... Hahahaha!! I think she asked him at least 20 times if he was being "for real"... It was really kind of cute. Well, like I said last night, even though I think Tony is too young to get married.... They are very much alike so I figure they got a decent enough chance at a good marriage.

It's Sunday night and other than my morning jog, today was pretty dull... But hey! I got 9.2 on my mile!! Not too shabby!! I'll teach Kevin yet!! The old bastard!! Hahahaha!!

Oh!! And your sister did hunt me down and force me to make my stir fry for her!! Too funny!! She's mean!!!!! But it's really pretty cute if ya ask me. I really do think she's making a mean little boy this time. Lord, if it is a boy he's going to have to have some meanness in him with two older sisters!!! Oh my God!! If he doesn't those girls will make his life Hell!

Enjoy this week as much as ya can JD!! You got a few more crazy weeks ahead of you, but soon you'll have your Eagle, Globe, and Anchor!!!

OooRah!!!

Chat at ya more tomorrow!!!
Sweet Dreams!!!!

Love, Mom

Wait!! I got a joke!

A Hunter walking through the jungle found a huge dead dinosaur with a pigmy standing beside it. Amazed, he asked: "Did you kill that?"
The pigmy said "Yes."
The hunter asked "How could a little fella like you kill a huge beast like that?"
The pigmy said, "I killed it with my club."
The astonished hunter asked: "How big is your club?"
The pigmy replied: "There are about 90 of us."

Nice!!!! Heh heh heh!!!

****

   I didn't just blindly listen to Gary in regards to all things in Boot Camp. Some things I did, others I researched or found out while researching other aspects of the Marine Corps.

   Drill and inspections really are a reflection of how well the DI is training his platoon. Those guys have so much on their shoulders though that for a recruit to not do his very best is really a slap in the face. So, while I wanted my son not to stress too badly over such things, I always expected him to perform as his DIs required. I could let JD in on these little secrets for one big reason; I knew he wanted to be the best Marine he could possibly be no matter what it took.

****

January 3, 2012

Howdy Baby!!

It's Monday night while I write!! Hahaha!
At least the post office will be open in the morning. I still don't get why
they have to have Monday off just because there was a holiday on
Sunday. But thankfully all that holiday mess is over and my letters
should be back on schedule!!

So I figure you're bombarded with mail today!! You should have my
letters from Saturday, Sunday, and tonight! Plus the card I put in the
mail earlier today. AND the package of bars I'll be sending in the
morning with this letter!!! Geez!!

I'm thinking for you it's probably Thursday already. That would mean
that the day you're reading this is the same day I will be sending even
more bars!!! Nice to know what I'm up to isn't it? Oh man, I'm so hopeful
that the packages move as fast as the letters. But somehow I doubt it...

Sadly, I'm having no luck with the recordable card idea... Ok... To tell the
truth, I destroyed them both trying to get them to stop playing the dang
Christmas song. Penny seems to think that I can have the lady at the
Hallmark store order one without music and that they can get it in a day
or two... So tomorrow I'm going to go over there and ask. I'll keep my
fingers crossed that Penny's right.

I was looking online to check up on what the graduation guide I got in
the mail was saying. It doesn't really match up, so I'm just going to do
more research until I find out if I'm to be on base that Wednesday or if I
need to wait till Thursday. Really, it doesn't matter if I have to wait, it's
not like I would be able to see you till that Thursday. And you're all I'm
really interested in anyway.

OH!!! I need to know, where in the platoon are you when you guys do
your runs and stuff? (How many guys are in front of you, and what side
are you on? Or how far on the inside are you?) If I know that it will make
it easier for me to see you when you guys go by on your motivational run
the morning of Family Day!

I am so excited!!!! I'm going to see you so soon!!! So if I'm talking about coming down there too much, well, sorry. I really can't help myself!

So, next week??? Is that belt fed weapons??? From the schedule, it looks like it could be.... They use so many abbreviations that it's really hard for me to be sure...
Lord, I hope so!!!! That should be mad fun!! There is just something about having that kind of weapon in your hands that makes the day seem so much brighter! Yup! If that's what next week is I know you'll enjoy it!!!

Your Dad sent me a creepy picture of himself!!! Hahaha! I hope you like it! That's one crazy beard he's got going on. I think he's hoping to join ZZ Top!!! I should tell him he needs more than just the beard... Too bad he can't play guitar...

It was way too cold this morning!! I forgot to take my robber mask, so my freaking snot froze in my nose again! That's ok though, I'll be a jogging robber tomorrow morning!!

I only jogged the 1.5 today and then walked the rest. Usually I jog a bit more, but a nose full of frozen snot slowed me down a bit! Shit, I'm actually proud of the fact that I didn't wimp out altogether! I swear it was warmer outside the house than it was at the park. But hey! I still jogged the 1.5 and then walked 5 more miles! And I did it in exactly 1 hour! SWEET!

Since you have so much mail today, I'm going to keep this one kind of short... I know you still got a mess of hard work in front of you JD. Just know that it's nothing you can't handle.
Yeah, it's that time again... The old lady needs her sleep. But don't worry! I'll write more tomorrow!! I love you!!!

Have sweet dreams!!! Soon you will officially be a Marine!! And we'll be out test driving those cars!!! Yay!!

Love, Mom

WAIT!!!

Joke time!!

A middle aged woman has a heart attack and is taken to the hospital. While on the operating table she has a near death experience. During that experience she sees God and asks if this is it.
God says no and explains that she has another 30 years to live. Upon her recovery she decides to just stay in the hospital and have a face lift, liposuction, breast augmentation, tummy tuck, etc.

She even has someone come in and change her hair color. She figures since she's got another 30 years she might as well make the most of it. She walks out of the hospital after the last operation and is killed by an ambulance.

She arrives in front of God and complains: "I thought you said I had another 30 years!!
God replies, "Sorry, I didn't recognize you."

****

I sent that picture of JD's dad to him because even though his dad and I don't see eye to eye, I know he loves his kids. And they love him too, so it was good for JD to see his crazy looking mountain man Dad with his new wild beard.

****

January 4, 2012

Hey JD!!
How is my amazingly kick ass, wonderful Son doing?
Was team week good?

It was freaking freezing out again today... Yep it was a whopping 18 degrees! Not to mention that the wind was whipping, and even with the mask my dang nose still froze. For all the good it did, I did indeed look like a masked mad person jogging in the park this morning! Heh heh heh!

Of course, I had to laugh at myself seeing as there was no one else there!! Nope! Not a soul to be found!! I was the only one crazy enough to go out there, everyone else was sane and stayed home or went somewhere heated. Even the 2 deer I saw were both bedded down together to stay warm. Alas, your old Mom has lost her mind and no longer has enough sense to come in out of the cold.

Thankfully I can take comfort in knowing that if you were home now you would have been out there with me. Yes Son, we share that special kind of crazy!!

I babysat the girls a bit tonight and I think Alexis really likes me now!! She didn't cry at all when Jackie left for work!! But, Jake still creeps her out... (Of course he does look like some crazy homeless guy, so I'm not sure if I blame the kid for not being so sure of him...) She didn't really freak out too bad at him, she just kind of kept her distance, stared at him a lot, and pointed every so often in his direction! It was cute! Her little accusing finger reminded me of how you used to point at your dad!! Hahaha! Audrey, on the other hand, was quick to try and force Uncle Jake to go play blocks with her. I guess she's always known that he just "looks" homeless and crazy.

I went to the Hallmark store today and asked if they could order a music free recordable card. The lady there said she wasn't sure if they still made them. The real bummer is that apparently they have thousands of cards they can order, and the recordable ones are not separated in their systems. So she said she would find out and call me tomorrow. I thought that was actually pretty nice of her, offering to go on that particular search for me.

Then I went to the post office! The ladies, Ann and Angie, both asked me to tell you hello in this letter. They really are very sweet, and they really do want to meet you when you come home. I personally think that's awesome! You've even got people who you've never met rooting you on!!

Ok, I'm thinking that you'll be reading this on Friday evening. So, in just 3 short, fun filled weeks, you will be smack dab in the middle of the

Crucible and less than a day away from getting your EGA pin!! Good Lord, I'm proud of you!!

Now, there is some stuff I really want you to realize and have embedded in your brain...

Just think for a moment about how far you have come. Yeah, you researched boot camp before you left, but the research is nothing like standing on those yellow foot prints in person! You have since lived, and excelled, through that POW camp known also as Phase 1.

Yes, in Phase 1, and in Phase 2, you passed every test they threw your way. You have stood tall, still and straight faced while being called names and even threatened. You have been forced to work out until you thought you had no more to give, and then somehow you gave even more. You've lived all that and worse!

Now you're in Phase 3. You have pushed and gone further than most people would believe possible for any human. You have literally fought your way, all the way. You are true Marine material. You never give up and you never give in. You're tough, smart, courageous, and persistent. You are both "Semper Fi' and "OooRah!" in the perfect mix.

Soon you will face your last rite of passage, and you will use every bit of what you have learned there, along with everything you are made of, to make it through to the end. You will be amazing! So much so that I'm sure you will even amaze yourself! Yes, it will be trying, it will wear you out, but you will succeed.

You have all that's needed and more inside you. You must trust me on this. You are my son, and I know you better than anyone. I believe in you, and if you believe in yourself just half as much as I do than you already know everything I have said is 100% true. You got this JD, soon you're going to reach your goal and earn your title along with all the respect that comes with it.

I, for one, will be thrilled to call you Marine.

Hmmm... I got all serious on ya there for a minute, but it's all true, and all stuff I want you to know.

On to a more amusing note!!

Jake and Brad are currently suffering! As in right this minute!
Yes, the worst has happened... The cable and internet have both gone
out!!! If that's not bad enough, Comcast says they can't be here till
Friday!!! OH NO!!!! Bahahahaha!!!

Maybe this blow will pull Jake away from the computer and Brad away
from the TV for a moment. But for right now they are both down stairs
staring at the black TV and making crazy plans to over throw Comcast!!!
For real, right now, as I type, your brother and Brad are plotting on
Comcast!! It's actually pretty damn funny. Brad's pretty buzzed and Jake
is pretty frustrated, so the shit they're coming up with is heinous! Poor
guys... Hahaha!! They've been cut off cold turkey from some of their
favorite addictions. Too funny!

Alas, now it's bed time for Bonzo.
I love you!!! And don't you forget it!! I'll chat at ya more tomorrow.
Sleep well JD! There are a lot of great adventures waiting for you!!!

Love, Mom

****

 Once upon a time there was no cable TV and no Internet. Back then if
the TV had no picture all you had to do was change the antenna
placement. Of course this may have meant that you had to stand there
and hold the antenna while everyone else watched the TV, or if you
were lucky you could add some tin foil to the mix and have a seat. If
none of that would work the TV was either broke or the power was
out. When that happened, we would usually go outside to play or
maybe read a book if it was dark out already.

 Thankfully, I don't recall ever staring at a blank screen and cursing the
TV Gods for my lack of entertainment. But times have changed, and
who am I to decide which way is better, the new or the old? All I know
is that I found my husband's and son's reactions to the loss of these
things pretty amusing. They ranted and raved to no avail and seemed

to suffer terrible pain and boredom until their technology was restored. In the meanwhile, I watched them and tried not to laugh too much.

Second phase was almost over and at this point I was really thinking about all the stuff JD would have to go through during the Crucible. From all the information I found I knew that the Crucible was a three day event, and in those three days these young recruits had to hike almost 50 miles. Really, 50 miles in three days doesn't sound all that bad, but the Crucible isn't just a long hike. No, it's a long hike that's filled with physical and mental tests along the way. Even better, they are only allowed enough food to sustain them and an average of 4 hours of sleep a night, if they can sleep, while making their way through this incredible test.

Fabulous! What made it even worse was reading the horror stories of the injuries some recruits had suffered during this trial in the past. Yup, I had read about all sorts of broken bones, and even a broken back! I had even spoken to a young Marine who broke his ankle half way through and knew he must continue on that ankle or he would be recycled back until he had healed.

The only good thing I had going was the fact that I knew what a physically fit, tough, and healthy beast JD was when he got to Boot Camp. Plus I had read that they would have their DIs and medics with them the entire way. So, at least I knew that if my son suffered some freak accident that he would be well taken care of on the spot.

Of course, that last bit doesn't ease too much of the worry for a Mom. But, it is a "rite of passage" for all of the recruits who make it that far. I'd say that the last day of the Crucible is one of, if not "the", best days of their young lives. After all, once they have made it to the finish line they can never be called that evil "R" word again.

On that amazing day they become Marines for life and are actually handed the EGA that they themselves have earned. So even though I knew I would be pacing the floor the entire time my son was making his way through that test, I really couldn't wait for him to just do it and get it over with.

****

January 5, 2012

Hi Baby!! Ya done finished another day!!! WooHoo!!

It's Wednesday night, so it must be at least Saturday for you!! I went and talked to one of the recruiters here today. Well, I originally went to tell SSgt. Ramos about how well you've been doing in boot camp. But he wasn't in so I chatted with the Sgt. at the window desk. (The one from Tennessee.) He was really impressed with your initial written and PFT scores!!

He also told me to tell you not to concern yourself with qualifying expert on the range. Apparently the weapons you guys get to use are freaking old and seldom shoot right. So, if ya did get expert, you probably got really lucky. He said he came out of boot as a marksman and has since been an expert and is currently ranked sharpshooter... Funny how that stuff changes all the time. But each time that you're tested throughout your career it could have a different outcome due to a million different reasons that have nothing to do with you or your skills.

Surprise! My jog this morning was freaking cold as Hell again!!! (Big shocker there!) I guess I didn't learn yesterday because, again, I was the only one nutty enough to be out there. But Hell, I can't stop now!! I'm just a little over a minute off from that 8 minute mile!! I'm so close! It's all good, seeing as it's supposed to be warmer tomorrow. But, even if the weather man is wrong, I'll still be out there again in the morning. Like I said so many times before, you can't stop and neither can I!!

Good News!!! I found coupons for the Pure Protein bars!!! Yay!!! $1.00 off each box!!! That'll save me $10.00!!!! SWEET!!! Now with that bit of info, I bet you can guess what kind of bars I'll be sending you guys tomorrow morning.

I say it all the time, but I really hope you guys are enjoying them and that they are helping some. I think it's nice to have a "good for you treat" every so often. Heck! I think it's nice to have a "bad for you treat" every so often too!! Heh heh heh!

I've been looking at more computers for you. The guy at Best Buy, who also happens to be a retired Marine, told me I need to get you a "Panasonic Tough Book." I checked them out and it sounds like a good plan to me. (He also told me to tell you, Semper Fi!) They claim the Tough Book can take a drop of 6 feet and can even withstand being run over by a car!! (Although, I personally wouldn't try it.) It also looks pretty sweet in regards to speed, storage, and graphics!! Plus, they have some kind of contract with the military for software specials. All in all I think that the retired Marine is right.

Well, since the Hallmark lady didn't call me today, I'll be going back over there tomorrow to question her thoroughly. I may even take a taser just so I can get the answers I want! (Ok, probably not...) I hope I don't have to get ugly... But I want a damn recordable card without music!!! Alas, Wednesday means Brad was off.... So after 1pm, when he woke up, the day turned..... Boring... LOL!!! At least the cable came back on so he had something to watch and keep him somewhat entertained.

Oh, before I forget... I'm still trying to get everyone together for a family picture for you. Soon I'm just going to photo shop us all in a picture or something. Seems every time Brad is here Jackie or Jake are either too busy to come over (Jackie) or sleeping (Jake)... Go figure!! The bums!!! Eh, if it's Photoshop you'll know because I'll put us on some strange back ground. Maybe the moon or Mars... It'll be beautiful!!! As the matter of fact, I think I'll do that tomorrow!! Heh heh heh!

Well My Dear, It's that time again...
I miss you!! Sleep well!!

And don't forget!! Eat, sleep, stretch, and go to church!!!
Keep going Recruit (soon to be Marine!)
Talk at ya more tomorrow!!!
Love,

Mom

Oh you know what time it is!! Today I have a fun joke list!! LOL!!

Useful phrases when dealing with the general population. Try to incorporate these into your conversations . . .

- Thank you. We're all refreshed and challenged by your unique point of view.
- I don't know what your problem is, but I'll bet it's hard to pronounce.
- I have plenty of talent and vision. I just don't give a damn.
- I like you. You remind me of when I was young and stupid.
- I'm not being rude. You're just insignificant.
- I'm already visualizing the duct tape over your mouth.
- Ahhh...I see the fuck-up fairy has visited us again...
- Yes, I am an agent of Satan, but my duties are largely ceremonial.
- How about never? Is never good for you?
- I'm really easy to get along with once you people learn to worship me.
- Are you a ray of sunshine every day?
- I'll try being nicer if you'll try being smarter.
- It might look like I'm doing nothing, but at the cellular level I'm really quite busy.
- At least I have a positive attitude about my destructive habits.

****

It still seems almost impossible to get my children along with my husband in the same place at the same time for a family picture. Alas, it never happened while JD was in boot camp. Instead, a few photoshopped photos did indeed make their way to him.

Thankfully, this was one of those few (and too far between) splendid days when my trusty mail man delivered another wonderful gift to our home in the form of a couple letters.

****

Hey Mom,

Today is the 1st of January, Happy New Year!

Well, on table 1 I scored 219, Sharpshooter. The thing that sucks is if I had scored 220 I would have qualified as expert. BUT I'll get it on table 2.

(I got your letter about the bank, go ahead and take the money back out.)

On a lighter note, YAY! I made it to team week. Now I just gotta get through this last month and then on with my life! Only 1 month away from actually TALKING to you every day! LOL!

The down side about this week is the platoon is showing signs of not giving a fuck anymore. It sucks.

As for the Propel drink mix, if you do send it, make it hidden. LOL! I'm like a drug dealer with that stuff! Hahahahaha!!

I hope this month flies by. But it probably won't due to a few idiots in the platoon. Unfortunately Grass Week only dropped 2 of them.... I also found out that our platoon is one of the most "punished" in all of 1st and 2nd battalion! That really sucks!! LOL! Well the others will all turn out to be wimps!

So, how was New Years? How is home? And how are you?
Oh hey, can you send me lyrics to the songs on my iPod?

Love & Miss You A lot,
JD

Mom,

I have time to kill right now, so I'll write you!
Thank God for Sundays! Only 4 more weeks and I can be called MARINE. It feels like forever-ago that I came here, and I am ready to leave. Right now I plan on doing my 5 years and then going straight into firefighting. I actually miss the station A LOT.

Please send more pictures of you all, I can still use the visual strength. I miss you Mom, when I get out we'll chill as much as possible.

Love, JD

****

It's crazy how you hate the fact that they miss you, but you love the fact that they miss you all at the same time. It's a catch 22, he's my son and one of my best friends so I totally expect him to miss me! But then again, he's my son and one of my best friends, and he had better things to do than think about missing anyone, including me. Missing someone, anyone, sucks. I know, I missed him too,

****

January 2nd ...
-Homesick-
I hate homesickness. Too much free time and it starts to take effect. I think that after my 5 years in the Corps I'll get out and get my medic and live somewhere close to you guys.

Dear God I miss you all! I know I'll be crying when I see you. Just a month left...
PLEASE Pray for me.

OH! Can you send inserts for a size 10R, hot and cold weather boots? I'd like some because the ones I have aren't that great and my blisters are pretty bad right now.

I love you Mom! –JD

January 6, 2012

Hi JD!!!

Yay!!!! I got your letters from the first and second!!!! Sharp Shooter is freaking fantastic!! Just 1 point from expert... Wow!!! And with those old beat up guns??!! I'm pretty damn impressed! I didn't think you could make me any prouder of you than I already am, but you've done it!!! I'm well BEYOND PROUD!!!

I got ya covered!! Yup, I got you the top of the line insoles!! The red ones go in warm weather boots and the black ones go in cold weather boots. (The black ones also have more padding.) Ok, they say to heat them up... BUT that's not necessary. As the matter of fact the guy at the store said they do not recommend heating them. The heat from your foot will shape them to you just perfectly. So even if they feel weird at first, wear them and let your body heat work on them, and soon they will feel freaking great!
(I used to use the same brand when I went hiking a lot. And Gary apparently has them in all of his boots and even his sneakers! They really are the best out there.)

Ok, so the box that I'm sending with this letter will only have the insoles and a card in it. (I don't want to chance anyone confiscating your insoles, because that would piss me off.)

***However, the next box that I'll send on Saturday morning will have Propel drink mixes and some Sweet Tarts hidden inside the flaps at the bottom of the box. You'll know it because of the X by my address.*
*Just be sure to open it at the top. **I'll put the addresses on the top.*
Inside it I'll put; a card, some pictures, the lyrics to those songs, some preprinted labels, a magazine, stamps, pens, another pad of paper, and 1 more package of mole skin. I doubt you need all of that stuff right now, but that way it looks like you need the box for a while. Then, (when the coast is clear) look closely at the bottom flaps. Taped inside them you will find an envelope on each side (some Propels in one and some Sweet Tarts in the other). All ya gotta do is pull off the tape from the edges and take the envelopes out of their hidey holes. If it looks like you're not gonna get to be alone with the box just toss it out. Since the stuff will be hidden inside the flaps, no one will see it even if you have to break it down.

It's funny, you said to go ahead and take out the money... The same day I got your letter, Brad got a check from work because the bank finally returned it! So, YAY!! There is no need for me to take any money out of your account after all!!! But thank you for being quick to say it was ok if necessary.

I certainly hope team week has helped with the platoons' morale. Ya know what's crazy? I wonder how many in your platoon are going into the infantry... It's my understanding that those who are will basically be continuing in Boot, the only difference is that they'll be able to have some, not much, time off and they can have cell phones.... Other than that, perhaps morale for them is down because after graduation they'll be heading for a lite version of the same shit different day...

You, on the other hand, will have all that training, and because you're not infantry, you'll go to MCT for 29 days. Aka, The fun bits of Boot...

Then it gets even better!!! You're off to an Air Force base for your school!!! (Good instructors, evenings and weekends off, good food, and good times.) Plus, Mom can visit weekends!!! Sweet!!!!! (Just look out, there are a lot of cute <u>crazy</u> chicks that hang around that AFB just dreaming to land themselves a military man who will take them away from their current lives. Notice the crazy bit...)

I also found out that if you graduate in the top 4 of your MOS school, they often give you an opportunity to pick if you want to go to the east coast, west coast, or overseas! That would be freaking sweet!!

I know you can do it! I'll help you study!!! It will be fun and you can teach me all about most of the stuff you learn!!! Hell yeah!!!!! (All but the "classified" bits which I'm sure will be just about all of it... Heh heh heh!)

Yeah, you say you're thinking about just doing your 5 years then going to fire and rescue... And you might just do that, or you might go with some kind of police force or government agency. (Remember, you'll have a clearance...) But I think once you're finished with the shit job of Boot and you get into your real job that you're going to love it!!! And I bet you'll make Sgt. within 3 years!! Heck, if you play your cards right in 5 years you could easily have your degree and be heading to OCS to become an officer!!! And you'll be able to volunteer for fire and rescue on the side if you want. Yup, your MOS will more than likely allow you that much free time.

Of course, since your first duty station might only be a 2 year assignment, your greedy Mom thinks that, if you can, you should pick the East Coast. That way I can easily come hang out!

No worries over shedding a few tears when I get there. I'm sure I will too! But, not too much, I don't want my mascara to run and make me look like a crazy crying raccoon with a big dumb grin plastered on its face!! (Because I guarantee I'll be grinning like a bird fed cat!!) That would be horrible!!! Hahaha!!!
I'm gonna hug the crap out of you too!! So ya better be ready!!!

I think I found me a LOUD jacket!! It's a bright red rain coat!! Really bright!! I'll get you a picture of me wearing it. You can't miss me in that thing!

My jog this morning wasn't nearly as cold!! 34 degrees is much nicer than 18 any day!!! Saturday I'll time myself again. I've realized it's a lot tougher to keep up a fast pace when it's super cold out, almost like you're just not getting enough air. But hopefully on Saturday it will at least be in the low 40's so I can get a decent time. What kills me is that I'm always hungry now. But I've only lost like 8 pounds!!! (Which I have deemed total crap!!)

Hey, it may very well be me losing fat and gaining muscle because I was able to go buy me a pair of size 4 jeans and have them not look painted on!!! Yay me!

Things are going just fine here!! It's a business as usual kinda thing. Brad is still Brad, Jake is still Jake, and Jackie is growing a nice belly and getting meaner all the time!! (But, in my opinion, it's about time that girl got some attitude!)
Gary is still in Florida at his folks, and we realized yesterday that we aren't sure if we should talk so long on the phone because he recently changed over to Verizon and now we don't know if his cell to cell is unlimited or not. If not, then he's probably going to get a big fat bill in a couple weeks!

Well JD, Momma has been running off at the typing!! Time for bed!! I'll chat at ya more tomorrow!! Till then, keep up the good work and don't let the bullshit get to you!!! You got this in the bag Mister!!
Sweet dreams!!!

Love,

Mom

Joke time!!

The Marine Drill Instructor noticed a new recruit and barked at him, 'Get your ass over here! What's your name?"
"Paul," the new recruit replied.
"Look, I don't know what kind of bleeding-heart pansy bull-shit they're teaching in boot camp today, but I don't call anyone by his first name," the sergeant scowled. "It breeds familiarity, and that leads to a breakdown in authority. I refer to my recruits by their last names only --- Smith, Jones, Baker. I am to be referred to only as 'Sergeant.' Do I make myself clear?"
"Yes, sir, Sergeant!"
"Now that we've got that straight, what's your last name?"
The recruit sighed "Darling, My name is Paul Darling."

"Okay, Paul, here's what I want you to do ....."

That's great!! Darling!! Bahahahaha!!!

****

That's right, I became a smuggler of candy, Propel drink mixes, jerky, and Fruit Roll-Ups! Thinking up new ways to get stuff in was the most fun I had in a long time.

****

January 7, 2012

Hi JD!!!!!

Another day is over!!! Yay!!!

Do you believe this is letter #60!?!?! It sure doesn't seem like that many!! But it tells me, YOU'RE ALMOST DONE THERE!!! Soon to be MARINE!!!! HELL YEAH!!!

I'm thinking that it's Tuesday the 10th as you read this!! Only 10 more days till you're an old guy!! YAY!!! I hope you got your Soles yesterday and your "special" box today. If not, I'm sure they will be there soon!! Please let me know how the hidey holes in the bottom flaps of the box worked out. If it was good, then I'll use that trick again!! (At least once, you're so close to done that the next "special" box would probably show up during Marine Week!)
But if ya just had to toss the box, or if by some strange twist of fate the DI catches the fact that the bottom is taped on the inside you can just play dumb and assume I did that so your stamps wouldn't accidentally get thrown out... After all, I ALWAYS TAPE THE BOTTOM WHEN SENDING THINGS LIKE STAMPS IN A BOX. See if I didn't tape the inside flaps down the stamps coulda slipped under them and been lost forever!!! I wouldn't want that, now would I?

I printed up the lyrics to all the songs I could find, I think I only missed 1, and a couple I had to print small so I could make them fit on a page. I hope you can read them... I also hope you like the magazine I got you! It has some nifty survival tricks in there. Like that bit about cooking a steak on a hot rock!! Honestly, I would have never thought of that, I've always just put it over the fire or embers and been stuck holding it till it was to my liking.... The rock sounds so much easier....

So! You should be doing Table 2 now! Are they the big guns?! Belt Fed Weapons! Oh Boy! I freaking hope so! I need to know so I can make sure I am appropriately jealous.

Ya know, I really hope you get to enjoy this week some and the DIs let you guys learn your shit out there on the range instead of fucking you all up constantly!! For crying out loud!! You'll be in Phase 3 on Monday! They're supposed to be building you up now!! Maybe they'll start easing up a bit on the jackass routine now and let you all catch a glimpse of who they really are... But I'm not sure if that even matters now, soon you'll be a Marine and they'll definitely be better to you guys then!!

I just find them confusing because I know you're awesome! I'm personally so proud of you that everyone I meet gets to hear about you!!! Yep, and all of them are equally impressed! So, I think your DIs should stand up and take notice!! It's not like they're a bunch of fucktards or anything... I think they should maybe take you to get ice cream and perhaps a steak or something!! But no!! Instead they bitch, scream, whine, moan, and work you guys like dogs all the freaking time!!! Hmmm....They must be taking the name Devil Dog a bit too seriously.... Eh! That's fine!! Their time with you is limited. We'll go get ice cream and steak when you get back!!!

My run today was pretty good! Tomorrow I hope to get a time of 9 flat... Somehow I doubt it, but there ain't nothing wrong with hoping!! What gets me is that here it is, January, and while it was down to 18 degrees at the beginning of the week, tonight I was sitting on the porch in 65 degrees!?! Now, don't get me wrong, I'm not complaining!! It's just kind of crazy... And tomorrow it's supposed to be warm again!! But it's January?!?! I can understand the weather being more or less a crap shoot in March, April, October, and even November!! Those are more or less seasonal "change" months... But January is supposed to be winter.... Isn't it??? Again, I'm not complaining, and I hope it continues to be warm, I'm just confused... But hey! That's nothing new!!

I tried to get Jake to take a picture of me in my new Bright Red rain coat... But my phone must not like him because both of the pictures he tried to take looked like there were 3 of me all kind of mashed together in a hazy mess!!
So!! I'll get Brad to take one tomorrow (Saturday) and send it to you

with my Sunday letter.

I hope you like the pictures I sent in your "special" box!! The ones of your girlfriends I stole off of your computer. I figured you might want them too. They are cute girls.

I've been thinking about your 10 days home. (I'M SO EXCITED!! I CAN'T WAIT!!!)
Ok, we need to make sure both of us don't slack off and get all soft!! So!! We'll have to continue my morning routine and probably go to the YMCA so you have some weights to work out with a few times! I'm still planning a day trip for us to Gettysburg too, so that day we won't have time for PT. But walking all over that big ass place ought to be workout enough!! Of course, I don't want to monopolize all your time though... (Ok, I'd monopolize your time in a heartbeat!! But people like James would get upset... Heh heh!) So!! I'm claiming the mornings and a day trip! (And all your other free time. Heh heh heh!) Don't worry, at things like your party, I'll try to share.

Oh, FYI I've already made sure that since you won't have a car right away, you can use the Saturn. Yup, I cleared it with Jake and Brad!! And both were actually happy to oblige!! So, seeing all your friends on the weekend and of course Monday night at the square will be easy!! You'll have some freedom!!! Yay Freedom!!!

You're almost home JD!! Don't forget!! I love you!! Eat, sleep, stretch, and go to church!!!!
See ya soon!!!
I'll chat at ya more tomorrow!!!!
Sleep well Son.
Love,
Mom

PS... Are they the belt fed weapons this week???

Hmmm.... Fucktards.... Ok, so I'm a really far cry from "politically correct." My language isn't always what you might expect from a typical Mom, but then I never was typical. And neither are my children. They know around who, where, and when they can use those "colorful" expressions, and around who, where, and when they can't. God forbid their Grandmother ever read this book, as she would indeed be shocked! I guess had best face up to this now, just in case....

Dear Nana,
Please forgive JD and I for our foul language. It's not meant to offend anyone, it is only meant to express a severity of like or dislike. I promise you neither of us will use such terms in your presence, ever.
Love, Hayden

Good! I feel better now. With that out of the way let's get on to the last letter I wrote JD in Phase 2 of Boot Camp.
****

January 8, 2012

Hey JD!!!!

I had a crazy dream last night!!!

You and I were driving down to the station, laughing and talking smack about people and stuff. Then you wanted me to pull into that park on Wide Water Road so you could show me a trick they taught you in boot camp! So we get to the park and you tell me that your new skill is a super-secret and I couldn't tell anyone... I agreed and then you just kind of pushed off with one foot and were suddenly freaking floating around!!! And you were laughing your ass off!! So I was like, ok now ya gotta show me how to do that!! You did, and I guess it was easy, because the next thing I knew we were floating around at night with masks on and scaring the shit out of people, then we pointed and laughed at them and just floated away to our next victims!!! Strange... LOL!! They aren't teaching you any crazy stuff like that.... Are they???

I went ahead and picked up some ZONE bars for you guys!! I caught them on sale and couldn't pass it up!! I don't think they are as good as the Balance Bars, but they aren't bad either. They kind of remind me of a peanut butter rice crispy treat covered in a little chocolate. (Just not as sweet.) But hey! They got 14 grams of protein along with some vitamins and minerals. Since I mailed them this morning, (I also mailed your special box) maybe you got them yesterday, or the day before?? The post office claimed they should arrive on the 9th... But somehow I doubt it... This whole "snail mail" thing can be so confusing!! Sometimes they go fast, sometimes they suck ass... Go figure...

Oh! And Neighbor Ralph asked about your party, he'll be there. But he can't get off for your graduation. I had actually forgotten that he had said he wanted to go... Sadly he keeps wanting to call you "soldier"... Hmmm..... No worries!! I firmly corrected him!! Now he knows when you get home to call you, Marine! (Ummm.... I also told him Leatherneck, Devil Dog, or Mr. Bad Ass will work too!! Heh heh heh!) You know he's a little slow, so forgive him if he slips up again.

So! I have searched high and low for a USMC blanket for your bed!!! And unless I win the lottery, the best I could have gotten was a stupid tiny thing!!! (4x5.5 they call them "throws") So!! I'm sad to say, I bought some material and am making you one!! Hahahaha!!

Now, your Mom is by no means able to sew like your Nanny could!! And I got to do it all by hand... So!! I'll do my best, but don't expect it to look store bought. (I'm hoping it turns out pretty nice though.) And when your Marine Corps buddies say, "Where did you get that old worn out blanket?" You can cry like you're all embarrassed and say, "My Momma made it for me!" (And each stitch was done with love and pride! Dag Nabbit!)

My run today was ok.... I got 9.36 on the mile... So, I still got a ways to go... But I'll get there. Honestly, I've been bad the last 3 days when it comes to my diet... I blame Penny... She MADE me eat off of McDonald's dollar menu!!! That Evil Harlot!! She started my downward spiral!!! LOL!!
But I'm back on track as of today. I think if Penny hadn't forced me to the dark side than I would have got my 9 flat... Yup!! It's all HER fault for sure!!

Ya know, it was actually warm, almost hot, out today!! I didn't even need my jacket! Someone told me that next week it's supposed to be in the 70's!! Yeah, I'm pretty sure 2012 is going to be an odd year.....

BTW! I was looking through the Parris Island Facebook pages hoping to see a picture of you and your platoon. Alas, you guys weren't there... But at least I have found a place to HOPE to catch a glimpse of you. That is, until I see you, IN LESS THAN A MONTH!

Oh!! Just so I get everything you want... I'm going to be bringing you a change of clothes, (sweats, just in case your jeans are too big, plus sweats will be more comfortable for the ride home) your phone, and contact lenses (with a case and saline). What else do you think I should bring?? Anything??

I suspect you'll have 2 or 3 sea bags to bring home, so I'm thinking all you'll need are those 3 things. And the sweats are questionable. I'm sure you have some nice olive drab colored ones with you.

Nevertheless, I figure I better ask these things now before it's too late and you don't have any time left to tell me what ya want or need.
I know you got a lot going on right now JD. So, just in case you forgot, I AM BEYOND PROUD OF YOU!!! SOON IT WILL BE FEBRUARY!! YAY!!! I CAN'T WAIT TO SEE YOU AND BRING YOU HOME SO I CAN SHOW OFF MY SON... THE MARINE!! Till then, KEEP KICKIN ASS!!! YOU GOT THIS!!! I know you do.

And with that, it's bed time...
I'll write more tomorrow!!
Sweet Dreams!!!
Love, Mom

****

Yes, there is a Facebook page for Parris Island and they do indeed post pictures of the recruits along with a bunch of other nifty things on there. You just have to make sure you're on the "Official" page. You'll know it when you see it, at least once a week or so they actually post a question to one of the DIs asking them why they chose to do what they do. It's a good question, and they all seem to give great, heartfelt answers.

Just don't expect to see your recruit on there. Think about it, there are an awful lot of people who pass through those gates each year and posting everyone's picture would be insane! Besides, if you don't expect to see them, then by some chance they actually happen to show up on there, you can be pleasantly surprised as opposed to getting let down daily.

JD had made it through Phase 2 and was about to enter the final phase of Boot Camp! I knew it was so because no one had called me to give me any bad news. My boy was still kicking no matter how hard they had kicked him! The chest cold he had acquired in 1st phase hadn't slowed him down, and thank God he had (so far) suffered no terrible injury. So long as he didn't get hurt, even though I knew Phase 3 was the most physically demanding of them all, I also knew he would make it. Soon JD would be walking across that Parade Deck and graduating from Boot Camp as a United States Marine. And I couldn't wait to see it happen.

****

Phase Three

The Final Phase of Marine Corps Boot Camp

From Basic Warrior Training, through the Crucible and across the Parade Deck to Graduation

JD now had 17 days left until he would embark on his journey through the Crucible and 20 days until he earned his title as "United States Marine." I, on the other hand, had 25 days left until I could hug my son again, only this time he would be a Marine.

It was nerve racking. The thought that he was so close and yet still had so many obstacles to overcome without sustaining a serious, or delaying, injury was driving me insane! I knew that no matter what, my son would finish what he had set out to do. It's just the way he has always been, and the Marine Corps had driven that home for him even more. But I didn't want to think of him possibly hiking almost 50 miles on a broken ankle or anything of the sort. So I stayed busy and as positive as I believe was humanly possible.

This is where the Marine Parents website I told you about back in Phase One can be a real blessing, or a real curse. Of course the site is set up so that the parents, spouses, siblings, or significant others of recruits in the same platoon can actually connect with each other. So you can go on there and get to know your recruit's new best friend's families. Plus, you can share all your fears and concerns along with all your high hopes and excitement with people who really are in the same boat as you.

Yeah, it was good to "get to know" the family members of the guys who were in my son's platoon. We shared stories of our sons when they were young and from the time they had been home before they left for Boot. We went on about what it was like to realize that we were about to become part of this wonderful Marine Corps Family thanks to the sacrifices made by our sons. Some people made plans to meet for dinner the night after Family Day. And some got together to make goodie bags for those few Stand Alone Marines (SAMS) who would graduate with no family there to see them. And we all prayed together, for our sons, their platoon, and every service member or family member that we felt needed a little lifting up. The dynamic was incredible.

But then sometimes we would hear about a recruit who wasn't going to make it through. Or one who was going to be held back due to an illness or an injury.

And we would pray for that person and their family while secretly we thanked God that it wasn't our son and became even more filled with worry knowing that the next time it might be one of us who got that unwanted phone call... Those seemed to have been the times when ignorance might just have been bliss after all.

At least everyone on that page knew that none of us would be truly blindsided, or left all alone in our time of need should tragedy strike one of us. And I have to admit, while the thought of it sucked, all in all it was good to at least be somewhat prepared for some sort of setback.

I was also pretty pleased with my own accomplishments at this point. Not only had I quit smoking, but when JD left for Boot Camp I couldn't even jog a full mile! (Yeah, I could walk until the cows came home, but jogging was a totally different animal for me.) However at this point, only 2 months later, I was not only able to jog a full mile, but I could do it in just over 9 minutes! Who knew that an old lady like me could make such progress in such a short amount of time!

Of course, JD is still stronger and faster than me, but he's over 20 years younger than I am, and he is a Marine! So in my opinion, it's all good.

*****

January 9, 2012

Hey Baby!!

*Alright!!! Another day down!! According to my calendar **you're starting PHASE 3 today**!! Of course you'll get this in 2 or 3 days... SO! How's table 2 going?? I hope it's at least a little fun!*

It's Sunday night, and a whole lot of nothing went on today.
My jog seriously sucked this morning because Brad was really sawing some logs last night!! I think he has a stuffy head and that made it worse so I only got about 3 hours of sleep... Ha! No worries!! I'll sleep better tonight, see I have a plan!!
  If Brad starts making that incessant noise again I'm going to smack him in the head with a spatula that I have conveniently placed on my night stand. (You know, the Rubbermaid one that had the sticker glue stuck on it through like 10 different washes..) Yup! That oughta stop him!! Heh heh heh!

I'm almost done with your blanket!!! It has actually turned out pretty nice!! All I have to do now is put some quilt ties in it so that when it gets washed the lining on the inside doesn't shift and get bunched up!! Yup, I'm pretty proud of my work on that!! I think you'll like it too.

I've officially decided have your party at the fire house. So I plan to send out a lot more invitations. I figure that since we'll be using the bingo hall, we'll have plenty of room!! I'd like to do it through Facebook. All I'll have to do is log on to your account and create the event, then I can send it out in one shot to the people you approve!!
So! I have printed up your friends list and just need you to cross out the people you don't really like (or don't really know) and send it back to me. (That's what the bigger self-addressed stamped envelope is for.)

Since I was up so early, I had extra time to snoop around on the web and realized that I can make a big sign to hold up for you during the Moto Run!! Hell Yeah!! I'll have that done today! Maybe I'll make Gary use his height advantage and hold it up super high!! Needless to say, I'll make sure it's extremely noticeable!

I also read a bunch of stuff on the message boards about a couple guys in different platoon... Sounds like they've had some guys get really sick, one of the parents on there was saying that her son was going to be at least 3 weeks behind in his training!! Poor kid... But she also said he plans to finish come Hell or High Water!! Good for him!!!

Alas, from the way she was posting updates, well, I have the feeling he was pretty babied to begin with. She has basically said he needs cool moist air to breath at night and she has always ran a humidifier in his room since he was a baby!!! Really?? There was a lot more from her as well about how she hates the fact that he's there, but guesses she has to respect it, and how she is just sick over the fact that up to 80 guys could share the same room!!! OH MY!! I wonder if she was still cutting the crust off his bread too.... (Ok, that was mean... I'm certain he'll be a great Marine. But I bet he really joined the Marines to escape her constant hovering... Can't blame the guy if that was the case...)

Of course, I know you're going to make it all the way through on schedule!! YOU GOT THIS MISTER!!

Well, I think you got this letter along with yesterdays, and today has been really long and boring...
Plus I've sent you the "oh so daunting" task of crossing out your "friends" that you have no need inviting to your party!
Hopefully this week is going good!!!
Keep kickin ass!!
They ain't got nothin on you!!!!!!
I MISS YOU!!!!!!!!!!!!!!!!!!!!!!!!!!!

Semper Fi (soon to be) Marine Son of Mine!!

I'll chat at ya more tomorrow!!!!

Love,

Mom

*****

I started becoming obsessed with the weather on Parris Island. All I could think about was the possibility of rain, snow, or sleet while these guys would be out in the field working their butts off. All it would take was one wrong step or one slick rock to spell catastrophe. Besides, no Mom wants to think of their kid getting soaked to the bone out in the freezing cold... I even stared sending JD the 7 day forecast on a regular basis.

*****

January 10, 2012

Howdy Baby!!!
You're a day closer to the finish line!!! And I'm a day closer to hangin out with you again!!!
     Yay!!!!! WooHoo!!!! Excellent!!!! Sweet!!!! Hell Yeah!!!!
You know it!!
 Looks like you guys are going to get some rain on Wednesday. (Was that yesterday or today?) I hope that doesn't mess with your schedules seeing as that looks like one of the qualification days out on the range. At least Friday (also looks like a qualification day) is supposed to be partly sunny with a high of 63 according to the internet.

I did some research and it looks like this is a fast paced and tough week for you guys!! It also looks like you guys are pretty much camping out all week!! I hope you have decent tents at least!!
On one of the message boards I read, to try and keep up with you guys, a number of people were saying that this week was harder than the Crucible!! Crazy!!

Of course, since it looks like a lot of outdoor stuff I know you'll do great! You might even jump clean out of the middle of the pack straight to the front, just be careful if you do, top dogs get beat often... Most of all, I'm just hoping that you'll find some enjoyment in it.
I'm gonna print out the page I found with the BWT week schedule on it...

Then you can tell me Sunday if it's right on the money or not. (I figure Sunday since it looks like that's the only day you might have a minute to write)

I hope I didn't throw you off by putting letter #62 in with your little package. I've been thinking about that all day. But that letter would have come with Sunday's so I figure worst case scenario, you'll get this letter before you get that one.... No harm done. I'm also wondering how that brown box bottom trick worked... Lord, I hope it went ok....

It's a good thing I get my jog in early... Today at around 11:00 it started freaking snowing!!! But get this, it's supposed to be in the mid to high 50's tomorrow... Mmmhhmm... Strange days indeed!! Nevertheless, it's not like a little snow will stop me!! I, my Dear, am on a mission!! A maddening and painful mission... But a mission none the less! I'm certain you, of all people, understand... There is NO STOPPING!! The freaking mailman, with his little chant about how not rain, snow, or sleet can stop them ain't got shit on us!! Hahaha! (Especially You!! You're Bad Ass Mister!!!)

Of course the snow made me realize that you guys could probably use some big zip lock bags to put your mail or pictures and stuff in... So!! Tomorrow when I go get your Balance bars, I'm also gonna get you guys a mess of baggies!! I hope the DI lets you all have them!! I can't even tell you how many of those things I've sent Gary while he was deployed... But I can tell you that they seem to be good things to have.

I met an old grisly retired Marine today. He was hanging out at the Fas-Mart over there by the 7-11 down the street hitting on the lady with the long dark hair. So as soon as I walked in she pointed me out to the guy and told him that my Son is in boot camp!! Ha!

It was cool. He went from hitting on her to telling me about the Marine Corps back in his day, and about how I had to be a good momma to raise me a Marine!! I told him about you and how proud I am!! And he told me he was a DI on Parris Island 30 years ago!! He said he hated being nasty all the time, but making Marines is serious business!! (I suspect it is!!! You guys are pretty damn important.) And then HE told ME about what a fine young Marine you're gonna be!!! Yup, just as if he had known you since you were a baby!! Hahaha! I let him go on, it was cute, and I agreed with everything he was saying so it was all good!!

I thought it was kinda funny, I had just got started bragging when all of the sudden he just kind of took over and started bragging for me!! All I had to do was agree!!! And as he talked, I swear to you, he started to stand taller and even looked younger!!! So JD, you saved a lady from being hit on and made an old Marine's day all in one shot without even being here!! Now that's impressive!!! Good job (soon to be) Marine!!!

I got your blanket 100% finished and washed!! I must say, its way better than any I could have bought!! Why you ask?? Well;
A. It's a one of a kind.
B. It folds down small but is still pretty heavy. (It's 3 layers of material, the bottom is a cotton blend like a tee shirt and the center piece is fleece. It should be pretty dang warm!)
C. It's a good size. (Ok on a full size bed, great for a long twin.)
D. Ok, my seams aren't perfectly straight, so you can tell it's handmade if you look closely, but they are double stitched and sturdy. (It came through the wash great!!!)
E. (And most important) I made it just for you. Not too shabby if I may say so myself!!

Hell, Tom thinks I could make blankets like that and sell them to make a pretty penny! So it must be ok!! Heh heh heh! (Of course, I'll never make another one "just like that"... That one is just for you.)
Ya Damn Skippy!!!

Sleep well!!! Stay as warm and dry this week as you can!! And be sure to change your socks regularly!! Those feet are damn important!!
I'll chat at ya more tomorrow!!! Till then, keep your head up (soon to be) Marine!!

Love, Mom

Joke of the day!!

Some retired deputy sheriffs went to a retreat in the mountains. To save money, they decided to sleep two to a room. No one wanted to room with Daryl because he snored so badly. They decided it wasn't fair to make one of them stay with him the whole time, so they voted to take turns.

The first deputy slept with Daryl and comes to breakfast the next morning with his hair a mess and his eyes all bloodshot. They said, "Man, what happened to you?"
He said, "Daryl snored so loudly, I just sat up and watched him all night."

The next night it was a different deputy's turn. In the morning, same thing--hair all standing up, eyes all blood-shot. They said, "Man, what happened to you? You look awful!"
He said, "Man, that Daryl shakes the roof! I watched him all night."

The third night was Frank's turn. Frank was a big burly ex-football player; a man's man. The next morning he came to breakfast bright eyed and bushy tailed. "Good morning," he said.
They couldn't believe it! They said, "Man, what happened?"

He said, "Well, we got ready for bed. I went and tucked Daryl into bed and kissed him good night. He sat up and watched me all night long."

HAHAHAHA!! Smart!!

****

BWT (Basic Warrior Training) is indeed said to be the toughest week of Boot Camp. Between the rifle range, combat skills, drill practice, land navigation, and a bunch more stuff, they are kept so busy it's sick!

Heads up, this is the week that your recruit probably won't have any time to write home. But don't worry… They're so busy that they won't even notice any homesickness. As far as I'm concerned, that's a definite bonus!

Just make sure you've sent them enough mole skin and ask if they need extra socks. Wet feet blister fast.

*****

January 11, 2012

Hi JD!!!

I hope you had a good time camping out this week!! And I hope the fresh air didn't get you guys sick but maybe helped you out a bit. I know some times camping in the cold can be a good thing and sometimes it's a very bad thing.... Let me know how it went.

I'm seriously hoping to get a letter from you tomorrow or Thursday. It seems like Thursdays are usually when they show up... Of course, I actually doubt you've had much time at all this week to do anything!!! Much less drop a letter off in the mail. So, no matter what, it's all good.

I got me an extra reservation for January 31st!! That's right!! Even though I won't be able to visit you until the 2nd, I WILL BE ON BASE BY THE 1st!! YAY!!!! That's right! Gary is coming with me and plans on showing me around the Island so we'll know what's there and where to park on Family Day. (No worries! I promise to try and control my urge to come hunt you down.)

You guys got another ton of shit coming up and coming fast!! Looks like Monday and Tuesday you have your CFTs! I hope you get a light weight buddy to carry around! (I have the feeling all of you guys are pretty light weight right now, but the smaller the guy the better!!) At least it looks like you only have to drag your guy a little bit, then it's a fireman carry all the way jogging back. So long as you got a good grip and he doesn't start to slide down your back that part shouldn't be too hard.

I know you're in great shape now too!! Sure, you guys have really been busting your asses, and I know you're tired, but I also know you are strong as an ox!!! Needless to say, I know you're going to get a great score on the CFT!!!

 Honestly, Every Marine I have talked to and given your scores to have told me that you are doing great!! But of course your DIs won't tell you that because they want you to do even better than great if at all possible. And surprisingly, I can actually understand that!

I also heard that for final drill the DIs have ways to hide the recruits with 2 left feet!! (Excellent!) So, I think you guys will stomp everyone on your final drill, final written, and final inspection!!! At least that's what I think!!

(Eh, I know not all the recruits there are as smart, sharp, and strong as you. But they too have come a long way, so if the platoon blows it somehow, I think it's only right to cut them some slack.
Just get to graduation so I can get you home to see everybody!!!!)

Oh!! I got a message from Chris! He got your letter and is thrilled!! They are sending you a nice graduation gift too!! He told me to be sure to watch my mail for it. Poor guy really wishes he could be there with you, or at the very least, be there to see you graduate!! But he's trapped with the pigmies in Australia.
I wonder how long his letters take to get to you... I believe he was saying he was writing you back, but if he is, I think you'll be at MCT by the time the letter makes it to Parris Island!! Hmm... Maybe he's going to write you at our home address?? I guess we'll see!!

A lady on the board I read said that her son told her not to write you guys after the 20th!!! Ummm... Nah, I'll write my last "Boot Camp" letter to you on the 28th. And you should have it by the 1st!! (I'll just try to make them shorter and solely motivational after the 20th! (Yep, after you're big 20 B-Day I'll try to make my letters just one or two paragraphs and the comics.) I know you'll be slamming busy!! And I know you guys won't get mail during the Crucible, so it will be a little *piled up. But I'm not losing all contact damn it!!! (Well... That is, unless you tell me otherwise.)*

By the way, I've decided that on the 15th I'm going to send you guys more of the Marathon bars, that way, maybe, you'll have them and be able to enjoy one for your birthday! (Even if you have to celebrate a little early or a little late, and only in your head, at least you'll know that's your special B-day treat from home.)

Wow!! It's all so close now!!! It's weird though, because it's like you said before... It kind of seems like you've been gone a long, long time, but then again it also seems like just yesterday we were walking through the park in almost pitch blackness watching strange lights in the woods, hearing distant conversations, and something run right behind us!!! Crazy!!!! Ha!! We'll have to do that again!!!

Well JD, before your old insanely Proud Mom heads off to sleep, you need to know what you've done Mister!! You have met the obstacles and kept going!! I am beyond proud! Keep up the good work!!

I miss you!! But I'll see you super soon!!! And I'm gonna call you MARINE!!!!
(But not all the time, you'll still be my Son ya know!!)

Sleep well JD!!
Semper Fi!

Love, Mom

*****

It wasn't too bad that JD missed Thanksgiving, Christmas, and New Year's because he was on the Island. What was going to suck was the fact that he wouldn't be home for his birthday.

I'm a firm believer that everyone deserves a piece of cake on the day they were born. That and I actually like birthdays! There are no crazy people to fight off in order to buy the right gift, no overblown hype, and no insanely loud music playing in the stores for birthdays. Birthdays are "personal holidays" that are supposed to include a cake with candles that you blow out after your friends and family have sung badly at you. But the best I would be able to do for my son was to send him some extra protein bars and hope that the DIs didn't find out about his "special day".

Yeah, if by any chance your recruit just happens to be in Boot Camp for their birthday, try not to make it obvious. If you think about it, you really don't want a DI giving your recruit their version of a gift. That is if you actually care for your recruit...

The clock was ticking, but the days actually seemed to slow down. Every day that passed seemed like an eternity to me! I couldn't wait for the sun to go down simply because I knew my son would be in bed, another day done, shortly after the moon had risen.

Thankfully I had my routine to keep me busy, just not busy enough. I also had some party planning to do, but that turned out to be all too easy for me... Even the blanket that I made JD didn't take up as much time as I hoped it would. So I moved on to redecorating his room in a nice Marine Corps Motif. That took up almost a full day...

It was like I was moving at some supersonic speed while the world was taking a snail's pace. But there was nothing I could do to change things; all I could do was wait... And waiting was maddening...

My life was a strange mix of emotions. On one hand I was so amazingly proud of JD, and I wanted him to be done! I couldn't wait to get on that Island and see my son graduate and bring him home for his 10 days of leave. Yes, truly I was like a kid who knew they were going to Disneyland.

But on the other hand, since I had read so many horror stories about that dang Crucible, if I could have yanked him out of there and not ruined everything he had worked so hard for, I would have done it in a heartbeat.

Oh, I knew he would be fine. Those horror stories are the minority. It was just a Mom thing I think. After all, people get hurt all the time, and they don't have to be going through Boot Camp to do it. But you give a Mom a little extra something to stress over in regards to her child and you can rest assured that she will stress like a champ! I know I did... (And still do sometimes.)

Finally another letter from my son arrived! And he needed help! The name tag on his "portholes", aka glasses, had come off and he needed a replacement tag fast!

*****

Hey Mom,

Sorry I haven't written much this past week or so. Team week sucked, but I kind of expected that. Table 2 and BWT is coming up soon! Only 3 more weeks and I'll be a Marine.

Hey, you should find a way on base during my recruit leave the Sunday after the Crucible. LOL!

Oh! Can you smuggle in jerky chew in an envelope or 2? I've been craving some. I miss the Propel... It was like money here.

By the way, we... once again... came in last for Company Inspection. The funny thing is that our platoon is still above average for the Regiment. (The whole company is above average in general.)

As for how I'm feeling... Still sore all over, still pretty stressed, but somehow I'm doing alright. Hey! I'm still alive!

They say Grass Week is the hardest, but the truth is it never gets easier in boot. The stress just seems to build up until the very end.

I have so much to show you when you get here! I'm going to show you where I suffered the most pain in my life!! LOL!

Home is less than a month away, THANK GOD. I'll be so glad to see all of you and to crush you with a giant hug.

OH! Can you send me some THICK Coyote Brown Boot Socks? More padding = Less blisters.

URGENT! The tiny tag in this envelope... Fell off my portholes. I need it in the same size and font... If they see that it's missing I'll get fucked up!! HELP!!!

I MISS YOU!!

Love, JD

The tiny tag was no more than ¼ of an inch high and about 2 ½ inches long. It was simply a small piece of paper torn in half, covered in a bit of tape, with his name and platoon number printed on it. The print was so faded in spots that it looked as though it had literally sweated its way off of his glasses.

Nevertheless, I set to work immediately! It took me about 15 minutes to find the right font and spacing. And then another 10 minutes to get it printed, cut, and covered with tape. Within 30 minutes of receiving his request for help I had 5 look-a-like tags, including the repaired original, at the post office and on their way to my son. I had even included small pieces of tape on some wax paper so he could easily put the tag in place as soon as he received my letter. The best part was that the mail man had come extra early that day. So even with my 30 minutes of repair time, his much needed tiny tag was on its way to him by noon that day. I just hoped he got it in time.

*****

January 12, 2012

Howdy JD!!

I got your letter today!!! Yay!!! I made your labels and you should have 6 of them already!! (I tried repairing the original, and sent it to you too.) Yup, I got to work on them immediately and ran them to the post office by noon today!!! (Finding the right font was a bitch!!! But I got it pretty quick!!!) I was worried that you might not have tape, hence the little envelope with wax paper strips of clear packing tape just in case.

I'll do my best to find you the Coyote Brown Boot Socks in the morning and maybe stash some Propels and shredded jerky in the box with them. I'll let ya know, I just can't guarantee the sneaky stuff yet. (I'm not too keen on trying to pack that stuff with something you actually need.)

Hell, I ought to see if Kevin is available to go get the socks at the Exchange on base for me in the morning. I'm pretty sure he's free, but if not I'll check Corkey's. No worries. Come Hell or High Water, I'll get you those socks tomorrow and put them in the mail!!!

Did you get your insoles and your "special" box yet??? I'm hoping you got them today at the latest. But, I'm not sure if they'd bring you your packages because of the fact that you weren't in the barracks this week...

Ok, I need to know....Do you still have your wisdom teeth or did they steal them? I wish we had just had them yanked while you were home and could have just laid around while you recuperated..... But what's done is done... Now I'm just hoping that they either left you alone or did an amazing job so you healed fast.

Oh man! I wish I could sneak on base for your liberty!!! But it would be my luck I'd get busted and banned or something... Then they'd make me miss family day and your graduation! (Umm... Yeah, I can't risk that. I'm afraid that kind of shit would probably trigger me to turn into the serial killer Dad always thought I'd grow up to be. Hahaha!)

In a few days I'll be sending you a calling card so you can CALL ME while you're on liberty!! I'll make sure it has plenty of minutes, so you won't be stuck talking to just me... I'll get you my number, Chris's, Kayla's, and James's... Let me know if you want anyone else's. (And I'll message Chris to let him know you'll be calling that day, due to the time difference, so he's right by his magic jack phone!)

See, that proves I love you!! Yep, I am actually pretty greedy, so if I didn't think you needed to talk to a mess of people, I'd probably try to keep you on the phone with ME till family day!!

I really can't wait to get there and see you. I want to see where you've suffered and <u>succeeded</u>!! I want to meet the friends you've made, and I want to meet the Marine DIs who made your life Hell!!

That way, when I go insane, I'll have a visual on some of the people I may want to punish. KIDDING! I'd actually be honored to meet them.

But most of all, I want to see YOU!! I've realized that I'm probably going to be visiting you just about every weekend possible while you're in your MOS school!! I seriously think that the people there are going to know me on a first name basis.

I think we should have been warned better!!! This no phone, no email, and no visits is bullshit!!!! At least that's my opinion on it. But I guess I understand... You need to be focused, and a visit might muck that up for you.

It's funny, I'm your Mom, and so I'm still going to tell you my opinion and thoughts on stuff, because I only want the best for you... But you're also one of my very best friends. And ya know, that's a pretty private club... I really only have a handful of people I actually like hanging out with, that I'd kill/die for, or that I really respect, trust, and think that much of... I guess I'm kind of snobby...Eh! The point is... I Miss You Damn It!

Ok!! It's Wednesday night... So, you should be reading this on Saturday the 14th!! I'm pretty sure that today has been a freaking long one for you guys.
But, tomorrow is church, and then the Red Cross will come and steal some of your blood! That isn't anything new for you. And it will give you at least 30 minutes to lounge in a decent recliner. I hope that they give you some good cookies in return for your blood! And orange juice!! Yes!! High in vitamin C orange juice!! All in all it looks like this Sunday might be pretty chill for you guys... At least I can hope!!!

(Speaking of vitamin C... I still haven't received the damn strips I ordered for you!!! The pharmacy website says my order is on "back order" and will be processed soon... It's been saying that for weeks... Their definition of "soon" and mine don't seem to be the same...)

Monday (F) and Tuesday (L) are CFT days! And you're going to do great!!! <u>Just remember, lift with your legs!!!</u>

I wish your platoon was at the top of everything, but as far as I'm concerned **<u>YOU ARE DOING FREAKING AWESOME!!</u>**

Yeah, I think your SDI wanted you guys to be on top so bad that he had his 2 little helpers take things too far and fucked himself over... Or, deep down in their tiny little hearts, his helper DIs hate his guts and did stupid stuff, like IT'ing you guys right before your initial PFT, to try and mess you guys up and thus make the SDI look bad... But it really doesn't matter or take away from your personal Marine Corps Awesomeness!!

By the way, I know I said I was going to send the Big Marathon Bars on the 15th, but that's a Sunday!! So, I'm sending them Saturday morning. That means you'll probably have them a bit earlier than your birthday... But that's all good!! Just remember they're you're B-day treat! I can't send cake, so this will have to do. It's much better for you anyways.

Tomorrow morning I'll also be sending either Zone or Pure Protein bars as well. Since I sent Balance bars yesterday I got to change it up! After all, I wouldn't want you to get bored with the same old thing!!

I have a confession to make... I was bad today.... I'm sad to say, I did not go for my jog/walk.... But wait!!! I have an excuse!! Brad had a doctor's appointment at 8am because he wasn't feeling well and thus I had to drive him there. Anyway, by the time he was done, (11am!) it was raining cats and dogs!! So!! I got out my little hand and leg weights and worked out a bit, then I went and killed zombies until I was good a sweaty!! Heh heh heh!! Hey! Whatever works, right? I also made a point to stay on my feet pretty much all day. So I should still be good.

Speaking of Brad, he broke his phone!! He claims he had slippery hands and dropped it in the garage. But, I saw it happen... Yeah... He meant to do it... Hahaha! It was kinda cool though; it hit the floor, bounced, did a flip, hit the motorcycle tire, bounced again, hit the floor, did a crazy cartwheel, and then slid directly under my car! I was impressed!!

Of course he tried to make it look like an accident, but I really do think he did it on purpose. Yup! It definitely looked intentional to me! I'm certain he just wanted a new one because his was a little scratched up! Oh but karma got him good!! His new touch pad apparently hates him and refuses to stop changing his words... Just today, in response to me texting him and asking if he wanted to go to Wal-Mart with me, he text me back with......

"No hands, I'm going to jail."

What he meant was... "No thanks, I'm going to bail."

Then his boss, Cliff, text him with, "Are you coming in tomorrow?" And Brad text him back with... "Got your wife on it!!" HAHAHAHAHAHAHA!!!!!

When what he meant was... "Bet your life on it!"

Cliff actually called him to clear that text up!!

Now Brad wishes he had his old scratched phone back!!!! Bahahahaha!!!! (I almost peed my pants I was laughing so hard!!! I wonder what Cliff was thinking when he read, "Got your wife on it!!!" Hahaha!! Alas, Brad didn't think it was all that funny... And that made me laugh even harder!! I guess I'm terrible!!)

Wow!! I've just been typing away!!! So, on that note, it's bedtime for your Wickedly Proud, yet Old, Momma!!!

Try and enjoy Sunday at church and at the blood drive. You'll be saving a life and reclining at the same time!

You're almost home!!!! Just keep going JD!! And remember, I will always have your back to the best of my ability!! (And better if need be!)

Now get some sleep (soon to be) Marine!! Rest well and have Sweet Dreams!!! You got a fast couple of weeks to handle!! I'll write more tomorrow.

Till then!! No worries! You got this shit!!!

Love,

Mom

****

OK, my Dad didn't really think I would grow up to be a serial killer. He just joked about it because I was a pretty rough "Tom Boy" when I was little.

No, I wasn't a bully, or mean to small animals, but I had no problem standing up to anyone who wanted to pick on me. I also had a bad habit, on occasion, of serving up my revenge cold.

The good thing is that while I'm still not afraid to stand up to anyone, I'm more direct and diplomatic in my approach now days. I have found that it really is much better to stay calm and talk things out when you can. But when that's not an option I have one simple rule; if no one hits, no one gets hit.

**Oh and just so you know, if you're looking at the Training Matrix for Boot Camp and you see (L) or (F) it's just to distinguish the groups that the recruits are in. See, if they have 6 platoons in a company they need split them up for training space purposes. So Platoons 1-3 might be (L) or Lead Series and Platoons 4-6 might be (F) or Follow Series. Neither series is better or different than the other; it's just a scheduling thing. Like I said before, the Marine Corps has this stuff down pat. Everything, and I mean EVERYTHING, is on a very tight schedule in Boot Camp.

*****

January 13, 2012

Hey JD!!!!

*In about 2 freaking weeks I will be on that island with you!! And in less than 2 weeks you will have **EARNED** the title **MARINE**!! Hell yeah!!!!*
In case you didn't know... I am proud of you JD. This is no easy path you've taken, and you knew that going in. Now your almost home, and

while I'm sure you still don't see it, you have done GREAT!! You will be a freaking Awesome Marine!!! You're a well-trained warrior!! If need be you will stomp the shit out of any enemy in your path!!! You will overcome any obstacles!!! And you will win!!! You will never be in harm's way because the **"MARINES ARE HARMS WAY!!"** *Damn Skippy Mister!!*

And once you're in the Fleet, many lives will depend on, and be saved pretty regularly, because of the calls you'll make.
Indeed!! You have an extremely important job waiting for you. If my life depended on someone making the right call, I would hope to God that it was someone like you who knew my life hung in his hands and would never let me down. Like I have said before, and will always hold true, the Marine Corps is lucky to have you. And I'm honored to have you as MY Son.
(Ah! That explains my incessant bragging!)

Just in case you haven't got the card I sent yesterday, I ordered your socks through The Marine Corps Shop today. They will ship them directly to you tomorrow! I hope you get them with this letter, but if not, I'm sure you will have them soon. Just try and let me know the week you get them. I also hope you got your "portholes" name tag taken care of!!

Is this month going by faster for you? I hope so!!! By the time you're reading this January will be over halfway gone!!
Your graduation gift from Chris and his family came in the mail today. It's pretty dang nice!!! I know you'll like it! (But I'm not saying what it is.)

I've been plotting and scheming on how to get you more propels and some jerky. I think I have the answer, but I have to test my idea... What I'm thinking is that if I take one of those padded envelopes and create a false inner lining then I can put the contraband in between the two layers. That way, when the coast is clear you can rip out the false lining and get the goods!! Heh heh heh! (Or if the coast is never clear, you can easily just toss out the padded envelope.)

I think it's funny that the Propels are like money there!! All I can imagine is some young recruit coming up to you all twitchy and itchy and asking if you could hook a brother up!! Like little Propel junkies!!! Hahaha!!

Ok, so we all know Audrey turns 5 on the 17th!! (Just a few short days from now...) Well, I was joking around with the Romanian Nick and told him about the "curse" HA! Get this!! He claims to have gypsy magic and that he can take that curse off me!! OH MY! I figure I'm too mean and have too much Cherokee in me for some Old Portuguese mojo to get me anyways! (Plus I totally plan on out living Brad!) But it was funny... The Romanian was getting all mystical and shit!! Hey!! I'll let him do his thing!! Why not? Maybe it will make me super lucky too and I'll finally win the lottery!!

Poor Tom... I guess he really liked this girl, Amy, he got her a pretty nice necklace for Christmas and then sent her flowers a couple days ago... But now she's just giving him the cold shoulder... She doesn't call and won't even text him back with any more than 3 words a day.... She seemed nice, but I think she's seeing another guy... She is, after all, a nurse, and sadly most single nurses play the field pretty regularly... But Tom's good at bouncing back!! He's already talking to another chick!! (And she is much prettier in my opinion.) Hey!! If his "girlfriend" can't even talk to him for a few minutes to find out that he's broke up with her.... Well, sounds like that's HER problem!!!

On another note, Gary was bragging today about it being 77 degrees down there in Florida!! (Yup, he's still there getting shit taken care of and hanging out with his folks.) Well, he stopped bragging when I informed him that while it may have been in the 60's here today, just a few weeks ago it was 18 degrees!! And that while he may be all warm and happy in Florida... HIS HOUSE with its possible busted water pipes was right here in the cold, cold mountains!! Yup, that stopped his bragging dead!

I hope you got the schedule I sent for the Crucible! It looks tough, but completely do-able with team work and the right attitudes!! I'll assume you have a few good guys there with you so you can all get that job done and out of the way with as little suffering as possible. You'll just have to think of it as one of your old night mission weekends!! A sleep deprived adventure!! Oh yeah, you've got that shit in the bag!!

AND SHORTLY AFTER THAT ADVENTURE I WILL BE THERE WATCHING YOU GRADUATE AND BRINGING YOU HOME!!!!! YAY!!! I'M SOOO EXCITED!!!
I miss you!!! And I'm makin plans for your 10 days!!! Hell yeah!!! We're gonna have a blast!!
I CAN'T WAIT!!!!!! WOOHOO!!!!!!!
(I think you're really gonna like the little things I've done to your room too!!! Heh heh heh!)

Ugh!! It's my bedtime JD!!! And I suspect it's close to yours too!!
So sleep well, have sweet dreams and don't forget!!! Eat!! Sleep!!! Stretch!!! And go to Church!!!
I'll chat at ya more tomorrow!!!
Love,

Mom

*****

The story goes that many years ago there was a witch in Portugal who got upset with the women in our family. I don't remember why, but as it turned out she supposedly put a curse on us to last through out the generations. Well, the curse is said to make it so any of us who have a granddaughter by our daughter will die the year she reaches the age of five.

Ok, knowing that, and the fact that I was 5 when my mother's mother passed, and Jackie was 5 when my mother passed, might make a person a little leery on what might happen to me now that my very own granddaughter, born to my daughter, was about to turn 5!

Fortunately I was born right here in the good old U.S. of A. I'm a Portuguese, German, English, and Native American mix. AKA, a mutt, and I don't believe in curses. Coincidence? Sure. After all it is a bit odd that my grandmother and my mom would both pass away when they did. But nevertheless, I seriously doubt some long dead witch's curse from overseas is going to get me. Besides, like I said to JD, as amusing as it may be to ponder the possibilities, I really am too mean to be concerned.

*****

January 14, 2012

Hi JD!!

Getting Closer to the FINISH LINE!! SWEET!!

I hope you guys did great out there for your Table 2 qualifications!!! And I hope you smoke the CFT!! (I actually know you will!)

SO! Now you know, and I know, last week had to be pretty freaking tough, but you made it!!! The few Marines I've talked to say that the table 2 week was harder and more stressful than the Crucible!! Shit, even that message board said it was!!! And you're still standing!!! (Even if every one of your muscles are aching like mad!)

Oh yeah, I bet relaxing and giving up some blood was a nice change! Whoever thought that someone could really enjoy such a thing!! Makes me think... Ya know, it's funny, the things we take for granted... A simple moment to just relax, (even if you're giving blood,) or a sunny day with just enough clouds to decorate the sky, or even a freaking idiot bird that keeps smacking into the back door window... (Yep, this afternoon there was a bird that kept slamming himself into the back door!! He must be brain damaged by now...) So many people miss moments, along with what's around them, assuming it will always be there....

Yeah, I imagine you're reading this on Monday or Tuesday. The days are racing now!! Before you know it those DIs will be referring to you guys as

Marines!!!

And you will have EARNED IT!!! HELL YEAH!!! THAT'S WHAT I'M TALKING ABOUT!!! YOU GO (soon to be) MARINE!!!

My jog today was really COLD!! It is tougher to get going and keep going when it's that cold... But I still managed to bust out a little over 1.5 miles jogging (slow) and I walked the rest to make my regular 6 miles. I still think it's amusing that I can break out in a sweat in 30 degrees and below weather!!! Yeah, it really wouldn't have been that bad if it wasn't so damn windy!! Of course all I kept hoping was that it wasn't that windy there on the island... (Lord knows the weather can mess with your shots! But I'm sure you did great anyway!!)

Every day that goes by makes me more excited to get down there and see you!! I thought about getting on base with Gary for your Sunday Liberty but he made a good point by saying that if we got caught meeting up with you it could still cause you trouble.... Besides I'll be spending the day with you just 4 days later! And you'll be able to call me!!!!! Yay!!!

Oh!!! Gary wanted me to warn you!!! Don't over eat or load up on sweets while you're on liberty, or during Family Day!! Apparently some DIs have been known to PT the hell out of new Marines right after they return from those days... And next thing ya know you're sick as a dog...

So, just be sure not to over indulge in anything!!!

I got you a calling card with 350 minutes on it... BUT, it says in the fine print that the rates on a pay phone aren't the same, so I'm not sure how many minutes it will really give you. I think I'm going to pick up a second one tomorrow too, just in case... I want to make sure you get to talk to people!

I figure I'll send the calling cards to you on Saturday the 21st, that way you'll have it a day or two before the Crucible, less time for you to have to keep track of them. On Tuesday the 17th I'll be sending you a "special" package!! I'm not 100% sure how I'm gonna set it up yet, but I'll let you know in my letter tomorrow.

I really want to know if the bottom of the box thing worked out ok....??? If you had to toss it out, that's ok... So long as it didn't get you in any trouble...

Let me know if there is anything else I can send!! It makes me feel better to do something, anything, to try and make your life a little better!! In the meanwhile!! You just keep going and kicking ass!! Never second guess yourself!! You got this JD!!! HAVE FAITH!!! You really are doing GREAT!!!

I LOVE YOU!!! Tis my beddy by time....
I'll write more tomorrow!
You sleep well and have sweet dreams!!

Love,

Mom

HEY! It's JOKE TIME!!!

A married fellow gets home early from work and hears strange noises coming from the bedroom. He rushes upstairs to find his wife naked on the bed, sweating and panting.

"What's up?" he asks.
"I'm having a heart attack," cries the woman.
He rushes downstairs to grab the phone, but just as he's dialing, his 4-year-old son comes up and says, "Daddy! Daddy! Uncle Ted's hiding in your closet and he's got no clothes on!"

The guy slams the phone down and storms upstairs into the bedroom, past his screaming wife, and rips open the wardrobe door. Sure enough, there is his brother, totally naked, cowering on the closet floor. "You bastard!!!" says the husband. "My wife's having a heart attack, and all you can do is run around the house naked scaring the kids?"

*****

I learned a valuable lesson that day when the mail man delivered a letter from JD that had been post marked 6 days prior...The same post mark that was on his last letter with the porthole emergency... Each letter or package really does travel at its own speed.

But hey! It was a letter and that meant, no matter when it was sent, it was like gold to me!

*****

Hey Mom,

I'm killin' time writing you again. Tell Penny that I thought her letter was funny as hell! LOL!

As for Tony, tell him I said congrats to him and his girl. And of course congrats to YOU on the running! One thing though, when I get out of here, I WILL smoke a Camel Light or maybe a Red. I think I have earned at least One!

It's crazy, I've been craving that shit this whole time! But I'll only have ONE.

On my 10 days we should definitely go jogging or walking at the park again.

Well, I'm getting killed again later today, so I gotta get ready for it.

Love you, tell everyone I say hello.

Love, JD

January 15, 2012

Hi JD!!!

*I'm gonna guess it's.... Wednesday the 18th!! Only 2 short weeks till
FAMILY DAY!!!! EXCELLENT!!!*
*I got another letter from you (post marked on the 8th!!) today! Just goes
to show how mucked up the postal service can be!!!*

*I'll let Penny know she made you laugh. And I'll tell Tony you send your
Congrats to him and Tara.*

*So, ya wanna smoke do ya??? ME TOO!!! Hahaha!! I tell ya what, I'll wait
for you and we can have ONE together. Then we'll probably get a buzz
and feel a little sick, but that'll be ok!! Heck!! I think you have more than
earned it!! But....The next day out at the park we'll probably be coughing
our fool heads off!! Hmmm... That coughing oughta burn more calories
and build up the abs!!! Right?? Heh heh heh!*

*What I think is really funny is you wrote that on your "10 days we should
go jogging or walking at the park again." And in the same 24 hours I
said, "Ok, We need to make sure both of us don't slack off and get all
soft!! So!! We'll have to continue my morning routine..."*
*(Letter #60!!!) You know my morning routine is indeed at the park!! Heh
heh heh!! Yup, it's that psychic link!!!*

*Ok!!! I got the jerky chew... It will be in with Monday night's letter, #70. I
put it in a zip-lock snack size baggy inside a small envelope that I have
conveniently stamped and self-addressed with a piece of paper included.
That way it really looks like nothing!! If I had known that stuff was so
easy to conceal, and that you liked it, I would have been sending some
each week!! It's excellent! That stuff squished down good and flat!!!*

*I have also concealed 20 Propels in a big envelope that I'll be sending out
on Tuesday as well. I just wanted you to get this letter first. **Ok, so I
made a false side inside the envelope by cutting off the side of an
identical one and using double sided tape to make it stay in place on the*

inside of the package. I'm going to send you a couple photos and more mole skin as an excuse for the package. I'm also going to slide a piece of cardboard in there as if to keep the photos from getting bent. (But really it's just to help disguise the firmness of the fake side that carries 2 long envelopes with the Propels in them.) The outside flap will be taped shut, just pull that tape to open it. (I mucked up the sticky stuff on the inside to make it easier to get into while being sneaky.) You don't want to rip into it if you can help it! If the DI has to look in the package all he'll see is what looks like a normal cushioned envelope!! If you look close you'll see the top lip inside has been carefully taped. (You'll also be able to feel that it's the thicker and more solid on that side.) When the coast is clear you can pull the fake side away and retrieve your stash!! And, of course if the coast never clears, you can toss it out without any suspicions being cast your way. No sweat!!

Just remember!! Open it by pulling off the tape!! Don't rip it open if at all possible!! (No X this time, but I will put #10 on the back to mark it.) Who knew one day your Mom would become a smuggler of snack stuff!?! Bahahahahahaha!!!

I decided to try out a different park today!! Ok, the trail claims to be 3.6 miles.... But I dare say 90% of it is uphill... It took me a full 45 minutes to walk the trail, and honestly, my legs seriously noticed the change in terrain!! The only thing is that the new trail had way too many roots sticking out of the ground for me to try jogging it... So!! I think, just to change it up a bit, I'll go to our regular park, where I can jog, every other day, and to this new trail on the opposite days!! Seeing as I cover 6 miles normally on a daily basis, it's obvious to me that I must need more of a climb... Or my legs wouldn't have gotten so tired from just a bit over 3 miles...
Yeah, honestly, that shit wore me out!!! Oh, I probably could have gone a lot further, but I was sure happy to see the car!! (It's also pretty creepy out there!! I think you'll like it!!)

Well!! It looks like this week is full of classes and the confidence course!! They must be getting you guys ready for your final everything!!

Hey, I'm sure you're already pretty good at going straight to sleep, but I really want you to practice falling asleep as quick as possible this week. You will need that skill the night before and both nights during the Crucible. 4 hours ain't much, but wasting time trying to get there makes it worse!!

*Ya know, i really, really, really, miss you!! I wish I could be there to cheer you on in person!! But you can be sure **I'm cheering you on from here!!! Every second of every day!!!!** Ya Damn Skippy!!!*

*You've always been a kick ass kinda guy!! And now you're a well-trained Warrior to boot!!! **I am beyond proud, and beyond confident.** You will smoke all your tests and the Crucible!! Between You and the Big Guy, you can't run into any real problems. Just remember to-*
Sleep Fast, Stay Focused, Eat all of your MREs, Stay Hydrated, Work as a Team, and Take Care of Your Feet!!!! (Use the mole skin and change your socks as needed!!!) As for the actual work, fights, hikes, obstacles and anything else, it's no sweat JD, you got that shit in the bag. I have no doubts.

Ha! Look at that!! Mom has jumped on her soap box and is tellin it like it is again!!! I'm like a creepy long distance boxing coach or something!! Hahaha! I'm just that cocky!! Like I said, you got that shit in the bag. On that note... It's bedtime!!! I LOVE YOU!!!! Keep going JD!!! I'll write more tomorrow!! (Don't forget your jerky chew will be in tomorrow's letter too!)

Sleep well (soon to be) Marine.

Love,

Mom

****

Looks like I'm giving away all my smuggling secrets!! Oh well, maybe you'll need them, and maybe you won't. Either way, they worked! JD never got caught with any of his special treats or drinks. Of course I was always careful to tell him just to toss out any packaging that might cause him issues.

Also keep in mind, these packages never had anything in them that could really cause him serious trouble. Had he got caught, his "would be treasure" would have surely been taken away and he may have had to face some extra brutal PT or maybe a bit of nasty clean up duty. But it wouldn't get him a NJP or anything of the sort.

Yeah, candy, jerky, and drink mixes were one thing, but if he had asked for something like an aspirin, I would have told him no on the spot. That's why they have their very own medical department. Anything and everything these guys and gals take to that effect needs to be in their medical file for a multitude of reasons. And yes, that really does include something as simple as aspirin.

So, if by chance it crosses your mind to use any of my little tricks to smuggle in anything that could possibly ruin your recruits career, keep in mind, his or her DI may have just finished reading this last night and are currently gearing up to double check those packages for sneaky hiding places. Better they find some beef jerky chew than some chewing tobacco. Trust me on this one.

Shoot, even just sending the stuff I sent scared the crap out of me! I knew it wouldn't destroy his dream, but it sure as Hell could have made getting there a lot more painful for him. I guess all I'm really trying to say is, good luck and be careful if you choose to get sneaky.

****

January 16, 2012

Howdy JD!!!

*It's me again!!! That's right, you still haven't gotten rid of me!!! AND YOU
NEVER WILL!!!
BAHAHAHAHA!!!! I'm the worst kind of stalker!!! A MOM!!!! That's right!
I'm your very own stalker Mom!
OK, So today was all in all pretty dang dull!! Yeah, as you know, Sundays
with good OLD Brad can be that way...*

*Oh Man! It was super cold this morning!!! I don't even think my car could
get fully warmed up!! I tell you I was bundled up like Nanook of the
North! I did my 6 miles, and even jogged the mile and a half... But it was
too cold for me to get a real sweat going... That's too freaking COLD!!!
Even in my gloves my hands were so cold they were too stiff to grab the
steering wheel until they had warmed up a bit!! It was horrible!! I was
almost a Nanook Icey!!!*

*So, I figure you'll get this letter with yesterday's. Since today was Sunday
the letter I dropped in the mail this morning won't move till tomorrow...
And this one goes out in the morning too!
I admit I was a bit long winded in yesterday's letter with all the details of
the "special packages" and, of course, my soap box preaching!! (**Just
tellin it like it is Son**!) So! I'll try to keep this letter a bit shorter.*

*I escaped Brad for a bit and had lunch with Kevin! He made me go to this
little sub shop and try a pulled pork Cuban sub... Ok, they put pickles and
mustard on what could have been a really yummy pulled pork sub and
turned it into something that was, at best, edible... I told Kevin it was
good though, because I didn't want to hurt his feelings... And I sure didn't
want to send him off on one of his rants... But now I'm worried he may
try to get me to eat there again!!!!! Eh, it'll be ok, it's not like he and I go
out for lunch all that often.*

*Cool news is that now Tom actually wants me to teach him a few swing
dance moves. He really thought it was a good idea for me to come down*

to the station and teach him! Uh huh, seems he's decided that dancing isn't just for girls after all!!! Hahaha!! From what I understand, the chick he is currently turning his attention to likes to swing!! It's amazing what a cute chick can get a guy to do!!! It's sweet, so yeah, I guess I'll try to help him out a bit.

Believe it or not, Gary is STILL in Florida!!! Yeah, he claimed he was going to head back today, but then his Dad got him to go out looking at sail boats!!! Hahaha!!! Silly Gary!! Boats are for guys who don't have 2 "project" boats already and a "project" house to boot!!! At least this evening when I talked to him he hadn't bought a new project... Yet... But damn if he isn't considering it!!!

I figure his house will be done in a few years, and his 27 foot sail boat can't possibly be sea worthy for at least another 10 years at the rate he's going!!! (Between you and me.... I doubt his 33 foot sail boat will ever be done... Even he has said that it's a serious hunk of junk...) So! I think he should save his money... And, while he agrees with me, I am certain he'll probably buy another boat... Poor guy just can't help himself!! (It could be worse... I guess...)

I hope you got your "friends list" and had the chance to cross out the people you don't want invited to your party. I'm also hoping you had the chance to drop it in the mail so I can get to inviting those people!! Time is running short now! As the matter of fact, the last date I'd say you could get a letter home before I leave to come down there (on the 31st) is Wednesday the 25th. (The day before the Crucible.) And by the time you get this, the 25th will only be maybe 7 days away!!!

Hell Yeah!!! You're only about 10 days away from being called MARINE by everyone FOREVER!!! *(Yeah, I think about that kind of stuff...)*

Well JD, it looks to me like you had a busy day!!! (As usual.) Oh and you got another one tomorrow!! BUT! Soon you'll be off that island and on to bigger and better things!! Yay!! I can't wait!! I know I say it all the time, but I'm so damn proud of you it's crazy!!

I'm really looking forward to coming down there to see you graduate and bring you back home!!!! WooHoo!!!

You know we're even gonna have a blast on the drive back!! Oh yeah!! I got Sgt. Gary all ready to give you the order to relax and have fun!!

Oh crap!!! I said I was going to keep this short!!! I better shut up now!! Can you tell I miss you? Well, I do!! Dag Nabbit!!! But not for much longer!!!!

Time for bed!!! I'll chat at you more tomorrow JD!! Semper Fi. Sleep Well and have Sweet Dreams (soon to be) Marine!!!

Love, Mom

Oh yeah!! I got jokes!!! LOL!!

A little old lady is walking down the street dragging two large plastic garbage bags behind her. One of the bags rips, and every once in a while a $20 bill falls out onto the sidewalk.
Noticing this, a policeman stops her, and says, "Ma'am, There are $20 bills falling out of your bag."
"'Oh, really? Darn!" says the little old lady. "I'd better go back, and see if I can find them. Thanks for telling me."
"Well, now, not so fast," says the cop. "How did you get all that money?' You didn't steal it, did you?"
"Oh, no", says the little old lady. "You see, my back yard is right next to the football stadium parking lot. On game days, a lot of fans come and pee through the fence into my flower garden. So, I stand behind the fence with my hedge clippers. Each time some guy sticks his thing through the fence, I say, '$20 or off it comes."

"Well, that seems only fair." laughs the cop. "OK? Good Luck! Oh, by the way, what's in the other bag?''
"Well, you know", says the little old lady, "not everybody pays."

LOL!!! Ok, that's wrong on soooo many levels!!!

****

Ultimately Gary did indeed buy another sailboat.

Sorry for busting you out like that Gary. I know it's good to have a hobby, but I still think you're some kind of crazy project hoarder. No worries, I love you anyway.

****

STOP!!! If you have not read letter #68 read it first!! If you haven't got it yet, do not open the small envelope in here in front of anyone!! It has very personal stuff in it...

January 17, 2012

Hi JD!!!

It's Monday.... And the freaking post office was closed today!!! (Dang them and their holidays!!!) So your Pure Protein Bars will be sent in the morning and, so long as you read letter #68 before this one, you know about the small return envelope in here and the shredded stuff inside. (Of course it looks more like powdered jerky to me...)

Alas, this has postponed my sending of the Propel "special" package by another day... I just want to make sure you know it's coming so you're ready to open it correctly. No ripping!! Just pull off the outside tape... It also means that you're probably slammed with mail today.

And you'll get slammed with more again tomorrow because, in my day after tomorrow, I'll be sending you your letter, "the package", and a card with your phone card in it! And the day after that I'll send more Balance Bars. (Great News!! I found the mint chocolate ones at Giant!! Just like the Girl Scout Thin Mints!!!)

Wow!! All this mailing has really kept me on my toes!! But it's the best I can do right now, so I'm damn happy to do it!!!

Ah!! The phone card!!! I took the 350 minute one back and got you one with 600 minutes instead. That way if you have to use a pay phone, and the rate is different, you should still have plenty of time!! (And you'll only have to keep track of the single card.) Plus with this card I can hop online and refill it if it gets low! Yup! I photocopied the back of the card so I could refill it without you having to read the pin and stuff off to me. Ahhh yes... The devil really is in the details.

So now I'm guessing that you're getting this along with my last 2 letters and it's already Thursday. Holy Shit JD! In one very short week you'll start your Last Right of Passage there!!! Sweet!!!! But before that!! Friday, you'll turn 20 years old!! Yeah, I bet you feel about 30 though!! Hey, 30 ain't so bad, heck, 40 ain't so bad!!! (Man, I hope you guys got your Marathon Bars and that you have already got to enjoy them!! An early birthday treat is much better than a late one.)

So! Since I saw this happening to another young Marine earlier today.... Just an FYI... If anybody, at any time, tries to claim they had anything to do with your success... I will personally punch their teeth in, rip their tongue out, and shove it up their ass!!!!
ALL the GUTS belong to YOU, and ALL the GLORY is YOURS!!! Oh yes, I will gladly go to jail, laughing all the way, for maliciously wounding anyone who tries to steal any of YOUR GLORY!!!!!

Ok, I really hate it when people try to do that shit... Even if they think they're joking.... And while I doubt anyone in your life is really that stupid.... Well, God forgive me... But, I'm always suspect of some people...

See, today I was getting me some lunch, and there was this guy, with his folks, who had apparently graduated from Parris Island a few months ago and was on leave from his school... Anyway, they were having a family lunch at Subway I guess... Well, I heard them while they were in line and his dumb Dad was basically saying that if they hadn't been so hard on him when he was growing up that he would have never made it through boot camp and that he "owed them" and should be thanking them and shit....

I eventually realized that they were joking. But it was pissing me off so bad!!! I could tell it was wearing on the young Marine's nerves too. Maybe I'm crazy, but their humor, in my humble opinion, was completely unacceptable!!! (Oh! Just so we're straight, it has to be me that mangles any idiot like that... You will have a security clearance to protect. And if I blindly attack someone it will make it easier for me to be declared insane and thus become your dependent and travel the world with you!!! Hahaha!!!)

Speaking of being insane!!! I believe I'm a bit nuttier than I originally thought... Yup, I was certain I was going to freeze solid this morning!!! I was so stiff from cold (15 degrees) that I was glad it was the uphill trail day and not my jogging day!!! I doubt I could have moved my chilled joints fast enough to jog anyway... Unless, of course, someone was chasing me, nah, even then I doubt I would have ran... It was so cold I'd probably be better off to just stand and fight!!

Poor Brad, he thought he had found a great deal for you... Some dude he knows is selling his 1994 Chevy S10 Blazer for $1500... But even though it "looks" clean, and the shop mechanic said it was sound, it has a freaking salvage title.... Brad went from being all excited thinking you'd really like that thing, to really bummed that it's a no go... He tried... But honestly, I'm glad the car fax was dirty... Yeah, the truck looks decent, but the gas mileage would have sucked... So I assured him that you'll find a car that you like and can afford, and all will be well in the world. But hey!! He was actually trying to do something thoughtful!

Wanna laugh at me? OK, I'm so freaking excited to get down there!! I got my stuff to make a sign for your Moto Run, my clothes and stuff are already packed and waiting to go, I had a recent oil change done on the car, and my reservations are set!! I even have your contacts, phone, a special little gift from me, and the one from Chris packed and ready to take to you!!!

Hell, if I thought I'd get away with loitering around the base I would just start heading down there now!! Yup!! I really am like a kid who knows they're going to Disneyland next week!!! But in my opinion, seeing you graduate from there is way better than some old amusement park. And bringing you home will be EVEN BETTER!!

Yep, I'm going to have fun re-introducing you to everyone as "My Son, JD, he's a United States Marine." Oh yeah!!! That's what I'm talkin' 'bout!!

I know, it will probably get boring to you, but I'm seriously proud of you and of what you have already accomplished... Not to mention what you will accomplish! (I know... I'm creepy proud... But it's not my fault! It's your fault!!)
Don't forget!!! Eat, sleep, drink, stretch, and go to church!!!
I love you!!!! See ya soon!!!
Time for beddie bye!!
Sleep well and have Sweet Dreams (soon to be) Marine!!

Love, Mom

Joke Time!!

The preacher's Sunday sermon was "Forgive Your Enemies." He asked how many of the congregation had forgiven their enemies. About half held up their hands. He then repeated his question. Now about 80 % held up their hands. He then repeated his question once more. All responded, except one elderly lady.
"Mrs. Johnson, are you not willing to forgive your enemies?"
"I don't have any."
"Mrs. Johnson that is very unusual. How old are you?"
"Ninety-three," she replied.

"Mrs. Johnson, please come down in front and tell the congregation how a person cannot have an enemy in the world?"

The little sweetheart of a lady tottered down the aisle and said, "I outlived every one of those bitches!"

(Hey!! That was my plan!!! LOL!!!)

January 18, 2012

HAPPY BIRTHDAY JD!!!!!!

(Yup, I'm assuming you got this on Friday!)
I hope they didn't beat you up too bad today... It was supposed to be a busy day anyway, but I know they tend to give "special attention" to recruits on days such as today... The worst part is I also found out that they tend to have that type of information right in front of them!!! So, even though I'm sure you tried to hide it... They knew anyway.... (Maybe you got lucky and they were too busy with the scheduled stuff to really lay it on you... I can hope!!)

Oh well... No matter how the day went, it's a done deal!! And now you're 20 going on 50! It's all good! I'm over 40 and going on 100!!! But hey! Now I can run a mile and a half in about 12 minutes!!!

I met your friend Marc!! Yep, I looked at his online profile and saw he works at Target. Funny, he's the same cashier that makes me pay for all those protein bars!!! (Believe it or not, the bars are cheaper at Target than they are at Wal-Mart.) So I introduced myself today. I asked if he had gotten my message about writing you, and about your party... He gave me "sad face" and told me he had indeed seen them, he had just been toooo busy to respond... I was cool and informed him that he needs to invite the people I told him to invite... After all, now I know where he works, it won't be hard for me to figure out where he lives!!

He asked how you were doing and I told him you were Kickin Ass!! (Because you are.) Then he said he's looking forward to sparring with you when you get back... Oh My! And I told him he's running out of time to get good enough to keep up with you now!!! After that he asked for my number so he could call me for more info on the party later... He seems like a decent kid, so I suspect that if he doesn't lose the number, he'll be calling.

I hope you were able to enjoy at least a little taste of the Jerky yesterday! But more important, I hope it didn't cause you any trouble... I'm always worried when smuggling shit in... Like the box with the secret bottom compartments I sent a while ago, and the big padded envelope I'll send with this letter.... Sneaky... And a little scary too... Of course, I'd rather find out you had to throw away the stash than find out you got the shit kicked out of you for getting it mailed to you from your incorrigible mother... After all, it's not like you have any real control over my actions.

Oh!! I also hope you liked your Birthday card!! I'm sure a river of beer, even if there's a talking rabbit involved, would indeed be a great dream!! It's signed by, ME, Brad, Jackie. Jake, Tom, Cole, Tracy, Mike, Penny, and even Neighbor Ralph!! And since Chris and his family couldn't actually sign it, they sent you the picture!! (That was pretty cool of them in my opinion.)

(Yeah, I could barely read your sisters signature, she's the one with the heart by it. Sometimes I think she writes with her feet. LOL!)

Today was Audrey's birthday!!! It's really hard to believe that she's 5 years old already!!!! Just goes to show, 5 years can go by pretty damn quick. I guess they took her out on the town, because Jackie's phone was off all day and she didn't call me until almost 8pm! And, well, your old Mom is normally on her way to bed by 8!! So, I'll see Audrey tomorrow, and she'll have 2 birthday days!!!

Yeah, you know, I think since I have been a Grammy for five years now that I should be able to get some kind of mad discounts on stuff!! Like a senior citizen, but better!! Yeah, I think I'll write congress and see if I can get them to hook me up with that... Hahahaha!!! (And by the time they read my letter I'll probably already be over 65 and a member of AARP!!)

It's also hard to believe that this is letter #71!! Only 10 more to go Mister!! And you'll be a Marine before you even get to read the last 5!!! I'll keep those short since I know they'll be piled up from the 3 days you're out doing the Crucible...Then that Sunday you'll have liberty!!!!

*AND YOU'LL BE ABLE TO CALL ME!!!! OH YEAH!!!!!! YOU KNOW I'LL BE
SITTING BY THE PHONE ALL DAY SO I BETTER BE YOUR FIRST CALL!!!
DAMN SKIPPY (soon to be) MARINE!!!*

*I gotta be the Proudest Mom in the whole freaking world!!!! You Better
be Damn Proud of Yourself too JD!!! Heck all you guys should be proud!!!
It's one tough road, but the truth is... Pain really is Temporary, and Glory
really is Forever!!
(And no Real Glory comes without Real Pain. That's probably why it's so
dang impressive!!)*

*Hmm.... Speaking of pain.... I hope you got your insoles and your socks by
now too!! Those socks are pretty cool!! It amazed me to find out that they
actually kill bacteria and aid in healing of blisters!!! Well, I shouldn't be
surprised... The military always does have the coolest stuff!! But now I
think I need to get me a few pairs too.*

*BTW, Gary is actually driving up from Florida as I write... I was really
starting to think he'd be in Florida until February 1st then he would just
meet me at the camp ground. But he finally broke away from his folks!!
And an even bigger surprise is that he did not buy a boat!! (At least not
yet...)*

*Ok! Ya got 8 more days and you'll be sporting your very own Eagle,
Globe, and Anchor!!! Keep Kickin Ass!!! You got this in the bag Son! I love
you!!!! I'll chat at ya more tomorrow!!!
Now it's bedtime for Bonzo!!
Sleep well JD!!!!*

Love,

Mom

January 19, 2012

Hey JD!!!
Yay for Saturday!!!
Ok, right now its Wednesday night... But! I figure its Saturday for you!!
You guys are really cookin with Napalm now Baby!!!

Brad was off today and we did a whole lot of NOTHING!!! I know you
must find that extremely shocking!! (But not really shocking at all.)

Ok, WE did nothing but I did some stuff...
I got my walk/jog in, and the weather was pretty decent. I also got to the
post office and sent you the package.... I couldn't get the picture I wanted
to send you and the one in there doesn't warrant any card board... So!! I
sent you an extra pad of paper. If you don't need it, I'm sure someone can
use it... Or you can toss it. I only put it in there to explain the firmness of
the package. Just don't forget, remove the outside tape to open it... And
go after the secret compartment later if you can...

I also went ahead and sent you guys your Balance Bars today. I'm still
thinking your packages take longer than your letters. So!! There are 35
Yummy Mint Chocolate ones (in the green wrappers) and 30 pretty good
Chocolate Brownie ones... If you get to pick, go for a green wrapper!!!
YUMMY!!!!

Gary showed up today with a U-haul from Florida and needed me to
help him unload it and get him home... Well, the first trick was to get to
the storage place before they closed at 5... It was almost 3 by the time he
got to our house and the storage is close to his house... Every bit of 2
hours away!! So the race was on!!!

I jumped in my car and he jumped in the U-Haul and well, we both had to
stop for gas... But as soon as the vehicles were both fueled we drove like
bats out of hell in a grand attempt to make it to the storage place before
they closed!!! It was actually pretty funny, we were chatting on the
phone while driving and every so often he'd mash on the brakes and yell,
"COP, COP, COP!!" Hahaha!!

I tried to explain to him that, although I had his 6, there were plenty of people behind me to take a ticket for the team!! And he wasn't even the lead!!! There was a maniac, possibly sent from God himself, who was driving Mach speeds right in front of Gary and his box truck almost the whole way!! (Poor guy probably thought we were following him.)

It was a good race, and we made it literally 1 minute before they actually locked the doors!! Then Gary begged, and pulled out the fact that he's military and recently returned from deployment... And finally the lady agreed to stay a few more minutes so he could rent himself a storage... (He's a pretty good beggar when he has to be!!!)
Only he tricked me!!!!!

After about 40 minutes of unloading the truck, I came upon the last item.... Damn if it wasn't an engine for a good size boat or something!!! Thank God it was strapped to a little platform type thing or we woulda never got it outta there!!! Yeah, good old Gary, my buddy, my pal.... Looked me straight in the face and said, "Umm... Yeah Baby, we used a fork lift to get it in here..."

What?!?! And somehow he figured we could get it out by brute force??? Uh huh, I knew that shit wasn't gonna happen without one of us, or maybe both of us suffering serious injury!!! So, your good ole Mom reassessed the situation!!! Then I found a couple good heavy duty tie-down straps and told Gary that we should just wrap those around either side of the engine's platform! Then we could drag it out and down the little ramp with minimal chance of injury!!! And what do ya know... It Worked!!!! No injuries and it only took us a couple minutes to get the dang thing where it needed to be!!
Ah yes, there is something to be said for working smarter, not harder. Silly Gary!! Tried to trick me into a sprained back!!! Ha!! I out smarted him!!!

Ok!! Like I said at the beginning, I'm guessing its Saturday. It looks like Monday is the Final PFT and Final Written!!! No, worries there, YOU ARE GOING TO DO GREAT ON BOTH OF THOSE!
(Gotta admit, I really, really like the word FINAL!!)

THEN, Wednesday is Final Drill!! Yeah, aka the last test to see how well your DIs have done!!

But honestly, some people just can't dance. And while Drill isn't exactly dancing, it does take the same kind of "ear to body" coordination as any choreographed dance. You guys listen for the order to be given the same way a dancer listens for the music to change... So, don't get too pissed if there is anyone who messes it up... Because:
A. That test really isn't about you guys.
B. Just because someone isn't a good dancer doesn't mean he's not a bad ass or that he won't be a good Marine. And
C. Thursday morning, only 2 hours after Wednesday's midnight, starts the Crucible, and you will all have to work as a team!! Including the bad dancers. Being pissed at them won't help with the team work.
(Of course, I'm pretty sure you guys are going to do great at Drill!! But, I only made you, so umm.... Yeah, I hope the rest do just as good as I know you will for your SDI's sake...)

Then, at 2 am on Thursday they will get you guys up and out to take care of the Crucible!!!! No worries there either Mister!! You are going to kick some Serious Ass!!! Hell Yeah!!!! OohRah!!!!!

(Just work smart as a team, take care of your feet, eat, drink, and sleep fast!!! It really won't be much different than what You, Robert, and Chris used to do for fun!!)

In just 7 days you'll have that pin!! And you will have earned your much deserved title... **United States Marine.**

And with that... Tis beddie by time!!! I love you and miss you!!! But I'm gonna be seeing you real soon!!! Yay!!! Semper Fi JD!
I'll chat at ya more tomorrow!!

Till then, sleep well and have sweet dreams!! You'll be home before you know it!!!!

Love, Mom

Joke time!!!

There was this fisherman that always had a good day fishing. His friend, the game warden, couldn't figure out how he did it, so one day the game warden decided to go fishing with his friend. The fisherman took the warden out to his favorite spot. Once there, the fisherman took a stick of dynamite out of his backpack, lit it, and threw it into the water. The dynamite exploded and a dozen fish floated to the top.

The game warden said, "That's illegal, you can't do that."
The fisherman goes, "Really?" He then lights another stick of dynamite and throws it into the water. The dynamite exploded, and a dozen more fish floated to the top.
The game warden said, "Stop that now, and take this boat back to shore...I'm going to have to give you a citation and confiscate all your gear."
The fisherman said, "Oh, really?"

He then lights another stick of dynamite, throws it into the game warden's lap, and said "You gonna sit there and keep flapping your trap, or are you gonna fish?"

Heh heh heh!

*****

Finally! I got a freaking hand full of letters from JD! I was starting to hate on my mail man, but all was forgiven on that day as I skipped into my house to read what my son had written.

****

Hey Mom,

Today is the 14th... Sorry I haven't written much. Table 2 had no belt fed anything...

BUT!! I did shoot about 500 rounds this week! So it wasn't a total loss after all.

THANK YOU for the insoles! (And your package worked!)

The next few weeks will be the hardest yet, so hopefully my feet won't be too bad off.

OH! BWT was AWESOME! I'll write more about it tomorrow.

Love, JD

Hey Mom,

Ok BWT was pretty fun. Something about crawling in muddy sand under barbed wire in the middle of the night while orange flares pop in the sky and smoke grenades go off seems to amuse me.

It was tough though. 5 hours of sleep on a freezing concrete slab in a hut with our gear and rifle in a sleeping bag didn't seem all that great.

As for table 2, I didn't do as well as desired. But there is always next time, and at least I passed.

I think I have the CFT tomorrow. Someone stole my schedule, so I'm not 100% sure.

Hopefully I pass with flying colors. (The only things in my way now are the; CFT, PFT, Final Testing, Prac App/First Aid, and the Crucible.)

How are you? Everything at home good?

OH! You can send your last shipment of bars on the 28th. (I think you already said that was your plan.) I'll pay you back for them when I get home.

AND for my Birthday… Send… would it be too much for those "Big 100" meal bars? If so, the Marathon Bars would be my next choice. And maybe sneak some more Sweet Tarts.

Have you been able to find a "card recorder" yet? I have 2 letters from you that I have yet to read. They're in my LB pack, so I'm not gonna get to read them till tonight…

The Crucible is 1 ½ weeks away, pray that I get through my requirements… I miss you a lot.

Love, JD

Jan 16

Hey Mom,

Graduation is right around the corner. I just gotta get through this last push. These last 3 weeks are going to suck though. The DIs have amped up the stress so we're almost always on the brink of snapping.

I know our platoon will get destroyed on the Crucible, so that kind of sucks, but it's whatever...

I've had many sleepless nights here and more to come, but God willing, I'll pull through this final endeavor... One eternal moment at a time...

BTW, don't worry about the sweats, I have a pair. Bring some pants, a belt, and a hoodie. I doubt I'll fit in my old jeans that I came here with anyway.

I hope these days fly by. I'm keeping a song in my head and the thought of home fresh on my mind. Today's songs are "I'm yours" and "Zombie"

So, the days are getting longer, shit is getting tougher... But I'm making it... Till the very end...

GAH! I miss home!! Miss you lots! Tell everyone I say hello and thank Jackie for the letters please.

Love You, JD

PS. I fucked a kid up from one of the other platoons. The dumb ass stood in front of me as I swung on a rope to get over an obstacle. Well, my foot flew out and freaking Spartan Kicked him right in the head. I sent him flying into the corner edge of the trench. Poor guy's portholes cracked into 3 pieces and his face was busted. I almost knocked the Kevlar off his head!

I asked him if he was ok, but he just stumbled to the back of his formation. Hahaha! SO I guess he was fine...

On another note, I actually found someone who plays D&D! Hahaha! Jake will be excited! He's a cool kid, his name is Calvin.

Miss you!! Love JD

*****

I could tell that the thought of the Crucible was wearing on him as much as it was wearing on me. And there was nothing I could do other than write him letters of encouragement and pray. But no matter what, even if I did nothing, I knew JD would do whatever it took to get that title. He wanted to be a Marine so badly that I was sure nothing in this world could have stopped him.

Along with his letters JD had also sent me my official invite to his graduation along with my very own parking pass!

*****

January 20, 2012

Hi Baby!!!!

WooHoo!!!! I got your letters today!!!! And the invite to GRADUATION!!!! HELL YEAH!!!!!

Yeah, I'm not worried about any of the tests you have coming up. I know you're going to do great!!!!

I'M SO DAMN PROUD OF YOU!!! AND SO DAMN EXCITED I'M GONNA SEE YOU REALLY SOON!!! Heck! By the time you get this, Monday or Tuesday night, you will have already passed the CFT, PFT, and Final Written!! The only thing in your way now is Drill, which isn't really about you, and the Crucible! (Which I think you might actually enjoy!)

As you know, I sent you Marathon Bars as your birthday treat! I hope you liked them!! Because, you guys are getting more Marathon Bars! I'm going to send them with this letter and hope you get to enjoy them before the Crucible!! Yeah JD, I'm sorry, but the Big 100 Meal Bars would cost me about $120.00... That's just a bit out of my price range... Especially since I like to send bars a couple times a week...The Marathon

Bars are like $80, and the others run between $55 & $65, plus shipping, so they don't hit my wallet too hard.

Not to mention, the Big 100's that Wal-Mart and Target sell are both kind of nasty... (Penny and I tried them earlier this evening.) And don't worry about paying me back!!! That's crazy!!! I'm doing this bit Dag Nabbit, and you can't stop me!!! As long as you and your brothers there are enjoying them and maybe getting a little bit of extra nourishment at the same time, that is payment enough.

Whew! I'm so glad my package worked!! Now I'm just hoping the jerky letter and the false sided bubble envelope worked too!!

Ok! In this letter, and all to follow, you will find a smaller envelope with a fruit roll up folded in it. If only I had thought of them before!!!! All I have to do is open the roll, fold it in half, and cover it with cling wrap. Then cover it again with a little piece of paper in a small envelope!! They're paper thin!! Utterly undetectable! And damn tasty!! Plus they'll give you a little more vitamin C.
(Of course that means you'll have a few roll-ups waiting for you after the Crucible!! Heh heh heh!)

SO!! I'm going to bring you the jeans you have here, a belt, a hoodie, your phone, your contacts, and I will have to find your iPod. (Heck, it could be sitting right on your dresser. I just haven't looked yet.) I'm positive the clothes you wore there probably stink to high heaven!!! After all, they have been stored in a box, in a room, with thousands of other recruits clothes!! Even if they did fit you now, there is no way you could stand wearing them, or I could stand sitting with you, for the long ride home!! So, I'm also bringing a little trash bag that we can close them up in until they can get washed.

I'm glad you had fun during BWT week!!! They say that's the toughest week of Boot Camp!! But, I thought you might like the actual "in the field" stuff!! Well, actually, I knew damn well that you would enjoy it! That's one of the many reasons why I know you'll do great on the Crucible!! Shoot, ALL the Marines that I have talked to (who are young *enough to have done the Crucible) tell me that BWT week is actually much harder than the Crucible!! So Yeah, I think your platoon will do just fine.*

I'm sorry you didn't do as good on table 2 as you wanted, but we go back to the FACT that the weapons there are old and over used. (aka, CRAP) You passed, and honestly, to me that means you did FANTASTIC!! (No worries, the weapons at MCT are way better!!!) Of course it's a big time bummer that there was no belt fed weapons... I almost cried a bit when I read that... But that's ok 'cause I checked, and the weapons at MCT are freaking great fun!! So, smile JD!! In just a few days, after you get off the island, you can come home, have some fun and then get on with the really fun stuff!!

Oh that poor idiot from the other platoon! Why on earth would he stand that close to someone going over an obstacle on a rope? Well, perhaps you saved him from a more serious injury by teaching him that he really ought to pay attention to were his face is!! What if you had a bayonet sticking out of your boot!! Silly boy woulda never seen it coming... Ah, no worries, he'll pay more attention now. Yes, I'm certain your kick to his face has saved him from a much shorter life!! I am proud of you Son!!

I will be seeing you, My Son the Marine, in about a week from you reading this letter!! In the meanwhile, if you need any extra confidence you can have some of mine!! 'Cause I got enough confidence in YOU for Me, You, and your whole freaking Platoon put together!! Hell, I'm down right cocky!!

Sleep fast!! Eat, drink, and take care of your feet!!! Remember I love you! And I'll be there soon!!
Keep Kickin Ass and get this DONE!!! Mama needs to travel!!
I'll chat at ya more tomorrow!! Sleep well!!

Love, Mom

January 21, 2012

Hi JD!!

It was your birthday today!! Yay!!! But, by the time you get this it will be... Hmmm... Let's see, I'm writing Friday night, printing and mailing Saturday morning, Sunday it will sit still, Monday it will move, and I think that means its Tuesday the 24th!!!
Tomorrow (Wednesday) you have Final Drill! Then tomorrow night you'll be woken up by 2am so you can go kick ass on the Crucible!!! Holy Shit!! You're damn near DONE!!!! Yep! The light at the end of the tunnel should be lookin pretty dang bright now!!!

I'm so DAMN PROUD of YOU!! In just a few days.......
YOU WILL OFFICIALLY BE A UNITED STATES MARINE!!!
OOHRAH!!!!!
I suspect you're slammed with mail today, so I'm going to keep this kind of short...
I hope you got the schedule I sent you regarding the Crucible... It sucks that someone took your training schedule... Well, even though I know it won't make much difference now, I'm including the days you got left, and another copy of the Crucible schedule with this letter. (Always good to have an extra heads up!)

Oh!! I found out that you guys will probably only have a few minutes to use the phone while you're on liberty. And that you'll more than likely be waiting in line for it... So!!! If you have time left on your calling card after calling ME, which I'm certain that you will, you could share some of the time with one or two of your buddies, then just save the card if you ever need it again. (Or you can just save it... I'm just saying that I think it would be nice of you to share.)

Also, I think a lot of you guys will be buying watches... If you do, get a good but cheap one because the "gift" that Chris sent you is indeed a really nice black G-Shock... (Yeah, I didn't really want to tell you so you'd be surprised, but I also didn't want you to start an expensive watch collection either!!)

Well JD, like I said, I'm gonna keep this letter short... You guys look sharp for Drill and take whatever spare time you get on Wednesday to rest, and power up!!!

You got this! I know it, and deep down inside you know it too!!!

All ya gotta do is look at it as one of your long hike weekend adventures!!! And try to actually enjoy it. I know you'll be sore, and you'll have to ration your MREs, so you'll probably get hungry too, but how many times did you and Chris find yourselves miles away from anywhere with sore feet and no food??? Often. And sometimes in the rain and snow!!! Yeah, how many cars did you dig or push out for people while cold, wet, and hungry?? Yep, you've been there and done that, and you even had a good time doing it!!!

<u>Keep a song list in your head, and your eyes on the prize!! (And take care of your feet!!! Use the mole skin even if you have to plaster it right over the blisters!!! Trust me.)</u>

I'll write more tomorrow!!!

I love you and I'll see ya soon, (in a few days) almost Marine!!!

Love,

Mom

<u>*Ha!! But there are always jokes!!!*</u>

A small town prosecuting attorney called his first witness to the stand in a trial -- a grandmotherly, elderly woman. He approached her and asked, "Mrs. Jones, do you know me?"

She responded, "Why, yes, I do know you, Mr. Burns. I've known you since you were a young boy, and frankly, you've been a big disappointment to me. You lie, cheat on your wife, you manipulate people, and talk about them behind their backs. You think you're a rising big shot when you haven't the brains to realize you never will amount to anything more than a two-bit paper pusher. Yes, I know you."

The lawyer was stunned. Not knowing what else to do, he pointed across

the room and asked, "Mrs. Jones, do you know the defense attorney?"
She again replied, "Why, yes I do. I've known Mr. Treviño since he was a
youngster, too. I used to baby-sit him for his parents. And he, too, has
been a real disappointment to me. He's lazy, bigoted, and he has a
drinking problem. The man can't build a normal relationship with
anyone and his law practice is one of the shoddiest in the entire state.
Yes, I know him."
At this point, the judge rapped the courtroom to silence, and called both
counselors to the bench. In a very quiet voice, he said with menace, "If
either of you asks her if she knows me, you'll be jailed for contempt!"

(LOL!! I hope she doesn't know me!!)

****

That was a hard letter to write... JD's birthday, with no JD, sucked! I really just wanted him to be done and home! Even though I knew that he would only be here for 10 days, then he'd be off to MCT for another 30 days of no contact... At least I'd get those 10 days! And once he got into his MOS school I could visit weekends if I wanted too. But, until then, the closest I could get to talking to my son was through the postal service...

Oh! Yes! You can even find a schedule for the Crucible on the Parris Island website. It's not a "by the hour" type thing, but it gives you a good general idea of what these recruits have to face in those last hours before they can be called Marines. It's all good information to have. And I know JD, along with his entire platoon, was very glad that I had sent it to them.

I also learned that excitement and concern is a very odd mix, because that's exactly what was going on, simultaneously, in my head. Imagine having a lottery ticket that you knew was the big winner, it's hidden in a safe and only you have the combination. But you have to wait for a thousand people to try and open that safe before you can go get the ticket. Although it's doubtful that you'll lose it, should any one of those people be lucky, or skilled, enough to get in there they will rightfully take your prize... Kind of unnerving if you ask me...

In the meanwhile home was a bit of a crazy place. Brad was not doing well with his back injury, Jake ended up having problems getting his financing straight for college, Tom's stalker had come right back after him once he and Amy broke up, Jackie and Dave were good but she was getting meaner than ever, and I was just about at my wits end!

But in the grand scheme of things, none of that mattered. What mattered was making sure JD had everything I could give him to help him reach his goal. He was the one out of my reach, so he was the one that was the most difficult to assist. He was also the only one about to face The Crucible.

JD had said that my letters took about 2 to 3 days to get to him. So I realized that my next letter should reach him on the night before the Crucible. I was banking on it. That night I wanted to give him as much of a pep talk as I could and maybe pass on some helpful hints that I had gotten from the multiple young Marines that I had talked to along the way. It would have been better if I had been able to look him in the face and tell him what I needed him to hear, but as you know, that wasn't an option.

I took every bit of information that I had gleaned from my multiple sources and wrote my son the best advice that I could give him. And then I prayed that he would read this particular letter at the right time... The night before The Crucible...

****

January 22, 2012

Alright Son, it oughta be Wednesday night... And 0200 is gonna come quick!!!
But before that, Mom is getting on her soap box to remind to you of stuff you already know... (And maybe one or two things that you didn't realize yet.)

The next couple of days are going to seem long at times, short at times, and downright insane!! But you must keep in mind, it's really just about 2 days!! (54 hours - 8 hours of down time= 46 hours.) You must do your best to sleep during those 8 hours!!! You have to stay clear and focused during your "go time", and a rested mind is what you'll need...

So, when it's time to sleep do not think of the mission you're on, instead you must clear your mind... Think of another time and another place; let all your best memories fill your head. This will help send you to sleep fast!

You have the ability to actually enjoy this challenge!! Do your best to do exactly that!! Use your imagination. Picture yourself and your team out to save the world, or maybe out to save some hot chick that's been kidnapped by people traffickers... Hey, whatever makes it fun.

Yep, think of it this way...
You and your team must all fight, make it over obstacles, through the swamps, and past the booby traps to take back the treasure that belongs to YOU!!

Ration your food the best you can. You don't want a full stomach during your travels anyway, just enough to power the machine. I know you're not allowed to put stuff in your canteen, so if they offer you any drink mixes or instant coffee, you'll have to pour some in your mouth then take a swig off your canteen and swish it around in there with your water. It makes it kinda strong, but it gets the extra electrolytes or caffeine in you so it's worth it...

Now, I cannot stress to you how important your feet are!! Please, use the mole skin. Use your best socks, and make sure you have enough socks to change at least a few times if your feet get wet. If you can, save a good pair of socks for the hike back... And if by chance they don't get wet, you can always double up your socks for extra padding on that last march to your EGA ceremony. Just keep the cleanest ones next to your skin.

While doing your night marches and maneuvers, try not to zone out. Listen to everything around you. <u>Stay Sharp</u> and be sure to step light as you can so if you step on a root or in a hole you will be able to adjust your step and avoid tripping or a twisted ankle.

On long marches, pick a good upbeat song, get it stuck and keep it in your head while marching. Let the beat of everyone's steps match the beat in your head.

When you guys come to an obstacle, the DI will NOT tell you how to handle it. Stop, assess the situation, discuss it with your team, decide on the best course of action, and act on it with confidence. Trust your team, and trust yourself.

You and your whole platoon will smoke this thing!! You are Pure Marine Material and you have been trained by the World's Elite! This is just another mission, a job, an event, that will lead you right to GLORY!! A life time of Earned Respect!! And that little pin that will mark you as a <u>UNITED STATES MARINE</u> forever! Yep, even after you've lived your life, you will carry the title to heaven with you. You are entering a Brotherhood of Heroes and Warriors. This is what you have worked so hard for all this time, and IT WILL BE YOURS.

I love you JD, and I am Overwhelmingly Proud of You and how far you have come already. You have worked so hard and come so far. To me, you already are a Marine. This is just the last step out of the proverbial tunnel and into the light.

I could go on and on about how strong, tough, courageous, and smart you are... I could even go on about how much confidence I have in you, your abilities, and your training. But I can say all that in 2 simple sentences...

If I ever need someone to go into battle with me, I want it to be you, or someone just like you. See, I know that to have you with me would mean certain victory.

No worries, no doubts. You got this. Your future awaits, and it's an amazing future!!!

<u>I give you my word.</u>

Ok!!! I know you'll probably get 2 letters from me today, and it's time to think of other things.... So, I'll tell ya all about my weekend trapped by ice and sleet in the next one!!! Yeah, yeah, I wasn't really "trapped", but had you and Chris been roaming the streets, I'm sure you could have made a few bucks pushing idiots out if ditches!!

Sleep well tonight Son!! I love you!!
(And since this letter should arrive with #76) I'll chat at ya in a minute!!

Love, Mom

January 23, 2012

Hello Again JD!!!

As I said in my last letter, you and Chris probably would have made some fast cash pushing people out of ditches this weekend!! It amazes me how many idiots actually drive!!

Ok, starting last Friday night through late Saturday night, we had a bit of ice and sleet, mixed with a touch of snow... Well, it was maybe an inch, but enough to make the roads pretty slick in spots. Of course, I know how to drive in that shit. But as I was on my way to Wal-Mart on Saturday morning, I kid you not, I passed 9 different cars that had slid into ditches!!!

I pointed and laughed at most of them, but I pulled over to give one couple a hand... It was this little old couple, and what really got my attention was the fact that it was the little old lady who was out trying to push the passenger side of their 1980 something Cavalier out of the ditch!!! So I pulled up about 50 yards past them and walked back to give them a hand... Turns out that while the old guy could still "drive", he couldn't walk anymore without his walker... He was a bit off too... Poor old guy felt horrible over his wife pushing, and was happy to see I had come to help "my mother"!!! And for some reason he kept asking me if I was going to make it home for dinner until I finally said yes... Of course she told me to "never mind him"...

So, I got her to get back in the car. Then I had him turn the wheel towards the road, and ease on the gas. It only took a couple minutes to have them back on their way. Then they stopped next to my car and when I got up there he was telling me that I had better make it for dinner and leave my low-life boyfriend at home!! Hahahaha!! I just smiled and said ok...

In the meanwhile, she was trying to get him to be quiet so she could hand me some cash!!! Yeah, I didn't take the cash, but they did give me a good laugh!! It was cute... But also scary to know that guy was driving anywhere!!! (Honestly, if he had just agreed to go straight for about 10-15 feet, he could have driven straight out... But hey! Then I wouldn't have known to steer clear of that particular Cavalier!!)

I'm sure I told you that I already had your Moto Run sign made!! I figured you might get a kick out of a sneak peek!! I realize, looking at that picture, that, well, I look really evil! I try to hide that, but I guess it doesn't really work... Oh well... There is nothing wrong with having an evil looking Mom cheering you on!!

Ok!! I had a crazy dream last night!! You, me, and Jackie were in a little bass boat and we were going to Portugal to pick Audrey up because Jackie said she had swam over there to see where Nanny was born. But, now she was too tired to swim back... There was a pay phone attached to the side of the boat and every time it rang the boat would speed up, so you and I kept taking turns calling it on our cell phones to make it ring.

After a short while Jackie said we were being chased by fucking pirates that she owed some money!! I'm not sure what happened, but the next thing I knew, you and I were on the pirate boat and kicking some serious pirate ass!! They just kept coming like the damn zombies in my game, and we just kept whipping the shit out of them and throwing them over board.

At one point I turned around and you were smiling at the last pirate and waving at him to come closer. But instead of trying to fight you he just screamed and jumped overboard on his own. Then we were over the edge pointing and laughing at them, and of course calling them names, as Jackie steered our new pirate ship towards Portugal...

Suddenly we were below decks. Jake was there behind a bar wearing a chef's hat and making us chocolate milk shakes... He asked you how you liked being a Marine and you took a drink then said it was good. Then Jackie was spanking Audrey for swimming off without her while we laughed about the stupid pirates trying to fight us and drank our shakes....

It really was as if Audrey swimming to Portugal was totally normal... I wonder what that dream might mean... Hahaha! But hey, stomping out some pirates was fun!!

I was looking at your jeans... I bet they won't fit you either... So I'm going to pick up a pair of 32/30s... (And I'll bring your old ones, just in case.) If you're smaller than a 32 I'm going to have to feed you like crazy till they do fit!! After all, Brad is a 30/31, and I wouldn't be able to stand the idea of my son being that skinny!! No way!! Uh huh... I'll force feed you brownies, cheesecake, fudge, steak, mashed potatoes, chicken alfredo, french fries and cheeseburgers!!! Until you fit in at least a 32!! Dang it!!

BTW, I found your iPod... Now I just need to find the charger.... Maybe, if I haven't found it yet, you can tell me where to look when you call me on Sunday.
Hell Yeah!!! I'm gonna see you so soon!!! I can't wait!!!
You're almost DONE, DONE, DONE!!!
And almost HOME, HOME, HOME!!!
Soon there will be No More Boot Camp for You Mister!!!

Sweet!!! Ok, since I suspect this is letter #2 from me today so I'm gonna keep it short. Enjoy the fruit roll-ups if you can, the extra vitamin C does a body good!!

Sleep well tonight!!! You got some serious ass to kick tomorrow!!
Have Sweet Dreams about all the cool stuff you're gonna do when ya get home!!

I WILL TALK TO YOU SUNDAY!! AND YOU WILL BE A <drum roll please> MARINE!!
OOHRAH!!!!!!!

Love, Mom

Yeah, I gotta get at least one joke in here... Heh heh heh!!

The Wisconsin State Dept of Fish and Wildlife is advising hikers, hunters, fishermen and golfers to take extra precautions and be on the alert for bears this summer.
They advise people to wear noise-producing devices such as little bells on their clothing to alert but not startle the bears unexpectedly.
They also advise you to carry pepper spray in case of an encounter with a bear. People should be able to recognize the presence of bears in an area by their droppings:
Black bear droppings are smaller and contain berry residue and possibly squirrel fur.

Grizzly bear droppings have little bells in them and smell like pepper spray.

LOL!! Pepper spray = bear bait?? Bahahahaha!!!

****

Those letters had exactly 2 to 3 days to get from the post office to his hot little hands. The first one was sent on a Sunday, the second on Monday. The Crucible always starts early on Thursday at around 2 in the morning. Since my next letter would be sent on a Tuesday evening, I figured there was no way he could get it until after he had completed the task at hand and actually had his EGA.

I wanted to prove how confident I really was to JD, so I decided to really roll the dice... His next letter would be pure congratulations on a job well done... I knew that JD would complete the Crucible and earn his Title so long as he was physically able.

Yes, it would take a seriously broken bone, or worse, to stop my son... And I was well aware that there was that slim possibility... But, I had to throw those worries to the side and go with my heart on this one.

It wasn't easy and the worry almost got the best of me. If I sent a letter congratulating my son, and something happened to stop him that letter could be devastating!

But then again, so long as all went as planned, how great would it be for JD to open that letter post marked days before he even set out to be tested? Pretty great!

I went to ask JD's recruiter his thought on it... Sadly, SSgt. Ramos wasn't in, but there was indeed a brand new recruiter in the office, SSgt. Jackson, and his words still ring in my head today... He gave me a huge smile and said, "Go ahead and send it! After all, I say if you have faith, you should claim it!" So I did!

*****

January 24, 2012

Congratulations JD!!
You did it!!!! I knew you would!!!
Of course I knew, it's Monday night, and I'm already congratulating you!!
Yup, by the time you actually get to read this....

You will officially be a **United States Marine***!*
I'm so Damn Proud of YOU!!!!
OH YEAH!!! You saw what you wanted and you did everything you had to do to get it!!

I know it was all up hill, but you never stopped and you never gave up. You have grown in many ways, and although there is always more growing to do, you have conquered some of the hardest things you will ever face right there on that Island.

I hope you had some fun during the Crucible. I know your body and your feet hurt like Hell!! But, just being out there, on the quest to where you are today, I pray you found some amusement somewhere!! After all, life in general is so much better when you can find a way to enjoy, or at least laugh about, even the shitty bits!!

So, now you know what I have known for a long, long time.... Yep, you have proved to yourself and to everyone, that there is nothing in this world you can't handle. Kind of empowering, isn't it?

It's a new birth of sorts. Now you are not only My Son, but you are also a Son and Brother to all the Marines who came before you along with all those who will come behind you and follow in your very foot prints.
YOU ARE A UNITED STATES MARINE!
If you look back to the first letter I sent you, you'll see, I knew it all along...
That really is you JD. You are a United States Marine and the stuff that legends are made of!!

I know my letters will be piled up today, so I'll keep this short. After all, now you know how confident I am, and always have been, in you. Yeah, I'm pretty cocky, but I'm right, so it's all good. Yup, you're one tough cookie!!

Ya got a few more letters to read!! Chat at ya in a minute!!!!

*I LOVE YOU! SEE YA SOON **MARINE!** SEMPER FI*

LOVE,

MOM

January 25, 2012

HELLO MARINE!! OOHRAH!!!
Ummm.... Can ya tell I'm a little HAPPY??? Well, I AM!!!!
Not only is My Son a Marine, but I get to see you and bring you home in just a few days!
Well, in "Writing Time" it's 8 days... BUT, in "Reading Time" it's only 5 DAYS!

What's funny is that I'm almost at a loss for words... Yeah, ME, AT A LOSS FOR WORDS!! I never thought that would ever happen!!!

I know I've told you again and again about how proud I am of you. But you ought to know, "PROUD" doesn't really cover it... It's like this.... I have always been proud of you, you're my Son, and I always knew you would do great things. Just like I know your brother and sister will too!!
(But, between you and me, in my opinion, you just leap frogged over both of them!! Shhhh...)

JD, I can understand your sense of accomplishment, and I can understand your pride. **You have earned it Marine!!!!**

But, I can only hope that you understand my pride in you, and how it really is so much more than the word, "proud", covers.

Of course, there is the simple fact that I'm your Mom, and I've loved you, and been proud of you, since before you were born. So I might be a bit biased... But not really, after all, now I know something more about you then I did back then...

You have grown up to be an inspiring and honorable young man. You're a fast tracker!! And you'll do way better than I ever did!!! You're smarter and stronger than I was at your age. And that is the best thing ever!!!

You earned your title!! Took your treasure!! And now you have so much opportunity and adventure in your future it's amazing! Your path is by no means an easy one, but it suits you, and you will excel in all things!! That's not a prideful Mom talking, that is a FACT! You will make a difference in many more lives than anyone will ever really realize. Because that's just what Marines do...

I'm not just proud, I'm impressed. You are indeed One Of The Few.
Oh, and by the way.... When you made yourself a UNITED STATES MARINE, You also made me a MMom!! (That's a Marine Mom!!) And I am extremely honored to take the job!!

Semper Fi JD.
I love you.
See you soon!!

Love,

Mom

****

The Crucible would actually begin the same day I wrote that letter. And as you can see, I was confident, but, perhaps not as confident as I portrayed myself to be.

That day I got my last letter from my son while he was in boot camp. It was post marked on January 23rd.

****

Hey Mom,

This week will be the most important week in Boot Camp. We have final testing, Drill, and The Crucible.

I got all your "secret" packages! They worked great!

I hope you'll be up early on Sunday because I'm going to call you ASAP when we get our liberty. (I'll probably just call you since we only get 4 hours off.)

We won 1ˢᵗ place against the whole Company in the CFT! And we, as a company, set the bar for Practical Application scores.

Now all that is left is…. Well, you know…

BTW, some of the recruits want to know when the party is, they'd like to come.

I must say, this week wasn't too bad. We didn't fuck up that much and for once the whole platoon didn't get IT'd. But, SSgt. Smith seems a bit moody, while Sgt. Jones has actually chilled out! Probably because our Platoon is back in the competition and might actually win at final testing and or Drill! (I can hope!)

Can you mail me some of my contacts for Marine Week? (I hate portholes!)

How are you? How's the family? Everything good? Audrey is 5 now so you gotta be extra safe this year! LOL! You're too tough to die from some stupid "curse" anyhow!!

Go ahead and give me a schedule of what all you want to do on my 10 days leave. I know I wanna go to Gettysburg, have the party, go to Jackie's restaurant, and wear my Bravos somewhere to show off! But that's all I really got so my days will be pretty free.

Also, please do me a favor, can you get me more info on my MOS School and on MCT at Camp Geiger?

The Crucible starts on Thursday, it's probably gonna suck because it's supposed to rain on Friday. But that's ok. I'll make it.

Oh! And by the way, I got a root canal because the nerves in my lower tooth were dead. Who knew? Well, that's all I have for now.

Love, JD

P.S. Thank you for all the protein bars and supplies!! See you after this last week of Hell! Soon I'll be in the Venza talking your ear off and heading home. It will be good to be back with my family and on the way to somewhere with FOOD!

- Love, JD

****

A root canal? Really? Because his nerve was dead? Ummm.... Ok...

All in all, that was the best letter yet! It might rain during the Crucible, but he knew he'd make it anyway! That's my boy!

****

January 26, 2012

Hi Marine JD!!!

I got your letter today!!! Yay!!! And I got you a pair of contacts, your case, and a little bit of saline in the mail. Just so ya know, I'm still bringing your boxes of contacts and saline with me to family day, just in case something happens with the ones I sent you today.

I'm so glad you guys got 1st in your CFT!! I think your whole platoon really needed a 1st place win to up the morale. And it was just in the nick of time!

Heck!! All of your MARINE buddies there can come to the party!!! Hmmm.... I have an idea!! I'll send you a mess of little business cards with the info on them!! That way you can just hand it on over to all those guys who you would like to invite!! (Of course, I seriously doubt they can ALL make it here...) We are gonna have lots of good food, good friends, and a live DJ!! And the DJ is not even gonna be me!!!

Hmmm... You got a root canal??? Because the nerve was dead??? Hahahaha!!! I love you, but I think you just got "practiced on" JD!! No worries, it's all good!! Almost all of my teeth have root canals! At least a tooth with no nerves never actually hurts. (As the matter of fact, sometimes I wish all my teeth were done!!)

Yup!! Audrey is 5!!! Oh no!!! Heh heh heh!! Yeah, if nothing else, you're right, I'm too mean to be taken out by some dumb old curse!!! Really, right now I am doing GREAT!! And I'll be doing even better once you're in the Venza talking my ears off!!!

On the message boards they say liberty is from 1300 to 1600, But you can bet your ass I'll be holding the phone from 0600 until you call!!!

I've done some research on your MOS... And, so far it's all good stuff. But I don't want to make this letter too long. I suspect you're over loaded with my mail today and probably too tired to understand everything you're reading anyway...

Plus, in "writing time" you will start the Crucible in just a few hours, in "reading time" you're done and a Marine!! Nevertheless, it's time for me to get to work!!! Yup! I have some serious praying to do!! (Even though I already know you'll finish and do great, any bit of help from The BIG GUY is a good thing!!)

Yup, Ya did good Marine!!! I'm damn proud of YOU!!

Now you get some well-deserved sleep tonight Marine!! (<~~ That's an order from a MMom!! Yeah, ummmm... Sometimes, MMoms trump all ranks! That is so long as they aren't counterproductive, or worse, downright insane!)

Semper Fi Marine!

Love,

Mom

*****

I woke up that night at 2 in the morning for no reason and couldn't get back to sleep to save my life until almost midnight. I paced, prayed, and stared at my phone willing it NOT to ring. The next day and night were pretty much the same thing. By the time Saturday morning came I was done! Thankfully my phone hadn't rang with any odd numbers so by 0900 I knew JD had made it! And I crashed hard! From around 0900 Saturday morning until about 1500 that afternoon. I slept like the dead! It was a good sleep because now I was more or less free from worry. JD made it, he was a Marine now.

*****

January 27, 2012

Howdy JD!

As I write, it's Thursday!!
You started the Crucible at 2 in the morning. And surprisingly enough, I woke up at the same time!!! It's 10:30 in the morning now, and I am still wide awake. I'm actually pumped full of adrenaline, like I'm fixing to fight!! I think it's that psychic link!!

My walk/jog went faster and further than normal, I only wish I had been timing the 1.5... I think I may have smoked my previous times!!

I'm so excited!! Oh yeah, Mom is looking forward to talking to YOU as a MARINE on Sunday!!! OohRah!

Of course, like I said, its only Thursday morning for me, so Sunday is still a few days away.... I wonder how long this adrenaline rush will last. I hope you have it too!!! If not I'll do my best to "think" it to you!!! YES!! I shall send you my power so you can add it to your own!! And you will be unstoppable!!!!!!!! Mauhahaha!!!!

I got you your old jeans, (and a new pair of 32's,) a new Adidas hoodie, your contacts with more saline, your iPod with a cable that I think you can use to charge it in the car, and your phone with 2 charged batteries! Oh!! I also have your gift from Chris in your little "civilian" bag.

I went to Loriella Park to swing on the swing set there and got caught by a couple little kids. It was actually pretty amusing, I'm certain they thought I was a crazy old lady trying to steal some kid!! They were hiding behind a big tree and just staring at me!! Then Tom called and since I have a little blue tooth head set now, I'm sure they thought I was super crazy and apparently talking to myself while swinging!! Hahaha!!

Yeah, they went running to their mommy and told on me!

I realized that swinging for like 30 minutes worked a totally different set of leg muscles!!! I was actually a bit wobbly when I stopped!! So, as long as the weather is clear, I'm going to add 30 minutes of swing set time to my days. Yup!! That means you and I will not only be hiking the trails, we will also be scaring the kiddies at the playground!!

After all, you need to keep up your PT on your 10 days!! Looks like MCT is very similar to Boot, but its more being out in the field, the DIs are more respectful, and you will be playing with the big guns!! I've found some good web sites for you to research all that. It's only 29 days long, and there is a good chance you'll be able to use your cell phone on Sundays. There is also another family day and graduation from MCT!! That way I get to see you again before you get on a plane and fly off to your school!!

I had my Thursday night date with Penny. Heh heh heh! That poor woman is a nut!! I think Mark's snoring has kept her from sleeping so much that she has totally lost her mind!! She was mid-sentence talking about her work when outta no where she asked me if I had ever really considered suffocating Brad because of his snoring... So I said that although it crossed my mind to suffocate him just a little, I've never seriously thought about killing him... So then she says... "Hmm... I guess Mark is just special..." And she goes right back into talking about her work!! Hahaha!!! Poor thing... But, she's so funny when she's tired.

Well JD, its 11:30 pm. Soon you'll be allowed to get some sleep!!! I pray you sleep quick and well. BTW, Tomorrow morning Jackie has a sonogram to see if the little one she's growing is indeed a boy or another girl!!! I'm hoping for a boy!! But I'll be sure to let you know the results!! If it's a girl... She's gonna be MEAN!! After all, whatever it is, it sure has caused Jackie to grow some BIG BALLS!! Hahaha!!!!

I miss you Marine!! But I'll be on that island Wednesday, AND I'LL BE HANGIN WITH YOU THURSDAY!!!! THEN FRIDAY WE WILL BE HOMEWARD BOUND!! WOOHOO!!!!
I love you!!! Sleep well and have Sweet Dreams!! See ya soon!!!

Love, Mom

They actually call MCT (Marine Combat Training) and ITB (Infantry Training Battalion) 4th Phase. So it would be important for JD to keep up on his PT while he was home for those 10 days.

While both schools are held at SOI (School of Infantry) they are a bit different. MCT is for those Marine who don't carry an infantry MOS. It's 29 days, and while all of them say it's extremely fun stuff, they all say it's hard work too! ITB is 52 days, a little more laid back than MCT from what I've heard, but still pretty tough stuff. Both groups hit the ground running so these Marines really need to stay in tip top shape! They'll be sorry if they plan on coming home and lying around for those 10 days off.

At this point I was more than ready to get to Parris Island and see JD! I had everything just waiting to be loaded in the car so I could get on down the road! It was actually kind of funny. My excitement was wearing off on other people! At least I think it did... But now that I'm looking back, it could've been that they were just excited to get rid of me and my persistent bragging for a few days. Who knows?

Brad wasn't going to be able to make it because there was just no way that he could tolerate the trip, much less all the expected walking around the island, with his back injury. So Gary would ride down with me on Tuesday. On Wednesday Jake and Jackie would ride down with her girls and Tom would come down by himself. At some point JD's grandparents would also be heading that way to their own accommodations.

The best part was that I was going to be a day early! I had Gary, a Marine, to show me around base and I prayed that I might catch a glimpse of my son on our early tour. But for now it was the 28th, I had one last letter to write, then on the 29th I would actually get to TALK to JD! If only for a few minutes...

*****

January 28, 2012

Hello My Son the Marine!!

I hope you're feeling better today!! I KNOW that was one intense ass kickin week last week!!!
I figure you're reading this on Tuesday!! So maybe you've gotten a chance to rest and recoup a little. Hey! I can hope!! And, if it is Tuesday...

Well then, I left the house around 1030 this morning to head your way!! Hell yeah!! I'll be on the Island snooping around tomorrow!! OohRah!!! You know! I gotta learn some more stuff and pick my prime parking spot for Thursday and Friday!!

Well, I gotta say... WOW!!! This is really letter #81!!!! It's kind of strange, because this is my last letter to My Son in Boot Camp.... I know that tomorrow night I'll want to write to you... But hey!! I'll actually get to TALK to YOU Sunday!!!! So it's all GOOD!!

Today has seemed soooo long... I've done my best to try and stay busy!! But the time seemed to be moving incredibly slow... I keep thinking it should be later, but it's only 2215... You still have almost 2 hours before you get to sleep... And I believe I've only prayed this much a few times in my life!!

Really, I already knew you had this under control. So even though you've been the topic of many prayers and all my thoughts, I never felt any real concern. I knew you couldn't lose. Of course, I also knew it wasn't going to be easy... I knew you'd be working pretty damn hard and taking a beating at the same time!!! So of course, I've been praying.
No parent likes to think of their kid in any pain... No matter how great the reason....

I've also been thinking about your 10 days!!!

How's this for a rough draft schedule?

0 - Thursday
WOOHOO!! FAMILY DAY!!!

1 - Friday
OOHRAH!!! GRADUATION!!!!
Drive home. Have fun!
Sleep in your own bed!!!

2 - Saturday
Go to the park for short hike. Go to the post office to meet your cheering postal ladies! Go get Moms hair cut short. (Yep, I'm tired of the long hair!! Besides, all I ever do is put it up in clips anyways!! So short hair it is!! But not as short as yours!) We'll have lunch at Vinny's.
You go hang out with James.
Later you can help Mom make fudge & cheesecake. Dinner at Logan's. Go swing on swing set at the park. (Weather permitting)
Sleep in your own bed!!!

3 - Sunday
Car church with breakfast. Go for hike. Go shop for clothes. Go to USMC Museum. Lunch at (museum) Tun Tavern. Go to base and shop for Tough Book lap top and other necessities. Play the rest of the day by ear. (Eat fudge and cheesecake!!)
Then go to sleep in your own bed!!

4 - Monday
Morning hike. Go to see recruiters and say hi. Terrorize the town!! Of course go to Wal-Mart! Get ice cream at Bruster's. Home cooked dinner of your choice. Go swing on swing set at the park. (Weather permitting). Go to the square. (Your buddy Marc plans on making sure people show up the Monday.)

5 - Tuesday
Day Trip to Gettysburg!!!

6 - Wednesday
Morning hike, then you tell me what ya want to do!! Of course, it's $5 movie night at the theater!

7 - Thursday
Morning hike. Go shopping. Go to lunch at the restaurant of your choice. Maybe test drive a few cars?? Then play it by ear. (Gotta leave time for James!)

8 - Friday
Morning hike. Go to recruiters to make sure you have all your ducks in a row. Go swing on swing set at the park. (Weather permitting) And the rest of the day is up to YOU!!

9 - Saturday
Whatever you wanna do!! Help Mom get punch and food ready for the PARTY!!!! Then GO PARTY!!!

10 - Sunday
Car Church! Breakfast!
And the rest depends on what your orders say in regards to what time you need to report to MCT on Monday.

11 - Monday
I'll drive you down so you can report to MCT for more fun under the sun!! Then I'll see ya in about 29 days Marine!!

(Let me know what you think of my 10 day schedule.)

I LOVE YOU!!! You Kicked Ass JD! Just like I knew you would!!!

I can't wait to talk to you MARINE!!!!! I wish Sunday would hurry the hell up!!

(BTW... Ya know, you should really trust me more... "When I said, no doubts and no worries, you got it in the bag," I was right on the money!!! As usual...)

Ahhhh... It's 2350. Past my bedtime!!! See ya soon!! But I'll TALK to you sooner!! YAY!!

You better get some good sleep Marine! You got a big busy future ahead of you!!!

Love,

Mom

After the Last Letter to Boot Camp

One phone call home and one awesome graduation on Parris Island

So there it was. My last letter dropped in the mail, and me anxiously waiting for JD to call home for the first time in 3 months.

Liberty isn't necessarily in the morning. For JD's platoon it started somewhere around noon. So it seemed like it was taking forever for him to call... I was just starting to get concerned when around 1330 on that beautiful Sunday afternoon the phone rang and I finally got to hear my son's voice again...

And he sounded horrible!

Don't get me wrong, he was in a great mood. He was a Marine! But his voice was so amazingly hoarse that I was certain he was on the verge of death! After hearing him say, "Hi Mom" I just kind of sat there in shock for a few seconds processing the shear strangeness of how he sounded.

After a moment of silence I managed to say, "Hi JD. How are you?" to which he said, "Well, I'm a Marine." Thank goodness he was still a bit of a smart mouth, he made me laugh. But what I really wanted to know was why he sounded so sick! So I straight out asked, "Well Marine, are you sick?"

He was quick to explain that he had been yelling for the past 13 weeks. Oh yeah, that'll do it...

Then he told me that there was a long line of guys waiting behind him to call home. So we talked for a whopping 15 minutes. But it was a great 15 minutes!! He told me about some of his experiences during Boot Camp, the Crucible, and what position he had in his platoon. I told him about how excited I was to come see him graduate and about how proud I was of him. Oh, and that according to his sisters sonogram she was going to have yet another girl! A very mean girl... And we both laughed a lot. After that he let the next guy in line use the phone along with the calling card that I had sent him. Turns out that since they didn't have to buy a card at the exchange they were able to get in the line for the phone, and call home, all the sooner!

I learned 2 valuable lessons from that short phone call.

1. Sending JD that phone card was an even better idea than I realized.
2. When a new Marine calls home, they sound really rough, and really happy.

The guys still had to make it through the Battalion Commanders Inspection to get across the parade deck and graduate. But that wasn't going to be a problem for any of the fine young Marines that the DIs there on Parris Island had made out of my son's platoon. As a matter of fact, even though JD had mentioned the Inspection, he had also said that they were beyond ready. It was all good...

In just 4 short days I would actually get to see my son live and in person! Maybe in 3 days if I was super lucky and caught a glimpse of him while Gary and I toured the base! To say I was excited is really quite the understatement, I was ecstatic!

Monday came and after my morning jog I cleaned the house top to bottom, washed the car, hung out with Brad, had dinner with friends, and then tried to get some sleep.

Then Tuesday morning, after my jog, I packed the car with some munchies, drinks, and the few things that I had yet to load. I drove over to pick up Gary, and by 1030 I was on my way to Parris Island! It was a good trip down and by 1800 we were checking into our lodge at Point South KOA Campground in Yemassee, SC.

Our lodge was only about 35 minutes away from the base, and just perfect for our group of 5 adults and 2 children. Clean, comfortable, and spacious! Not to mention, the owner of the campground is a wealth of knowledge when it comes to the rich history of Parris Island itself. We had a great time talking with him our first night there.

On a side note, if you're on your way to Parris Island and have never had a milk shake from a place called "The Cookout" I really think you should take a moment and try it out. I can't vouch for the food there, but the shakes... Oh My! I had the banana fudge shake, and it was beyond marvelous! I gave that shake 5 out of 5 stars!

Wednesday we were on Parris Island! Gary took me all over that base! But honestly, other than the Museum, and the fact that it was a beautiful day, I don't really remember too much. I was too busy looking at all the groups of young recruits and Marines searching for JD's face. It didn't take long for me to see the difference between the new recruits, 3rd phase recruits, and new Marines. Of course the DIs were the easiest to spot. And they were everywhere!

I think Gary was afraid I might run right up to my son if I saw him because it seemed to me that every time we would pass close to a group of new Marines, Gary would quickly try to steer me away from them! I actually confronted him on the issue, and of course he denied any such thing. Alas, while the island was a really neat place, I didn't see JD anywhere that day... We went back to the lodge that evening, got all of our new arrivals squared away, had a nice dinner and hit the rack early because I had big plans to be back on base no later than 0600 for the Moto Run and Family Day.

Ok, we may have hit the rack early, but I'm pretty sure I didn't sleep a wink! I really was worse than a kid on Christmas Eve.

Finally! It was Thursday morning! Family Day! And we were there by 0600 just as I had planned. After we made it through the gate and got some much needed coffee at the Visitors' Center, it was time to get out on the side walk with our flags and signs to cheer on our Marines while they ran in the Moto Run.

I finally saw JD! Yep, he had lost weight, but I'd know his face anywhere! (It helped that I knew what his position in his Platoon was as well.)

The cheering crowd was one to rival a stadium full of football fans at the Super Bowl! But it seemed to me that no sooner did the Marines pass by as they were gone again. It was like a teaser view! Really, it was an amazing, spectacular, and motivational peek at our new Marines. Then another 2 hours would pass before we would be briefed by the Battalion Commander and our sons and daughters would be released for a day of base liberty.

There was a good deal of ceremony and information at the Battalion Commanders Brief, but the real show stopper was when all these new Marines marched into the hall. Once they were all in their places and standing at attention, you could have heard a pin drop. These were the new Warriors of The United States, and they were awe inspiring.

There right in front of me stood my son. He was a good kid when I saw him off in that hotel lobby 3 long months ago, but now he was something even better. He stood taller, straighter, and confidence literally radiated from him. I could actually see it from my seat in the bleachers! It was incredible!

When they were finally release for liberty I dashed over to JD and got the best hug ever!

Then we spent the rest of the day as a family again. He introduced us to a bunch of his new friends along with his DIs. (I'd like to single out one DI and say that he was a monster, or that he was startling, but the truth is that they were all perfect gentlemen who had more than earned my respect.) He showed us all the places he had suffered and all the places he had succeeded. We ate much more than we should have and explored parts of the island that even he had never seen.

It was a whirlwind 5 hours of stories, laughing, and learning. Even little Audrey and Alexis were enjoying themselves! (Which is pretty impressive if you think about it, after all how many 1 year olds or 5 year olds do you know that would enjoy starting their day at 0430 after an 8 hour drive the day before?)

I realized what had really happened to my son. The Marine Corps had taken him, taught him a great deal of new information and skills, changed his vocabulary a bit, gave him a lot more confidence with a dash of humility, and polished him up like a fine gem. He was still JD, he was just the New Improved Marine Version.

At 1445 liberty was pretty much over. So we returned JD to the parade deck where he and all the other new Marines would practice for their graduation ceremony. We stayed a while and watched them practice, but ultimately had to head back to the lodge for some much needed nap time.

Friday morning was a little more laid back. This time we were on base by 0630 to get some more coffee and to see the Morning Colors at 0745. (I really wanted to beat traffic. The line at the gate can get pretty ugly if you try to get there at the last minute.) Besides, I figured watching Morning Colors would get us all ready for the Grand Finally! GRADUATION! And it worked well. Just standing there watching the ceremony of the Flag being raised in the morning, hearing the band play, and seeing all those people standing together in that moment of reverence, is indeed more than extraordinary.

By 08:30 we were seated at the Parade Deck watching all the other seats fill up fast. Then at 0900 sharp the Marine Corps Graduation began.

I could go on and on about how I felt and what I experienced on that day sitting in those bleachers. But I would never be able to do that graduation ceremony the justice that it deserves. From the first bugle call to the swarm of people running out to greet their Marine, it was breathtaking. But even that is selling it short. It smoked every event I have ever been too, and I have been to many.

This is where this part of the story ends.

It's been good sharing with you and I hope you've gathered a little more insight into what it is to become part of the Marine Corps Family. It's tough, but it's one of the greatest things in the world. If it were easy there'd be no reason to brag.

I like to think of Parris Island as a place of miraculous change and growth. Yeah, change isn't easy, and growing often hurts, but the end result is worth every bit of it.

They Make Marines. And they do it very well.

My son is a United States Marine; he fights for our freedoms, our families, and our country. Without the men and women, just like him, who have given up so much to serve in our military, I believe we would be a Nation Lost. But thanks to all of them, we are a Nation Proud.

Semper Fidelis,

Hayden Hodges

A Proud Marine Mom

Printed in Poland
by Amazon Fulfillment
Poland Sp. z o.o., Wrocław

32277956R00172